CITIBANK

A Century in Asia

CITIBANK

A Century in Asia

text by
PETER STARR

special photography by

LUIS ASCUI, AMIT ASHER, JON BURBANK, CHIRODEEP CHAUDHURI,

GARETH JONES, HILDA TING, PRESCIANO YABAO

EDITIONS DIDIER MILLET
Singapore . Paris . Kuala Lumpur

Designed and produced by
EDITIONS DIDIER MILLET PTE. LTD.
121 Telok Ayer Street #03-01
Singapore 068590

www.edmbooks.com

Project Director
TIMOTHY AUGER

Editor
SHARON HAM

Art Director
TAN SEOK LUI

Designer
NELANI JINADASA

Production Manager
SIN KAM CHEONG

Color separation by
COLOURSCAN CO. PTE. LTD.

Printed in Singapore by
TIEN WAH PRESS PTE. LTD.

First published 2002 by Editions Didier Millet
© Citibank, N.A. 2002

ISBN 981 4068 29 2

Photographs on pp. 1–15
p. 1: Close-up of a metalwork grille, part of the International Banking Corporation branch at Tianjin,
China; p. 2: First National City Bank of New York, corner of Ice House Street and Queen's Road
Central, Hong Kong; p. 5: Citibank Corporate Banking, Salomon Smith Barney and Travelers
Insurance Company offices in Beijing, China; pp. 6–7: Calcutta staff, 1920s; p. 10: Citibank branch in
Shinjuku South, Tokyo, Japan; pp. 14–15: Citibank Philippines' head office in Makati City

"Our highest single priority remains people—the employees, customers and shareholders that make Citigroup the most regionally committed financial services company in Asia"

Sanford I. Weill

FOREWORD

As the most successful financial services company in the world, Citigroup owes much of its achievement to those early pioneers who transformed America's first bank in Asia into what is now the region's leading financial institution.

In 1918, we employed less than 500 people in the six countries and territories that are celebrating their centennial this year. Today, we have over 22,000 employees in these locations alone. For our entire Asian network across 13 countries and territories, we have over 30,000 people servicing over 11 million accounts, generating revenues in excess of 4 billion dollars.

When we opened in Shanghai and other Asian cities in 1902, Americans were newcomers in a part of the world that was long under European influence. So we initially hired Europeans to compete with Europeans, although there was a sprinkling of American and even Cuban-American staff. By the late 1920s, however, we began promoting local staff in branches from Japan to Singapore, a very unusual policy at the time. This grooming of local talent accelerated, particularly after the 1960s, when dedicated training programs set up in the Philippines eventually led to local managers assuming some of the top positions in our company, not just in Asia, but in other parts of the world as well.

Over the past century, the companies that make up Citigroup were involved in many financial landmark events in Asia. In the 1920s, we arranged international bond issues for governments in the region; and some 40 years ago, we arranged the first listing of a Japanese company in New York. And over the past 20 years, we have played a leading role in Asia's infrastructure development while also building a consumer business for customers across the entire wealth spectrum.

Asia is a strategic focus for our new business model, which builds on existing strengths by concentrating on our broad distribution channels, unparalleled global footprint and unmatched range of products and services. At the same time, our highest single priority remains people—the employees, customers and shareholders that make Citigroup the most regionally committed financial services company in Asia.

In fact, I would like to pay a special tribute to the hundreds of current and former employees from more than a dozen countries who contributed to this book. We deeply appreciate the legacy left behind by our former colleagues who often were forced to exhibit considerable courage to perform their duties. The pioneering spirit of those early days is matched only by the great technological developments now sweeping our industry.

This book is a unique record of our achievements in Asia over the past 100 years and demonstrates our commitment to customers in good times and bad. We are honored to have played a small role in shaping the history of this part of the world. In the financial services industry, we never stop learning. Every year brings new challenges that require new innovations. We hope that our second century in Asia is as exciting and successful as the first.

SANFORD I. WEILL
Chairman and Chief Executive Officer
Citigroup Inc.

CONTENTS

NAMES IN THE TEXT

In this book the names of Chinese cities and historical figures have generally been Romanized using the pinyin system of transliterating Modern Standard Chinese *(putonghua)* based on the pronunciation of Mandarin in Beijing. The main exceptions are the names relating to Taiwan, where the older Wade-Giles system of transliteration is adopted, and Hong Kong, where prevailing Romanizations of Cantonese are used. Chinese names in other countries, for example Singapore, where several dialects occur, appear in the form by which they are most widely known. Names pertaining to Myanmar (Burma) appear in the form by which they have been known for most of the period covered by this book. Names of cities in India are given in the form appropriate to the date—for example, Bombay is given as Mumbai from 2000 onwards. With the exception of those who use European names, the names of Chinese and Korean individuals are written in the traditional format, with family names followed by given names. Japanese names appear with the given name followed by the family name, in accordance with the practice prevailing in Japan. The most important spellings used and variants used in English appear below.

PLACES

Beijing	Beiping, Peiping, Peking, Pekin	Lushun	Port Arthur
Bombay	Mumbai (recently renamed)	Macau	Aomen
Burma	Myanmar	Madras	Chennai (recently renamed)
Calcutta	Kolkata (recently renamed)	Mongkok	Wangjiao
Cheung Chau	Changzhou	Nanjing	Nanking, Nankin
Chongqing	Chungking	Qing	Ching, Ch'ing
Dalian	Dairen	Qingdao	Tsingtao
Guandong	Kwantung	Rangoon	Yangon
Guangdong	Kwangtung	Repulse Bay	Qianshuiwan
Guangzhou	Canton	Shandong	Shantung
Hankou	Hankow	Shantou	Swatow
Hong Kong	Xianggang	Shenyang	Mukden, Moukden
Jiaozhou Bay	Kiaochow Bay	Sri Lanka	Ceylon
Kowloon	Jiulong	Tianjin	Tientsin
Liaodong	Liaotung	Tokyo	Tokio, Edo
Liutiaogu	Liu-t'iao-kou	Tsuen Wan	Quanwan
Lugouqiao	Lukouchiao, Marco Polo Bridge	Xiamen	Amoy

PEOPLE

Chiang Kai-shek	Jiang Jie-Shi	Sun Yat-sen	Sun Yixian, Sun I-hsien
Mao Zedong	Mao Tse-tung	Yuan Shikai	Yuan Shih-k'ai
Puyi	P'u-i	Zhang Xueliang	Chang Hsueh-liang
Soong T.V.	Soong Tse-ven, Song Ziwen	Zhang Zuolin	Chang Tso-lin

THE NAMES OF THE BANK

When it was incorporated in 1812, the bank was known as City Bank of New York, becoming The National City Bank of New York in 1865. After a merger with The First National Bank of the City of New York in 1955, the bank became The First National City Bank of New York. In 1962, the name was shortened to First National City Bank, which was sometimes abbreviated to FNCB. In 1968, the bank became a subsidiary of a holding company, First National City Corporation, shortened to Citicorp in 1974. The name of the bank itself was changed to Citibank, N.A. in 1976, the abbreviation standing for "National Association." Following the merger with Travelers Group in 1998, the holding company changed its name to Citigroup Inc. For more details of the predecessor companies that went to make up Citigroup, see pp. 202–203.

In late 2001, the Citibank and Compass Device logo began to be joined by the new Citibank Red Arc Design logo, linking the company more closely with the Citigroup family of products and services.

The International Company, chartered in Connecticut, changed its name to International Banking Corporation (IBC) six months after it was incorporated in June 1901. Citigroup's first century in Asia started with the arrival there of the International Banking Corporation. Although National City Bank acquired a majority stake in IBC in 1915, and full control in 1919, the IBC name was retained until 1927, when all the Asian branches except for those in the Philippines adopted the name of the parent (the Manila and Cebu branches changed several years later).

Information on the bank's Chinese-language name is given on p. 99.

1812–1865	*1901–1919*	*1919–1927*	*1865–1955*	*1955–1962*

1955–1962	*1962–1976*	*1976–present*	*1976–present*
			2001–present

1998–present

Introduction
The 19th century: a new interest in Asia

"It is as a base for commercial operations that the islands seem to possess the greatest importance. They occupy a favored location not with reference to one part of any particular country of the Orient, but to all parts."

Frank A. Vanderlip on the Philippines

When, in 1901, industrialist Marcellus Hartley joined with corporate lawyer Thomas Hubbard to establish the International Banking Corporation (IBC) in Connecticut, the United States of America was showing a new interest in Asia.

In Beijing, an uprising by Chinese peasants against Christian missionaries and their converts had just been quelled by a foreign expeditionary force. The Manchu court had fled the capital. The insurgents had worn red headbands, and, because of the martial arts they practiced, came to be known as "Boxers." The aftermath of the Boxer Rebellion was to be important to the banking community: a number of foreign banks, IBC included, participated in the receipt of the reparation payments that ensued (see p. 31).

The suppression of the rebellion came after six decades of sporadic conflict between China and foreign powers going back to the First Opium War of 1839. The settlements of these disputes, sometimes dubbed "unequal treaties," are a sensitive matter in China to this day; but the fact is they profoundly influenced the pattern of foreigners' commercial involvement in China in the decades before IBC's arrival. Under the terms of the Nanjing Treaty of 1842, China ceded the island of Hong Kong to Britain and agreed to open five coastal cities to direct trade. These included not only Shanghai and Guangzhou, but also Xiamen, Fuzhou and Ningbo. France and the United States

soon obtained similar concessions. It was in many of the so-called "treaty ports" that foreign banks first set up their branches. British pressure for new concessions resulted in another war in 1858. Under a new treaty, a further 10 ports, among them Tianjin, Shantou and Haikou, were opened up to foreign trade. At the same time, Britain and other powers were allowed to set up diplomatic missions in Beijing and Christian missionaries were permitted to travel in China. Further concessions over the next three decades culminated in the opening of the great inland city of Chongqing in the southwest in 1890.

Japan, too, was eyeing promising ports abroad. After the restoration of direct imperial rule in 1868, Japan sought to expand its influence in Korea, until then a tributary state under China. In 1876, a fleet of six Japanese vessels forced the Koreans

Opposite: Chinese residential quarter in Hong Kong at the end of the 1860s. The architecture shows a mixture of Chinese and colonial influences. Right: The Temple of Heaven in Beijing, dating back to the 14th century, as it appeared in a mid-19th-century photograph

to sign the Treaty of Kanghwa, giving the Japanese access to three ports including Pusan. Events in Korea led to tensions between China and Japan, culminating in a declaration of war by Japan against China on August 1, 1894. The Japanese seized Port Arthur (Lushun) in November and destroyed the Chinese fleet at Weihaiwei on the Shandong peninsula in February 1895. Under the Treaty of Shimonoseki signed later that year, China ceded the island of Taiwan and the Liaodong peninsula to Japan and agreed to pay an indemnity of 200 million taels of silver.

Enter latecomers Russia, Germany and, to a lesser extent, France. Russia had recently begun building the trans-Siberian railroad, which would ultimately link Moscow with Vladivostok, a major Russian port on the eastern coast near Korea. Germany, unified for barely two decades, had started to look east as well. Together, Russia, Germany and France exerted pressure on Japan to relinquish its territorial aims in Manchuria and restore the Liaodong peninsula to China in exchange for increased indemnity payments of 30 million taels.

Japan reluctantly complied but then, in 1898, Russia obtained from China a 25-year lease on Port Arthur and Dalian, located on the southern tip of the same peninsula. The Japanese were incensed. At around the same time, Germany forced China to grant a 99-year naval lease on an area in Shandong province which included Jiaozhou Bay and the port city of Qingdao. France successfully pressed for a new concession as well. Not to be outdone by these relative newcomers, the British now pressed China for further concessions at Weihaiwei and for a 99-year lease on "new territories" adjoining Kowloon across the waterfront from the island of Hong Kong.

As a British diplomat in Beijing remarked, a "general and not very edifying scramble" was underway—not only for ports but also for concessions to build railroads across China. However, at the root of all this activity lay a sense of the almost unlimited promise of China as a huge potential market for many of the manufactured goods now being produced in the industrialized countries of Europe and North America.

Naval engagement in the First Opium War: Chinese war junks under attack by the British paddle steamer *Nemesis* in January 1841

The American steamer *Williamette* at Henan. Foreign merchants shifted here after the burning of the Guangzhou "factories," or warehouses, in 1856

Further south, another storm was brewing. In the neighboring islands of the Philippines, more than three centuries of Spanish colonial rule were finally coming to an end. Although the local economy had flourished after the galleon trade between Manila and Acapulco was discontinued in 1815, by the end of the century things started looking bleak. Manila's port activities had been affected by the opening of the treaty ports in China. The price of cane sugar was dropping on world markets as the cultivation of beet sugar expanded in Europe and the United States, protected by high tariffs on imports of the tropical variety. In the 1880s, the local coffee industry was ruined by disease. The government was in debt. Political repression rose with the arrest and exile of reformist leader Jose Rizal in 1892.

Crude sugar at a factory in Pampanga Province, the Philippines

A revolution against the Spanish erupted in the Philippines in 1896. Even with its leader Emilio Aguinaldo exiled to Hong Kong the following year, skirmishes continued. In early 1898, after the American battleship *Maine* blew up and sank in the Spanish colony of Cuba, the United States declared war on Spain. American warships led by Admiral George Dewey sailed into Manila Bay and destroyed a Spanish squadron. Aguinaldo returned to the Philippines aboard an American vessel only a few weeks later.

Emilio Aguinaldo, leader of the Philippine revolution

Although the Constitutional Republic of the Philippines was declared in June 1898, in December Spain ceded the Philippines, Guam and Puerto Rico to the United States in exchange for 20 million U.S. dollars. Guerilla warfare soon ensued, and Aguinaldo was eventually captured by the Americans in 1901. President William McKinley, who was re-elected with his running mate Theodore Roosevelt in 1900, admitted that he had been "criticized a good deal about the Philippines. But I don't deserve it. The truth is ... they came to us as a gift from the gods."

The "British Century" was drawing to a close. The European powers had fought the "battle of concessions" on the Chinese mainland; at the same time, Japan and the United States had, between them, managed to acquire the Pacific island gateways to Asia in the space of a few years.

The clipper *Lady Egidea* loading in Calcutta, 1875, toward the end of the age of sail

Nineteenth-century Calcutta

The earliest branches of IBC were set not only in the treaty ports of China and Japan, and in the American colony of the Philippines, but also in India and Singapore, both parts of the then British Empire. Indian ports provided a staging post in the trade with the "Spice Islands" of the Dutch East Indies (Indonesia), and India's exports and re-exports included silk and cotton textiles,

Old Court House Street, in the European commercial center of India's greatest 19th-century port city, Calcutta

which could be used as barter goods further east. Until the mid-19th century, British trade interests—and to a substantial degree its political interests—were in the hands of the East India Company. By the end of the 17th century, the East India Company was operating in what later became Calcutta and Bombay. By the end of the 18th century, the company was in effective control of the entire subcontinent, although local royal houses still wielded political power in theory. After the Indian Mutiny of 1857, the reins of power were taken over by London directly.

Calcutta was the economic heart of India in the early 19th century. By then, there were already a few private banks operating. In 1806, the first semi-government bank in India, the Bank of Bengal (later known as the Bank of Calcutta) was established. In time, while Calcutta remained influential politically, the focus of commercial activity shifted to Bombay. Two more semi-government banks were established: the Bank of Bombay and the Bank of Madras. By the mid-19th century, India had ceased to be a major exporter of high-quality textiles and the export trade concentrated on opium, raw cotton, jute, tea and coffee.

most fertile, best cultivated, most industrious and most populous countries in the world" and "a much richer country than any part of Europe." But its potential was not realized, and, according to a recent study by the Asian Development Bank (ADB), by 1820 China's income per person had fallen to around half the level in Western Europe.

Like China, the rest of Asia had fallen behind Europe after 1500. Japan largely closed itself off from the world from 1603 to 1868 during the military rule of the Tokugawa Shogunate. Foreign trade was strictly limited to Dutch and Chinese merchants in Nagasaki, leaving the Spanish to dominate trans-Pacific trade between the Philippines and Mexico. In India and Southeast Asia, the Portuguese were replaced by the Dutch and British as the dominant powers with the advent of their respective East India companies.

It wasn't supposed to have been like this. China was politically unified as far back as 221 B.C. By the time of the Sung Dynasty (960–1279 A.D.), commercial sophistication and technological advances had brought to China pre-eminence in the world economy. But with the suspension of expeditions and much foreign trade in the 15th century, China stopped building ships and lost its lead in navigation. As late as 1776, Adam Smith described China as "long one of the richest, that is, one of the most fertile, best cultivated, most industrious and most populous countries in the world" and "a much richer country than any part of Europe."

Between 1820 and 1870, the economies of Western Europe and its offshoots (Australia, Canada, New Zealand and the United States) grew at an average annual rate of 1.1 percent per person while Asia, Latin America and Africa barely grew at all, at about 0.1 percent a year. The resulting economic and military dominance of the western powers gave them increasing influence in Asia, either through direct colonial rule as in India or the imposition of treaties on favorable terms, as in China.

Entrepôt Singapore

The intentions of Sir Stamford Raffles, an official of the East India Company, in founding Singapore were to establish "the emporium and pride of the East," bidding fair to be "the next port to Calcutta." Raffles' motives were no doubt commercial rather than imperialistic, and it was he who set the tone of a free commercial environment that laid the foundations of the prosperity of Singapore that exists to the present day.

Throughout much of the 19th century and the first half of the 20th, migrants flooded in from the southern provinces of China itself. By the time the East India Company handed over control of the Straits Settlements (Penang, Malacca and Singapore) to the colonial authorities in London—they became a Crown Colony in 1867—Singapore was a predominantly Chinese city.

Singapore became a major center not only for European commerce, but also for traders from the Dutch East Indies (Indonesia), Siam (Thailand), China and the Malay Peninsula. The opening of the Suez Canal (which the sailing ships could not use) worked to Singapore's benefit, as the main east-west shipping route now ran through the Malacca Straits, and Singapore became an important link in a chain of coaling stations for shipping both further east to China, and southward to Australia.

Singapore demonstrated the validity of the three cardinal principles held dear by modern dealers in real estate— "location, location and location."

By the end of the 19th century, the main business was no longer in exotic spices, but in primary products such as tin, sugar, and later rubber. The benefits from the expansion in the American canning industry, and later the demand for rubber by the American automobile industry, were huge. By 1902, the island of Bukum, off Singapore, was the oil supply center of the East.

By the turn of the century, several European banks had established branches in Singapore. Subsequent decades were to see not only the first American arrival, but also the growth of a very substantial locally owned banking sector, reflecting the presence and achievements of a prosperous community of merchants, particularly in the Chinese-born population.

Above left: Fortune teller in early Singapore
Right: Chinese merchants in Singapore in the early 1900s
Below: Chinese residential quarter in the 19th century

Commodore Matthew Perry, the United States naval officer who reopened Japan to the western world in 1853

Among the Asian countries, Japan alone made the dramatic breakthrough to modern capitalism in the 19th century. With the overthrow of the Shogunate, Japan restored direct imperial rule in 1868 under 16-year-old Emperor Mutsuhito (known posthumously as Emperor Meiji—the name means "enlightened rule"). The capital of Japan was shifted from Kyoto to Tokyo and the country's new leaders quickly set about ending feudal privileges and creating markets for land, labor and capital.

The reforms led to several changes, including updating the tax system, setting up a central bank with the gold standard as the basis for money, introducing a company law and a commercial code based largely on European models, and establishing a political system based on constitutional rule and cabinet - government. Agricultural reforms dramatically improved productivity, thereby releasing surplus labor for manufacturing.

To be sure, Japan had suffered its own share of "unequal treaties" imposed by the United States, Russia, the Netherlands, Britain and France. In 1853 an American expedition led by Commodore Matthew Perry had sailed into Edo (Tokyo) Bay, demanding to establish commercial and diplomatic relations with Japan. While initial negotiations led to the opening of smaller ports in Shimoda and Hakodate, subsequent treaties opened to foreign trade several major Japanese cities, including the big ports of Kobe near Osaka and Yokohama near Tokyo. As in China, it was at these "treaty ports" that western banks were initially to establish themselves.

Japan's rapid industrialization in the later part of the century was in actual fact enhanced by these treaties, as tariffs were kept below five percent. According to the ADB study (see p. 20), "Openness brought many benefits; for instance, many

Banking in Shanghai

The Imperial Bank of China was set up in 1897 as China's first bank. It was also the first to issue notes. Other Chinese banks opened over the next decade, notably the Bank of Communications, although the development of local banks did not really take off until after the 1911 revolution.

Foreign banks had begun to appear in Shanghai much earlier, soon after the First Opium War in the 1840s. The British-chartered Oriental Banking Corporation, later renamed Asiatic Banking Corporation, was set up in Shanghai in 1847. It was followed 10 years later by another British bank, the Chartered Bank of India, Australia and China. With France expanding its influence in Indochina, the Comptoir d'Escompte de Paris opened a Shanghai operation in 1860, followed five years later by the British-controlled Hongkong and Shanghai Banking Corporation.

By 1894, there were nine foreign banks in Shanghai, including a newly established German concern, the Deutsche-Asiatische Bank, as well as Japan's Yokohama Specie Bank (later known as Bank of Tokyo). Within five years, a Russian institution, the Russo-Chinese Bank, was also operating, as was Paris-based Banque de l'Indochine.

Foreign banks not only aided in financing trade, they also led the development of Shanghai's financial markets in the late 19th and early 20th centuries, issuing their own bank notes and dominating the foreign exchange market, then focused largely on silver transactions.

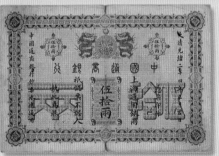

Hundred-tael note dated 1898; the Imperial Bank of China was the first Chinese commercial bank to issue paper money

Japanese diplomatic mission being given a spectacular welcome on the streets of New York City, 1860

of Japan's early technological advances were based on imported technologies brought in through foreign machinery and foreign experts. ... Private capital subject to the discipline of the international market overwhelmingly dominated Japan's export sector. The government focused on creating the conditions for modernization."

All these developments were not going unnoticed in the United States. In 1860, an 81-member Japanese diplomatic mission to Washington received a grand reception in New York City and paraded down Broadway in horse-drawn carriages. Expanding trade was accompanied by educational and cultural exchanges. By the turn of the century, Japan-related courses were being taught at the University of California and baseball clubs were mushrooming at universities and high schools all across Japan. At around the same time, Japanese exports of raw silk and tea were beginning to find bigger markets abroad. Imports were dominated by products such as cotton and machinery, two items that America was especially well placed to supply.

Japan's banking system

At the turn of the century, Japan was the only Asian country with a well-developed banking system. Under currency regulations passed in 1871, Japan began minting new money called "yen," whose value was pegged to the Mexican dollar, the standard unit for East Asian trade at the time. The Bank of Japan was set up in 1882 and within three years it was issuing its first yen banknotes convertible into silver. Under a new currency law passed in 1897 and after China paid the equivalent of 230 million taels of gold as reparations for the

From top: 20-yen gold coin, 1871; 1-yen gold coin, 1872; 1-yen silver coin for foreign trade, 1871

Sino-Japanese War of 1894–95, Japan moved to a gold standard. Another consequence of the war was the Japanese government's formation of the Bank of Taiwan in 1899 as a central bank for the island—Taiwan had been ceded to Japan as part of the peace treaty.

In the commercial banking sector, Dai-Ichi Bank was formed in 1872 as Japan's first state bank while Yokohama Specie Bank (later known as Bank of Tokyo) was set up under government auspices in 1880 with the twin objectives of acquiring silver and promoting Japanese exports.

Convertible banknotes were issued when the exchange rate between silver coins and banknotes was stabilized. This first Bank of Japan note, issued in May 1885, was convertible to silver coins

In the private sector, the well-established Mitsui merchant house, former bankers to the shoguns, set up a bank in 1876 and enjoyed exclusive use of tax revenues until the central bank was formed six years later. In the main commercial center of Osaka, the Sumitomo trading house set up a bank in 1895, although its money-changing roots went as far back as 1743. Mitsubishi Steamship Company, a relative newcomer, branched out into finance in 1880, the same year as the establishment of Yasuda Bank, later known as Fuji Bank.

Lyman J. Gage (seated center) and
Frank A. Vanderlip (second from right)
on board a revenue cutter in 1897

Among the Americans keenly following developments in Asia was one Frank A. Vanderlip. A former farm boy from Illinois, Vanderlip had risen to become financial editor of the *Chicago Tribune* before being brought to Washington in 1897 to work for Treasury Secretary Lyman J. Gage. Within six weeks, President McKinley had approved Vanderlip's appointment as assistant treasury secretary and after a few months he was put in charge of arranging a 200-million-dollar government bond issue to finance the war with Spain.

Shortly after the Spanish defeat in Manila Bay, Vanderlip wrote a magazine article on the Philippines, particularly on its commercial importance along with that of Japan's new colony in Taiwan: "It is as a base for commercial operations that the islands seem to possess the greatest importance. They occupy a favored location, not with reference to one part of any particular country of the Orient, but to all parts."

Following Japan's victory over China, "we buy more than 32 percent of Japan's exportable products, and we supply 12 percent of all the empire buys abroad," he wrote. But the United States' overall share of trade with the whole of Asia, estimated to be at two billion dollars a year, was only about seven percent, offering considerable scope for expansion. "There is a promising field for our manufactures of cotton in almost all countries of the Orient. Within a few years our exports of raw cotton to

Silver, gold and paper

After two and a half centuries of Spanish galleon trade between Manila and Acapulco, the silver Mexican dollar was the main unit of exchange for East Asian trade during the 19th century. But by the turn of the century, various government authorities in Japan, the Philippines, Singapore and India were minting their own coins, although the production of silver rupees at the Indian mints was temporarily halted in the 1890s. Hong Kong gave up minting its own coins and shipped the machinery off to Japan.

In China, both silver dollars and locally made ingots resembling Chinese shoes were in circulation. Silver ingots were measured in "taels," the word foreigners used for a Chinese weight which varied from city to city and market to market.

Both central banks and commercial banks issued their own notes. Although central banking was essentially limited to Japan and Taiwan in the early 20th century, a similar role was being played by the Imperial Bank of India. In China, both local

Hundred-dollar (Straits-dollar) note issued by The Chartered Mercantile Bank of India, London & China

and foreign banks were issuing notes; British colonial financial institutions were printing banknotes in Hong Kong and Singapore. Japanese yen pegged to the Mexican silver dollar were also circulating.

Around the turn of the century, silver prices began fluctuating wildly.

The Philippine monetary system was particularly confused, with daily fluctuations in gold-based and silver-based American and Mexican silver coins.

The first gold coin minted in the Philippines

A single monetary standard was clearly desirable. "With the villain identified as silver, all were agreed that the single standard must be gold—all except a few diehard bimetallists and the Chinese," wrote Frank King in his history of the Hongkong and Shanghai Bank. So, while monetary authorities from Japan, Thailand, Singapore and the Philippines adopted a gold standard, China and Hong Kong stuck with silver.

Total assets (1834–1901)

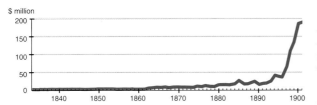

$ million

The balance sheet expanded tenfold in the first decade of Stillman's tenure, as he developed ties with big business and the Federal Treasury, and focused on investment banking and trade finance

Source: annual reports

James Stillman, president of National City Bank in 1891

Japan have doubled, and our trade with China has shown a marked tendency toward expansion. We have the bulk of the trade in mineral oils, although there is a growing competition with Russia, which may be greater when the trans-Siberian railroad is completed. American flour also has gained a foothold, and the growers of the hard wheat of California, the best shipping wheat in the world, look to the Far East as a future market for their exportable surplus."

Vanderlip recalled years later that when America and Spain signed their peace treaty, the same article was reprinted as a government pamphlet "so that the people would know what those things were for which we were paying the Spanish government 20 million dollars. As a matter of fact, it was probably with the same pen with which I wrote the article that I signed the five checks for four million dollars each."

While the eyes of the American public were now focused on Theodore Roosevelt—the assistant navy secretary, later vice president and eventually president—someone was watching Frank Vanderlip as well, as he later recalled. As he worked on that 200-million-dollar bond issue, unknown to him there had been fixed "the sharp and piercing eyes of James Stillman, the head of the biggest New York bank, the biggest bank in the United States."

Founded in New York in 1812, The National City Bank of New York had in 1898 led one of two syndicates that guaranteed the mammoth issue of war bonds arranged by Vanderlip, which he later described as "the most intensive clerical undertaking in which the government had ever engaged."

The City Bank of New York, as it was originally called, was a highly unlikely candidate for greatness: "It seemed more likely during the first quarter-century to earn a place in history by being one of the first banks in New York to fail," according to Citibank's official history. "The merchants who directed the bank subordinated its welfare to their own, using it to finance their own firms. This endangered the bank, ultimately pushing it to the brink of failure." What the bank did have going for it was location—New York was destined to become the financial capital of the United States and indeed the world. Demand for funds from New York merchants was a driving force behind the bank's establishment—in the early 19th century, finance had been more readily available in the old money centers of Philadelphia and Boston than it was in New York.

Prospects for setting up a new bank in New York greatly increased in 1811 when Congress voted against renewing the charter of the Bank of United States. America was about to go to war with Britain and many of its shares were held abroad. The vote reduced the number of banks in New York from six to five. Amid political

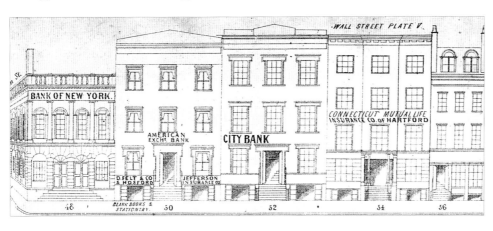

City Bank's office in 1850, as shown in the *New York Pictorial Business Directory of Wall Street*

Moses Taylor, president of City Bank of New York for 26 years

wrangling over chartering a new bank, republican statesman Samuel Osgood stepped in and proposed that the new bank should aim to "harmonize" the republicans who were then dominating politics in New York. The deal was such that there should be six directors from each of the two factions sitting on the board. The presidency was to go to Osgood who already had some banking experience. So on June 16, 1812, the City Bank of New York began life. Two days later, the United States declared war on Britain, and the new bank vigorously responded to the government's demand for funds.

After the war ended in 1815, the bank had difficulties adjusting to a peacetime economy. This led to a change of ownership in 1825, with merchant Charles Lawton acquiring a majority stake. But even with Lawton's involvement the bank failed to take advantage of the industrial development taking place in New York, and it was hit hard during the financial panic of 1837. At this point, Moses Taylor stepped in.

Taylor was a leading merchant and, after joining the board, soon began to diversify into commodity trading and shipping. He eventually became president of the bank in 1856, acquiring a controlling interest after that. But even under Taylor the bank failed to grow. "In sum," the official history said, "the bank acted largely as a treasury for Taylor's companies, taking deposits from firms with temporary cash surpluses and lending to those with a deficiency." By the time of his death in 1882, Taylor's personal fortune exceeded 33 million dollars—more than twice the assets of the bank. By 1891, the bank had slipped to twelfth place among New York's banks in terms of size. With the passing of the National Bank Act in 1864, City Bank of New York surrendered its state charter and became The National City Bank of New York in 1865.

It was under James Stillman that the bank really began to move forward. Stillman was the son of a wealthy cotton broker and a businessman in his own right. He joined the board of the bank in 1890 and became president the following year. He quickly set about building the bank into a major financial institution by expanding into the booming business of underwriting and distributing securities while forging close alliances with leading industrialists, notably William Rockefeller, the president of Standard Oil of New York. After a banking panic in 1893, Stillman actively supported government efforts to maintain the gold standard and he became an adviser to President Grover Cleveland. By 1897, the bank had set up a foreign exchange department and was also the biggest holder of government deposits. Stillman also enjoyed close ties with Treasury Secretary Lyman Gage, who was Vanderlip's boss.

President McKinley's first term was to expire in 1901. In early 1900, Gage informed Vanderlip that Stillman was keen to hire him at National City Bank. Vanderlip resigned from the treasury in early 1901, initially going on a four-month tour of Europe to meet bankers and finance ministers. When he got back, he joined the bank as vice president.

Working for the bank
• The office will open at 7 a.m. and close at 8 p.m. daily except on the Sabbath. Each employee is expected to spend the Sabbath attending church.
• Each employee will bring in a bucket of water and a scuttle of coal for the day.
• Make your pens carefully. Whittle the nibs to suit your taste.
• Men employees will be given an evening off each week for courting purposes, or two evenings if they regularly go to church.
• Any employee who smokes Spanish cigars, uses liquor in any form, gets shaved at a barber shop or frequents pool or public halls will give us good reason to suspect his worth, intentions, integrity and honesty.

Set of rules found in Citibank archives (from Walter Wriston, Risk and Other Four-Letter Words)

While the aspiring banker was traveling in Europe, a new bank had been chartered by the General Assembly of the State of Connecticut. America's victory in the war with Spain and its acquisition of the Philippines focused attention on the possibilities of developing trade with Asia. Among those whose interest was sparked was Marcellus Hartley, a successful merchant who had acquired the Remington Arms Company in 1888.

Marcellus Hartley, first president of IBC

Hartley first came to prominence during the American Civil War, when he was commissioned by the government of President Abraham Lincoln, made a brigadier general and given millions of dollars to buy arms in Europe through British merchant bank Baring Brothers. On his return to America, Hartley began his business in manufacturing arms and ammunition in Connecticut. He later founded an electric light company that he merged with the Westinghouse Electric Company, of which he became vice president. In around 1866 Hartley had also been associated with Moses Taylor in financing the first successful Atlantic cable, and was also chief investment officer of the Equitable Life Assurance Society.

The new bank that was chartered in Connecticut in June 1901 was called the International Company and Marcellus Hartley was the founding president. Four days before Christmas in 1901, it was renamed The International Banking Corporation. Its board of directors included prominent corporate lawyer Thomas Hubbard, who was also chairman, and several other businessmen, among them investment bankers Jules Bache and William Salomon, and representatives of the Equitable and Metropolitan insurance companies. After Hartley's death in January 1902, the IBC presidency went to Hubbard, who also remained chairman. Hubbard had earlier served as financial officer of the Southern Pacific Railroad.

As the next chapter will show, it was the establishment of a number of overseas branches in 1902 by the International Banking Corporation that formed the initial basis for Citigroup's first century of operations in Asia.

Wall Street at the turn of the century. The New York Custom House (left) was later remodeled and became the head office of The National City Bank of New York

1. The Early Years
1902–1929

"With the acquisition of the branches of The International Bank, we will have more branches and cover a wider territory than any bank in the world."

Frank A. Vanderlip

In March 1902, two months after the death of its founding president Marcellus Hartley, the International Banking Corporation (IBC) advised shareholders that developments were finally starting to take shape which would make it the first American bank with overseas branches. The timing was favorable. Stability seemed to be returning to China. The Empress Dowager and the imperial court, who had fled Beijing in the wake of the tumults of 1900, had just returned to the capital. Paving the way for the court's return was the signing of a peace treaty between China and the eight-nation military alliance of Europeans, the Americans and the Japanese. Among the terms of the treaty, signed at the Spanish legation on September 7, 1901, was the payment of an indemnity to cover the cost of the military expedition and the destruction of property associated with the Boxer Rebellion.

Although the agreement permitted the Allies to station military forces at 12 points along the Chinese coast, no territory was to be ceded. The outlook for the Qing Dynasty looked brighter than it had for years. The future Republican president Sun Yat-sen was in exile in Japan and a spirit of reconciliation between Chinese and foreigners was in the air.

The new century brought with it the promise of stability in the Philippines. After two years of fighting, the American William Howard Taft arrived in 1900 to set up a civilian administration, and quickly set about reforming the education system and improving sanitation, helping to check an outbreak of cholera that had probably been brought on by the war. "In the same year, as if to signify the re-establishment of a comfortable bourgeois routine, the Americans opened the first ice cream parlor in Manila," Philippine historian Raul Rodrigo observed. "The Americans were here to stay."

Resistance among the revolutionaries was fading. Attempts by their Japanese supporters to send arms had failed when the ship sank before reaching Manila. And in America, noisy opponents to the war suffered a major setback when President McKinley won a second term. America's "manifest destiny" of rejecting isolationism and becoming a Pacific power was starting to become a reality. In four years, the Philippines had suffered more than 250,000 casualties. General Martin Delgado, the rebel government leader who led a series of daring raids

Opposite: Interior of IBC's Harbin branch in northern China during the 1920s. Right: The swearing-in of William Howard Taft as the first American governor of the Philippine Islands

IBC president Thomas Hubbard, who oversaw the bank's early expansion in Asia

Five-yuan note issued in 1914 by the Bank of Communications, Shanghai

against the Americans, surrendered in early 1901. In March that year, self-proclaimed president Aguinaldo himself was captured and told his people to lay down their arms. "There has been enough blood, enough tears, enough desolation," he said.

In New York that same month, IBC president Thomas Hubbard advised shareholders that the bank had secured premises on Wall Street and would be moving there in April. Hubbard, who after the death of Marcellus Hartley had become president, announced some appointments: a general manager and an assistant general manager in New York, and a manager for one of the bank's first branches in Asia.

Two of the new appointees were experienced bankers from a well-established British bank, the Chartered Bank of India, Australia and China. Set up in 1853, it had been operating in Bombay, Calcutta, Shanghai, Hong Kong and Singapore for more than 40 years. John Lee, the new general manager in New York, had spent 22 years with Chartered Bank, including 19 in Asia. His colleague, R.W. Brown, selected to run the proposed IBC branch in Manila, had been with the same bank for 15 years. These initial hirings set the pattern for one of IBC's common practices in its early days in Asia—emulating the structure and raiding the staff of the British overseas banks. Indeed the general culture of the bank was similar to that of its British competitors, until significant numbers of American staff arrived in the 1930s, and until, later in the century, the bank pioneered the policy of promoting staff recruited in Asia to senior positions.

Apart from recruiting new staff, Hubbard had another piece of good news for shareholders. This involved a proposed branch in Shanghai and would prove to be historically significant. "The International Banking Corporation has been appointed fiscal agent of the United States government in China and is now acting on that appointment," he wrote. A week after the bank's London branch opened on April 15, 1902, Hubbard wrote a second letter to shareholders advising that "matters are progressing favorably in Shanghai" and that IBC had already appointed an agent, James Fearon, a respected merchant who then became Shanghai's founding manager.

When the Shanghai branch opened on May 15, 1902, IBC became the first American bank to have a presence anywhere in Asia. But it was one thing to have a bank—finding bankers to run it was an entirely different matter.

Candido Ozorio, who worked as chief clerk at the Shanghai branch, observed that while Fearon was a "highly respected merchant, he was not equipped with the knowledge of a fully-fledged banker." Being unfamiliar with the intricacies of foreign exchange transactions, he initially ran the business under telegraphic instructions from New York. Links were gradually extended to London and other new branches in Asia. Fearon left

The IBC branch in Shanghai opened in 1902. The first branch of an American bank in Asia was located in a converted warehouse on the corner of Fuzhou Road and Sichuan Road

Interior of IBC's Shanghai branch

Setting the books straight

The first Asian branch of an American bank took quite a few months to get into effective operation. So recorded Candido Ozorio, chief clerk at the Shanghai branch of IBC and National City Bank for 32 years.

The branch was first located in a converted warehouse on the corner of Fuzhou Road and Sichuan Road. Off the main room was a side room with an office for James Fearon, the founding manager. Yuen Yuen Kee, the first comprador (see p. 33), ran his own department in the back where the cashiers were.

Neither Fearon nor Edward Quelch, the branch's accountant, had any real idea how to run a bank. And none of the five clerks who completed the team were familiar with banking routines. Ozorio, a Portuguese veteran of the well-established Chartered Bank of India, Australia and China, decided to set things straight.

"To give an idea how crudely everything was carried on, not a single book was balanced for months. ... The first thing I asked for was a ledger. ... Of course, it was not produced. Then I

Ozorio in 1932 when he retired, after 30 years with the Shanghai branch

began to examine all the books they had. When the general ledger was brought to me, I found it to be a huge book requiring two coolies to carry. It was not a bank ledger but a commercial one—calculated to last a quarter of a century." After "some considerable work," Ozorio managed to balance the ledger before he turned to the bank's other books. "After putting every book in a spic and span order, a proper set of books—correctly ruled—arrived from London. ... They were all modeled after the Chartered Bank method. It was easy to transfer all the books ... as I was familiar with them, being in the Chartered Bank for 14 years. ... Having knowledge of the entire routine of bank work, I trained the International Bank staff to adopt and work with the system brought to them."

When, in 1940, Ozorio looked back on half a century in banking, this self-confessed "quill driver" was intensely proud of his achievements. "When I left the bank on retirement, the system of bookkeeping had reached its perfection."

IBC Shanghai as debt collector

As the only American bank in China at the time, the new IBC branch in Shanghai was designated to receive, on behalf of the United States government, indemnities payable by China for the costs of the Boxer uprising.

Under the 1901 treaty, Beijing agreed to pay the gold equivalent of 450 million taels of silver (equivalent to 67.5 million pounds, roughly 335 million U.S. dollars at the time).

The biggest claims came from Russia (29 percent) and Germany (20 percent), followed by France (16 percent) and Britain (11 percent). The American claim of 32.9 million taels was only seven percent of the total, about the same as the Japanese claim. Under the agreement, matters relating to the indemnities had to be handled in Shanghai, with each bank sending its foreign manager and its local comprador (see p. 17) to receive payments.

In 1908, the United States government decided to forgo outstanding payments from China. In exchange, the Chinese government agreed to send students to study in the United States, initially at a rate of 100 a year. Among those who went to America was Soong T.V., who graduated from Harvard, briefly worked in 1915 for IBC, and later became China's finance minister.

Indemnity-receiving banks

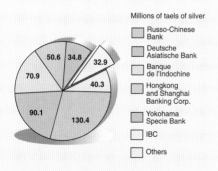

Millions of taels of silver

- Russo-Chinese Bank
- Deutsche Asiatische Bank
- Banque de l'Indochine
- Hongkong and Shanghai Banking Corp.
- Yokohama Specie Bank
- IBC
- Others

Source: People's Bank of China, America's Flower Flag Bank in China

Staff of the Hong Kong branch in 1906. Standing left to right are Tam Yiok Cho, Iu Chiu Chung, Iu Siu Boo, Iu Shau Sheang, Iu Ku and Ho Siu Po. Sitting are Mak Ysung Kai, Chan Cheuk Ting, Iu Ku Un (see p. 87), Kwok Yam Kai and Cheung Ho Kuen

A Portuguese legacy: the comprador

To some, compradors combined streetwise and patrician qualities, offering opium to prospective clients and highly motivated when it came to conducting business dealings. They were an essential lubricant between East and West.

Harbin branch comprador Key Mousen in 1921

"Comprador" is a Portuguese word which literally means "buyer." Portuguese traders first started appearing on the coast of India in the late 15th century. They captured Goa in 1510 before sailing south to take the Malay port of Malacca the following year. Within three decades, they had landed in Japan and in 1557 they established an important outpost on the south China coast. Over the next two centuries, Macau was to become an important hub for Portugal's maritime empire across Asia.

By the late 19th and early 20th centuries, compradors were not just buyers but also intermediaries. Each bank branch had its own comprador, a highly trusted individual in charge of the local side of the business. In fact, one of the most famous of IBC's earliest compradors looked after Japanese affairs. Kan Tong-po was the first comprador at the Kobe branch, which opened in 1904. He later founded the Bank of East Asia in Hong Kong, which by the end of the 20th century was the territory's biggest locally owned bank.

"The comprador pledged to mortgage his house and his kids or anything else, made … and guaranteed all the loans," said Walter B. Wriston, the bank's chairman in later years. "Because they [the compradors] were so short of capital they basically invented the way to handle acceptances.

Keeping customers satisfied

"On entering our bank or any other bank in China, foreign or native, there was always a sweet smell hanging in the atmosphere. This was opium," Daniel De Menocal wrote in his memoir.

"Our comprador had a small office where he received his daily customers and they were offered a drag on the pipe—just as he might tender a highball, cocktail or glass of beer under similar circumstances. This was a custom of the country and generally accepted without criticism."

According to De Menocal, opium use was "very rare" among the actual Chinese employees, as opposed to customers. "No foreigners ever smoked opium in our circle of friends—except some screwball who would be likely to do the same sort of thing in secret wherever he might be."

Staff, including the comprador (front row, third from left), in the main doorway of the Guangzhou branch around 1915.
The foundation stone on the left was laid by De Menocal. The building was still standing at the end of the 20th century

It started with a bill on London before that time obviously. But these guys turned it into a fine art."

Raymund A. Kathe, one of the first Chinese-speaking managers, had first-hand knowledge of the role of the comprador. He spent the greater part of his long career in Asia, before retiring in 1984, the same year as Walter Wriston. He noted that the comprador system was not limited to banks.

Torture

In the chaos surrounding the fall of the Qing dynasty in 1911, the Chinese comprador at the Beijing branch disappeared for several months. In the words of the American banker Daniel De Menocal (see p. 35),"He was a loyal and devoted member of our staff, and I was much disturbed." It turned out that he had been thrown into jail and tortured, although he was eventually released and returned to the bank.

"Most of the foreign businesses had compradors—the oil companies, the trading companies," he recalled. "Business to a foreigner was so mysterious in Asia that the comprador system was considered a necessity. As a result, in northern Asia and even Japan, there was a comprador system. … The latter was so mysterious and so different that we used Chinese intermediaries to deal with Japanese in their own country.

"The comprador usually put up a fairly good amount of collateral. He was a man of some means, normally. He would pledge a certain amount of his assets—maybe most of them—then he would go out and find clients and bring them in. He'd take his cut from them. We never really knew what he was taking and we'd finance them.

"The comprador also took care of the cash department in our branches—the tellers. He guaranteed all the tellers so we never had frauds or losses." As a result, most of the people working in the cash department were related, "something we

never permitted in the bank in the U.S. … So all those people were loyal to the comprador and therefore they didn't cheat or steal. And it worked just fine—he would bring in the large, native clients that we didn't know very much. And he guaranteed them. But we had to have some kind of idea because the comprador wasn't necessarily rich enough to guarantee everything. He would tell us so-and-so was all right, and we did a reasonably good business if the comprador was competent."

For Kathe, trading companies performed some of the same functions in post-war Japan. "For Japanese banks, to some extent the trading company stands in between and takes the risks of the marketplace. … Many of the transactions you finance in the banks today really are nothing more than pass-throughs in the trading companies to the ultimate users of funds," he recalled.

Compradors also provided valuable continuity. While the bank's Shanghai branch had more than a dozen managers in its first 38 years, it had only three compradors in that time: Yuen Yuen Kee, Wong Ching Chung and Woo Pei Choo.

Song Kim Pong

Mr. Song Kim Pong

The comprador in Singapore was born on the island in 1865. He worked as assistant cashier for 16 years for another bank before being appointed comprador of IBC's Singapore branch on its establishment in 1902. This photograph was taken five years later.

the bank in mid-1903 but obviously made a mark, real banker or not. "During the period he was at the helm, the bank was prospering every month and business in all departments increased slowly but surely," wrote Ozorio. "More assistants were employed, more brokers called for business, more inter-branch transactions were done, more clients patronized the bank and the International Bank became a real live institution."

Silver Mexican dollars

In Shanghai, Fearon was succeeded by John Lee, who arrived as the general manager from New York on an inspection tour in 1903 and decided to stay on for a year. "He was a live wire and a perfect wizard in finance. The business increased by leaps and bounds," Ozorio wrote. Lee was apparently obsessed by the foreign exchange market, especially by opportunities for arbitrage. In addition to trading in sterling and other currencies and precious metals, he shipped silver Mexican dollars to Singapore and imported bars of silver from India. "It made one dizzy to witness his transactions. ... In all this business he never lost a cent. His subtle mind never missed a chance to make a profit."

Lee was evidently a hard act to follow. John Longmire, the next manager, was a "cautious man" and he was succeeded by J.K. Moor, described as a "steady plodder" who never took any risks. But business grew at a reasonable pace and profits rose during the three-year period after Lee's departure.

As the foreign exchange business was developing in Shanghai, IBC's head office in New York had hired Wilhelm Pannenborg and Bernard Duis, two brilliant and experienced traders from the Berlin-based Deutsche Bank. At that time IBC's rented offices were located on the second floor of a drugstore, and were reached by a dark and narrow wooden staircase, according to Daniel De Menocal, one of the first employees. There were two windows overlooking Trinity Church and another two overlooking Broadway. The small space had offices for John Hubbard, the president's son and the bank's treasurer, and Chas Palmer, a West Point graduate and

A non-performing loan

The early activities of the Manila branch weren't limited to acting as fiscal agent for Washington or just doing trade finance. One of the first clients was a small traveling circus. It was already in debt to the bank when it was stuck by a typhoon that destroyed most of its assets.

"The branch management concluded further funds would have to be advanced ... if the original loan was to be salvaged. So to protect the bank's interests,

Boies C. Hart, later vice president in charge of Asian activities

a young officer was assigned to be ticket seller and cashier," recounted Boies C. Hart, who had joined the bank in 1916 and traveled widely across Asia on visits to various branches. "The star and mainstay of the circus' attraction was a charming woman trapeze artist whose popularity gave every promise of paying off the debt. This lovely performer and the ticket-seller-cashier fell in love and promptly began 'infanticipating.' That canceled the trapeze act and the circus blew up."

Staff of Hsing Cheng Bank in Shanghai, the first commercial bank established by the Chinese

Rosario Street in the old Binondo district, Manila. IBC began operations at No. 86 in July 1902

retired army captain. Palmer had just returned from the Philippines and was helping to get the Manila business established. Neither had any banking experience.

"The rest of the premises provided a stage for these two remarkable Germans to rush about, to shout commands to everyone within earshot, to battle over the telephone with brokers, dealers and competitors in the foreign exchange market," Daniel De Menocal wrote in his memoirs. "Their speed, their fury of their attack on the days' problems was unlike anything I had seen before." De Menocal was impressed by "their sure knowledge of the arbitrage of exchanges and bullion throughout the world, their confidence, their accuracy, their speed, their impatience (it seemed) with everybody else and their drive."

The son of Cuban and Spanish parents, De Menocal was attached to the two traders as an assistant in his early twenties. What he found and experienced in New York was similar to the situation described by Ozorio in Shanghai. "There was a great purchases and sales register that had never been totaled. So I was put in a room for three days and I added and added all day long from page to page from morning until evening. At times, I became so exhausted I could hardly bear to look at the figures. But the lesson was learned. I supposed this is the way these men had been trained by German drill sergeants." De Menocal said his apprenticeship lasted about

IBC's first Singapore premises: No. 1, Prince Street. In 1923 the bank moved to nearby Ocean Building

12 hours every day with "cables to be recorded, most intricate calculations in the arbitrage of international exchanges to be verified, errands to be run and great piles of drafts and great piles of shipping documents to be examined instantly on delivery." Duis was to head the foreign division of IBC's future parent, National City Bank; Pannenborg ended up running Deutsche Bank in the Netherlands. De Menocal was shipped out to Asia.

Two months after the Shanghai branch began operations, IBC opened a branch in Singapore on July 1, and another in Manila in the same month. The fourth followed in Yokohama on October 8 and a fifth in Hong Kong on December 15. Calcutta was next, with a second Indian branch opening in Bombay at the beginning of 1904. Also in 1904 a second Straits Settlements branch was opened in Penang, although this was soon closed. In August 1904, second branches were also opened in Japan in Kobe, in China in Guangzhou, and in the Philippines in Cebu.

After that, no further branches were opened in Asia until 1909, when the third and fourth Chinese branches were established in Beijing and Hankou; Hankou later became part of the inland industrial metropolis of Wuhan.

De Menocal was the first American recruit to be trained in New York and sent to Asia. He set sail for Hong Kong in early

Hong Kong branch in 1909. The building was located on the corner of Ice House Street and Queen's Road Central

"Admired and respected"—the abacus

1904. The 31-day voyage from San Francisco took him to Honolulu, several Japanese ports, and Shanghai on the way. "It was surprising at Nagasaki to see the ship coaled by little Japanese girls and women in an endless chain carrying the coal from the pier to the bunker in small wicker baskets," he wrote. "Nearby, there was a Japanese naval ship guarding two Russian vessels captured off Shimonoseki Straits just the day before, which was the overt act of war." (See p. 37.)

In Hong Kong, De Menocal found himself working under branch manager Charles Scott with about half a dozen London-trained British who had already completed their apprentice-ships lasting several years. The branch also had about a dozen Chinese employees who reported to the comprador. "The Chinese handled all the cash and at the close of business, reconciled their balance with that of the European-controlled ledgers," De Menocal recalled. "I had a high stool before a teak wood desk upon which rested several ledgers which I had to post and to keep in balance. It required some time before I even understood how these various books—when combined—reflected the overall position of the bank. All entries were made in pen and ink, and these young Britishers all had extremely good handwriting."

Adding machines "were generally looked upon with contempt as noisy, probably inaccurate"—unlike the abacus, which "never ceased to be admired and respected." Clear handwriting was absolutely compul-sory, as a group of fresh American graduates soon found out when they

Umezono and Umezono

One of the first employees of the Kobe branch, opened in 1904, was Hirozo Umezono, who became the biggest foreign exchange trader in western Japan. His son Tatsuo joined the bank some 40 years later, eventually becoming the first Japanese manager of Citibank in Japan.

In the early 20th century, Kobe was the main entry for imports of cotton from the United States and India and wool from Australia—Japan's major textile mills were in nearby Osaka. Yokohama, where IBC had its first Japanese branch, was more an export center for tea grown in nearby Shizuoka. Another big export was raw silk from Maebashi, the huge spinning center north of Tokyo.

Umezono senior spent more than two decades with the bank, moving to the Osaka branch after it opened in 1925. "My father probably decided to move to Osaka because the foreign exchange market was bigger," the younger Umezono recalled more than 70 years later. "He left the bank in 1928 to become an independent broker, although most of his business was still with IBC and the Yokohama Specie Bank."

Tatsuo Umezono said his father, during his time with the bank, dealt mainly with the big Japanese trading companies based in Osaka, such as Itochu and Tomen. The latter was formed in 1920 when Mitsui decided to spin off its cotton-importing business as a separate company.

Harbin in 1930. Russian signs were common in this northern Chinese city, which had a large population of emigrants from the Soviet Union

Black dragons and bears

Russians call it the Amur River. In Chinese, it's the Heilongjiang, or "Black Dragon River." In 1901, a group of ultra-nationalist Japanese named themselves after this river, which forms much of China's long border with Russia. Founded in 1901, the Black Dragon Society pressed the Japanese government to oppose Russia's growing influence south of the river. It also supported revolutionaries such as China's Sun Yat-sen and Emilio Aguinaldo of the Philippines.

Although China ceded the Liaodong peninsula to Japan at the end of the Sino-Japanese War in 1895, pressure from Russia, France and Germany forced Tokyo to relinquish the southern Manchurian claim, its greatest prize in the war. Many Japanese were furious when in 1898 Russia obtained a 25-year lease on Port Arthur and Dalian, on the southern tip of the peninsula. Over the next three years, Russia exacted Chinese consent to extend the trans-Siberian railroad across northern Manchuria through Harbin, gaining a shortcut to Vladivostok. Russia pushed to extend the new northern Manchurian line to the south through Shenyang (Mukden) and its new possessions at Port Arthur and Dalian.

Russian expansion divided the Japanese government. One faction wanted Tokyo to accommodate the Russians in exchange for Moscow's respecting Japanese influence in Korea. But an anti-Russian faction believed Japan's interests would be better served through an alliance with Britain and it was this group that prevailed. After the Anglo-Japanese Alliance of 1902, Russia promised to withdraw its troops from Manchuria but failed to comply. In early 1904, Tokyo severed ties with Moscow. Two days later, the Japanese navy attacked the Russian fleet at Port Arthur and war was declared. Although the Japanese army had limited successes, the Imperial Navy scored a major victory with the destruction of the Russian Baltic Fleet in waters off Korea and Japan in 1905.

Under the Treaty of Portsmouth signed later that year, Japan gained exclusive rights over Korea (which it annexed in 1910) and the southern half of the island of Sakhalin. Most importantly, it got Russia's leases on Port Arthur and Dalian plus control over the southern Manchuria railroads.

Only a minority of Japanese opposed the war, which cost 1.5 billion yen—mostly financed by banks in London and New York. For most Japanese, the war embodied the independence that had been the national goal since the Shogunate was overthrown in 1868. For British writer H.G. Wells, the war was "an epoch in the history of Asia, the close of the period of European arrogance." Only a decade earlier, Russia, France and

Germany had refused to recognize Japan's renaissance. In their "pursuit of new Indias in Asia," they prevented Japan from reaping any fruits from the war with China. But now, "the European invasion of Asia was coming to an end and the retraction of Europe's tentacles was beginning."

Russia's defeat by Japan was followed by Germany's withdrawal from the Chinese port of Qingdao at the outbreak of World War I in 1914, leaving the city under Japanese influence for the next three decades.

Although IBC had only two branches in China when Russia was defeated, Japan's expanding influence in Manchuria and Shandong province became a focus of new business opportunities. After opening in Tianjin in 1916, IBC set up new branches in Harbin and Qingdao (1919), followed by Dalian (1923) and Shenyang (1928). The last two were on the South Manchuria Railway, run by a Japanese company which eventually dominated economic life in the area until the Nissan conglomerate took over local heavy industry in the 1930s.

The IBC branch building in Harbin (see also p. 108)

The IBC clubhouse on Cheung Chau island, an hour's ride by ferry from Hong Kong, in 1922. According to *Number Eight*, the bungalow, high on the rocks overlooking the sea, was "equipped with all the things necessary for holiday and weekend parties"

arrived in London for a year's training before being sent east. "Their handwriting was so bad that London office could make no use of their services and they were all sent to an English school to be taught how to write before they could touch pen to paper," De Menocal said. At the close of business each day, the Chinese cashiers would quickly count the Hong Kong colony's bank notes before weighing sacks of silver coins from all corners of the world. "Every individual coin would be sounded to test its purity in silver. This tinkling and ringing would go on for an hour or more in the afternoon and practically every day some half dozen counterfeits would be returned to the sending bank."

After learning the ropes in Hong Kong, De Menocal moved up the Pearl River to Guangzhou where in 1904 he opened IBC's second Chinese branch. Initially housed in a small building, the bank later shifted to a newly constructed, more palatial headquarters located on the islet of Shamian. "All the American missionaries in the district were depositors, and we did an active business negotiating bills of exchange, financing shipments of raw silk and other native exports," he said. "We imported substantial amounts of bar silver from San Francisco, which the Chinese bankers melted down."

Americans and Russians

The American consul general in Hong Kong was finding it difficult to adapt. "He came from somewhere in the deep south," Daniel De Menocal recalled. "He wore his hat in his office, and soft high boots almost to his knees were visible as he kept his feet resting on the consular desk. He spat a great deal and appeared to be generally angry about everything."

There were other reminders of the United States, very appealing to lonely Englishmen and Scotsmen far from home. "Up the street provided for every need," according to De Menocal, who described a "commodious house" with a bar, a piano, newspapers and "a collection of bonnie and seductive lassies practically all from California."

The Russians were relative newcomers to China too. De Menocal recounted how the bored foreign residents of Guangzhou were "always delighted" when American, British or German naval vessels anchored in town. There were also occasional calls from the Russian Navy "who after 24 hours would find almost all their crew in their white naval uniforms spread all over our bund and gardens, completely unconscious."

Russian diplomatic behavior in Beijing was even more colorful than that of the American. When posted to the new Beijing branch, De Menocal described the minister at the Russian diplomatic mission as an "evil-looking man, abrupt, short of speech" with a beautiful wife and daughter. "He was supported by a motley crew. The first secretary had a great hole in his head between the eyes and the hairline resulting from poor aim with his revolver in a suicide attempt." The minister entertained guests in a "barn-like" mission where nothing was served except tea and standard drinks.

But the work was light and the heat was intense for most of the year—which may explain why Guangzhou had the longest bar in China at the time outside of Shanghai. "Drinking at the close of the day was likely to be somewhat overdone," he said. But "there was never any overt drunkenness as we were all young, in our late 20s, so we could carry a tremendous amount of whisky and gin without slopping over." De Menocal ultimately went to Beijing, where he witnessed the collapse of the Qing Dynasty in 1911 and the inauguration of China's first president.

Daniel De Menocal in Guangzhou

During this period, IBC was consolidating its position in Asia, particularly in the area of trade finance. In Japan, the Kobe branch financed Japanese imports of cotton from India and wool from Australia while the Yokohama branch financed exports of raw silk and tea. From India, the Calcutta and Bombay branches financed shipments of cotton and jute. In the Philippines, the Manila branch had been acting as a depository for the American colonial government, although this role was eventually transferred to a bank set up by the Philippine government itself. At the same time, IBC in Manila also played a major role in financing imports from the United States as well as exports of local commodities ranging from hemp and copra to sugar, tobacco and coconut oil. The Singapore branch focused on exports of tin and rubber from neighboring Malaya, although here the bank acknowledged that competition was "exceptionally severe" among the British, French, Japanese, Dutch and American banks.

In the new Republic of China, export opportunities were beginning to grow, although foreign exchange trading in Shanghai would remain the paramount business. The new

Revolution

As the political situation in Beijing grew tense, there were reports of Manchus leaving the capital in big numbers.

"We knew the revolution was slowly and steadily putting on pressure. But both sides wanted to cultivate good relations with the foreigners who had the money. So we were not too uneasy," wrote De Menocal. The remnants of the Qing Dynasty were holed up in the palace under the protective custody of General Yuan Shikai, who became China's first president after the dynasty's collapse.

"The political situation was chaotic. The revolution was advancing from the south. ... In the evening after sunset, there were every day now some sounds of gunfire. ... Then one night about ten o'clock, the firing became really heavy. Over our heads there was the constant whine of streams of bullets crossing our courtyard, accompanied by the thump of exploding shells and a general uproar in the main street in brilliant light as flames from apparently everywhere seemed to surround us." When the banker and his wife climbed on to the roof of their gate house, they saw Chinese soldiers looting shops and smashing kerosene lamps.

"The entire city as far as we could see was blanketed by fire and smoke," he said. The looting turned out to be a mutiny by General Yuan's soldiers whose pay was long overdue. "I made my way to the Chinese Ministry of Telegraphs, found it still open and sent on to our head office probably the first cablegram to get through to New York to reassure them at home that their assets and our own personal safety had been protected."

The Spanish-Filipino Bank in Manila

Staff from IBC's Beijing branch

branch in Hankou was particularly well located as the area was a major tea center, and also an important producer of cotton, leather and oil seeds. Hankou also had a Japanese-controlled ironworks and it was linked by rail to both the Japanese and Russian railroads in the north. In the south, where the bank now had two branches, the main items for export were raw silk, tea and cotton from Guangzhou, and textiles, sugar, flour and metal from Hong Kong.

The year 1914 was significant in the history of IBC. In the United States, the Federal Reserve Act came into effect, and introduced a new era of American overseas banking. The histories of IBC and National City Bank began to converge. Until then, federally chartered banks had been prevented from operating abroad or making acceptances. IBC was a state-chartered bank—it was allowed to open branches anywhere as long as they weren't in Connecticut. Furthermore, the need to finance the World War in Europe also fostered the expansion of American banks abroad and the creation of an American market for acceptances. Indeed, there might not have been very rapid progress in either had it not been for the war.

In 1901 National City Bank president James Stillman had brought former assistant treasury secretary Frank Vanderlip to New York to join him as vice president (see p. 26). Vanderlip had rapidly expanded the business. In 1908, Stillman offered him the presidency, becoming the bank's first chairman and retaining financial control. Stillman took himself off to live in Paris, leaving Vanderlip to run the bank's operations.

Vanderlip played a major role in writing the legislation for the Federal Reserve Act, although the initial draft did not get through Congress. Even before the legislation was actually passed at the end of 1913, Vanderlip had been interested in the idea of foreign banking and had sent an assistant to South America in 1909 to assess the potential profitability of branch operations there. Interestingly, he had also written to Stillman the same year about the possibility of eventually acquiring control of IBC, although it is doubtful whether this would have been legally possible at the time. Stillman himself had invested personally in a Cuban bank established by a group of

Banking for Amex

One of IBC's first correspondent banking relationships between the United States and Asia is believed to have been with the American Express Company.

Correspondence from 1908 reveals the American Express Company confirming arrangements for local-currency drafts at the Hong Kong, Yokohama and Manila branches of IBC. At the same time, the New York head office of IBC agreed to supply American Express with daily foreign exchange rates for yen in Yokohama and Kobe, for Hong Kong dollars in Hong Kong and Guangzhou, and for both pesos and U.S. dollars in Manila and Cebu.

Trowel used by Daniel De Menocal in 1908 to lay the foundation stone of IBC's new building in Guangzhou

American financiers in 1905. He also had a stake in the Farmers' Loan and Trust Company, like IBC a state-chartered institution, which had opened branches in London and Paris.

With the passing of the new legislation, Vanderlip decided to move quickly to gain an edge on his competitors. In November 1914, National City Bank opened a branch in Buenos Aires, the first foreign branch of a federally chartered American bank. A second branch opened in Rio de Janeiro in April 1915 and a third in Montevideo in August.

As Vanderlip ·was expanding his Latin American branch network, the IBC president Thomas Hubbard died, having overseen the IBC's development for 13 years. His death occurred on May 19. Stockbroker Jules Bache, among the original shareholders, was apparently one of the first to sell his stock. By October 21, Vanderlip was able to cable Stillman in Paris with the news that he had· completed the acquisition of a controlling stake in IBC. "Nothing will be done probably for the present, or at least as long as I can keep it quiet," he wrote to Stillman the next day. "Just how it will be best to handle it I have not yet decided and will do nothing at all for the present— except to go on accumulating the stock but quietly keeping in touch with the management." A week later,

Left: Early premises occupied by IBC in Calcutta. Above: Staff at work in the Bombay branch

Manchu pearl fever

With loud rumbles being heard from Chinese revolutionary forces in the south, the days of the Manchu dynasty were numbered. "One day, a decree was issued from the palace which removed from the court full-dress uniform the pearl that had always decorated both the officials and their wives," wrote De Menocal. Foreign banks in Beijing were immediately advised of large letters of credit being opened, mainly in francs but also in dollars and pounds.

Before long, "principal dealers in jewelry from all the great markets of the world" began to arrive in Beijng. "In our own bank, we set aside one room exclusively for their

use, and even had the ceiling at one end replaced by a glass studio window to provide them with the desired light. Most of these experts were French and soon the market was boiling. At the French Banque de l'Indochine, they were taking in millions.

"One of these buyers ... show[ed] me what he had purchased ... pearls—perfect in shape and large to very large in size, and of many varied and beautiful shades. ... It was curious to think that these very jewels— which we had perhaps seen decorating these noble ladies from the Forbidden City—might one evening have greeted us with a smile of recognition as they adorned the neck of some avid American beauty."

feet. It has a serviceable and well tried-out staff, although not a brilliant one, and it has a machine that we will be able to develop and make great use of."

In January 1916, Vanderlip wrote to Stillman that the IBC "is coming on most satisfactorily and is working in harmony with the bank in mutual advantage." Six months later, it was "doing better than it ever did before. It is obvious that we made a very advantageous purchase." Vanderlip said he wanted to bring IBC's New York office to National City Bank headquarters as soon as possible. "But it is now fairly clear in my mind that we will continue the organization, at least for some time, rather than attempt to absorb it directly into the bank. It must work, however, in the closest cooperation with the bank.... That is going to be helpful to the bank, and greatly strengthen its own position."

By 1917, it became apparent that the investment was paying off. IBC profits accounted for three-quarters of foreign branch earnings of two million dollars in 1916, with the remainder coming from branches set up by National City Bank itself. And by the end of 1917, overseas assets had grown to 177 million dollars, almost a fifth of total assets.

however, news of the purchase leaked and it was widely reported in New York newspapers. Vanderlip believed the purchase was "substantially below the book value" and was extremely enthusiastic.

"We are going to have a development beyond anything either of us have dreamed of in former days," he wrote to Stillman on October 29. "With the acquisition of the branches of the International Bank, we will have more branches and cover a wider territory than any bank in the world. I can see how it is possible and very probable that within a short time comparatively, the City Bank will have a well ordered branch in every important center in the world outside the United States. We have got it at a time when it has really gotten pretty well on its

With the outbreak of World War I in Europe in 1914, the bank rushed to make sure that cotton exports from the United States were adequately financed. It also made use of its new acceptance powers, with total acceptances outstanding rising to 20 million dollars by mid-1917. However, in the financing of wartime trade, it remained well behind its

A Japanese war loan

In 1908, the Japanese consul in New York forwarded to National City Bank president James Stillman a diploma for a Third Class Distinguished Order of the Rising Sun. The letter mentioned that the order was conferred on Stillman "some time ago" but the consul didn't elaborate, apart from saying that he was forwarding the diploma on behalf of Japanese Foreign Minister

Tadasu Hayashi. Stillman's biographer, Anna Robeson Burr, suggested that the order was "probably in recognition of his assistance in floating a Japanese war loan through the City Bank," and Hayashi's background indicated this was almost certainly so. As minister at the Japanese embassy in London from 1900, he played an important role in negotiating the Anglo-Japanese Alliance which paved the way for the war with Russia.

Ten-dollar and one-dollar notes issued by IBC in 1918 and 1919 respectively

arch-rival J.P. Morgan, which was the purchasing agent for the British and French governments.

In the event, the war delayed National City Bank's attempts to buy out the minority shareholders of IBC. Although amounting to less than one percent, the biggest single outstanding stake of 304 shares was that formerly held by Belgium's King Leopold. But he had died and the stock had been transferred to a baroness who had in turn transferred the stake to a Belgian village now occupied by the Germans. To complicate matters, the share certificates were in London in the Bank of England vaults and could not be touched until after the war. German ownership was claimed but this was challenged by the Belgian government in exile. Lawyers were called in but by 1919 the war was over and new negotiations had begun with the Belgian Finance Ministry. National City Bank finally acquired the stake held by La Fondation de Niederfulbach in mid-1919 for 91,200 dollars. The offer of 300 dollars a share was three times their face value. The price valued IBC at 9.75 million dollars, almost 40 percent more than the previous year's earnings of National City Bank as a whole.

IBC corporate seal after The National City Bank acquired a controlling interest

The IBC acquisition soon brought an exotic air to the staff magazine in New York. Until now *Number Eight* (the name came from National City Bank's numerical designation by the New York Clearing House) had been a largely parochial affair. The opening of new branches and the construction of new branch buildings—frequently palatial affairs with classical façades—provided the perfect opportunity to acquaint the American readership with the mysterious Far East.

Six years after acquiring control of IBC, National City Bank became increasingly global in outlook. Apart from the 1913 law permitting federally chartered banks to operate internationally,

America's public interest in China was also fueled by political developments following the establishment of the Republic of China in 1912. The number of Chinese students coming to the United States also increased. And America's trade with China was filling the gap left by Europeans distracted by a devastating war at home.

In February 1921, *Number Eight* announced that its "distinguished visitors of the month" had included a large Chinese silk mission to New York. Among the delegates from the three Shanghai and Shandong silk guilds were Ting Juling, owner of Yung Yue Silk Filature Company, and May Zungsung, owner of May Han Yue Silk Company. During the visit, the Americans attempted to standardize the reeling and grading of Chinese silk for American importers, who preferred Japanese grades and had therefore been reluctant to buy the Chinese product.

IBC basketball champions in Manila, 1920

Left: The Yokohoma branch before the 1923 earthquake. Above: Red Reed (left) and a colleague survey the damage the following day
Right: Reed at the entrance of the bank's temporary tent accommodation

A tough afternoon in Yokohama

A devastating earthquake struck the Yokohama branch as it was preparing to close one Saturday morning in 1923. John T.S. ("Red") Reed was among the survivors.

"It was just three minutes to 12 when the first shock came. It was more violent than any we had experienced before. ... When I looked up from my desk—and saw a large pillar supporting the upper floors start to break in two—I knew the building was coming down. ... I can remember running up the floor as though it was the slanting deck of a ship. Then everything went black.

"When I came to, I was in darkness, covered with debris and suffocating from the dust. For one instant, I thought it was all over with me ... The whole building had collapsed flat as a pancake. It was a mass of jumbled brick and timber."

With fires spreading across the city, Reed and other survivors headed for the waterfront two blocks away, diving into the sea when the heat became unbearable.

"It was a tough afternoon," Reed recalled. "We clung to a log, pretty well exhausted. Worst of all, we were drifting to sea." Just when it seemed impossible to hang on any longer, they hailed a lifeboat which took them to the *Empress of Australia* tied up at the end of the dock. The ship was "crowded to the gunwales with survivors, most of

whom were separated from husbands, wives or children—all missing and probably dead. On top of that situation came another harrowing experience. The entire surface of the water was covered with a heavy layer of black oil from the large tanks of oil companies that had burst open. Sometime during the day, we noticed what appeared to be a pillar of fire, perhaps 200 feet high, moving along the water close to shore. A barge had caught fire and ignited the oil. This column of flame moved along the shore until it reached the dock to which we were moored and then proceeded toward the ship. Frantic efforts were made to cast off. But the anchor chain or hawser of the steamer next to us had got caught in our propellers and it was impossible to get the boat away.

"Meanwhile, the dock—which was tilted at a crazy angle—was fueled with refugees who by now were cut off from the shore. Finally our steamer cast off her moorings and began to edge away from the dock. The fire was so close that it was too hot to stand on that side of the ship. Efforts by the crew to keep the fire hose playing on the woodwork were almost useless.

"It was a terrifying spectacle to

watch—people left screaming on the dock, our boat drifting slowly, so slowly, away from this tower of flame bearing down upon us. It was only by the narrowest of margins that the big steamer drifted out into the bay ahead of the fire."

The tent was upgraded to a shack (above), which was in turn replaced by a temporary concrete-and-steel structure. A new permanent branch building was completed in 1930

"The great European powers, which have such a strong hold on the Chinese trade, are concentrating their attention on matters close to home," wrote a Commerce Department official who accompanied a Chinese Trade Commission visiting in 1915. "The United States, which has always been considered by the Chinese to be their friend, is therefore in a position to take over a large part of the trade which has heretofore gone to its competitors.

"Aside from the practical business results," the official enthused, "this trade visit has done more to awaken among the American people an appreciation of the sterling qualities of the Chinese race than any other event in the relationship of the two republics."

By 1915, when National City Bank acquired its majority stake in IBC, there were already a dozen IBC branches in Asia— four in China, two each in Japan, the Philippines and India, along with another two branches in Hong Kong and Singapore (the second Straits Settlement branch in Penang had since closed). After the opening of a fifth Chinese branch in Tianjin in 1916, the bank moved to tackle the Dutch banks on their home turf rather than competing in Singapore. Two branches were set up in 1918—in Batavia (today's Jakarta), and in Surabaya, eastern Java. IBC then further challenged the British banks by establishing a new branch in 1919 at Rangoon, at that time administered as part of British-controlled India.

The opening of the new branch in Rangoon coincided with Mahatma Gandhi's entry into politics, and the start of his campaign in opposition to the British colonial rule. The same year, 1919, saw a further strengthening of IBC's network in China, despite growing unrest among students protesting against the expansion of Japanese influence. In August, a new branch was opened in the northern frontier city of Harbin on the Japanese-controlled railways, where thousands of anti-Bolshevik Russians had fled following the Soviet revolution in 1917.

In October 1919, IBC opened another branch in Qingdao, a former German naval port which Japan had occupied at the beginning of the war. Under the Versailles Treaty signed at the end of World War I, Japan had obtained the former German lease to Qingdao, triggering massive protests by Chinese students in Beijing in May. Among the student leaders was a young Mao Zedong, and the so-called May 4 Movement would reverberate through Chinese history for the rest of the 20th century.

Four years later, in 1923, IBC finally opened a branch in the Japanese capital. The timing was fortuitous: eight months later the nearby Yokohama branch was reduced to a heap of rubble after a massive earthquake centered on the area south of Tokyo. Nearly 143,000 people lost their lives.

The bank opened its fourth Japanese branch in 1925 in Osaka, the big western metropolis near Kobe. The growing Japanese economic presence in northeast China had meanwhile prompted the establishment of another branch at Dalian on the South Manchuria Railway line in 1923.

The relationship between James Stillman and Frank Vanderlip dramatically soured in 1917 as a result of losses of millions of dollars sustained by National City Bank in Russia.

Staff numbers then and now		
	1918	2001
China	131	188
India	125	3,155
Hong Kong	74	3,384
Japan	74	10,212
Philippines	74	1,601
Singapore	20	3,518

Note: in the 1918 figures only, Guangzhou is counted in with Hong Kong

Messenger boys of the Surabaya branch in East Java. Left: Branch interior in Batavia (today's Jakarta), capital of the Dutch East Indies (Indonesia). The Batavia branch in West Java opened in 1918 (the same year as the Surabaya branch). Located at No. 4 Kali Besar, West, it was one of the oldest foreign-style buildings in the city. Below: The exterior. The wood carving above the door was considered one of the best specimens of wood carving of its period

A cautious note

In June 1919, the IBC vice president, Lawrence Morton Jacobs, explained to his National City Bank colleagues just what those mysterious international bankers did for a living—and what they did not. "IBC is not an infant prodigy. In foreign banking, it is not a novice," he wrote in *Number Eight*. "It is more like a bronzed and hardened mariner. For 17 years, it has been sailing upon uncertain seas and possesses a breadth of experience of unusual character."

The vice president went on to correct "several misconceptions regarding China" following the overthrow of the Qing Dynasty and the establishment of a republic.

Americans had been "deluded" into thinking that trade opportunities were suddenly more favorable because of political changes. In fact, "fundamental conditions" remained the same as they had for the past 15 years. "China is still only a very loose agglomeration of provinces, seething with political intrigue," he said, noting that there was still no rule of law outside the foreign concessions and that foreigners virtually monopolized trade. Direct trade between Americans and Chinese in the interior "is surrounded by many difficulties and the risks involved are not to be lightly regarded."

The vice president dismissed the media hype about Chinese holding Americans in higher regard than other peoples. "This is twaddle of the most time-worn character."

Jacobs also dismissed talk of a "golden opportunity for America to meet an unusual banking need," adding that the role of a bank was to underwrite, not invest in projects using its own capital. "IBC has considered it wise never to pose as a reservoir of American capital," he said. "Its policy has been to present the exact truth to its Chinese friends and it has been saved from the harmful reaction of an unfulfilled promise."

Staff at the Rangoon branch around 1928. Seated behind the office boys are (from left): junior typist Miss Brown, chief cashier Desai, deputy manager Alexander Drysdale, manager J.J. Milne, officer William M. Simmons, chief clerk Guan Sing and Miss Brown's sister, a stenographer. The next row is mainly the Sino-Burman clerical staff except for those with black hats who were relatives of Desai and worked in the cash department. The back row comprises Indian messengers known as durwans. Brass medallions attached to their red bandaliers bore the bank's initials

Realities of banking in Asia

After telling his readers what the bank was not doing in Asia (see opposite), Jacobs described what it *had* been up to for all these years. "The outstanding feature of the activities of the IBC and other foreign banks in Eastern countries is the buying and selling of exchange, bills, drafts and telegraphic transfer," he wrote. Foreign exchange was "so important" to the overall business. "As silver has risen 100 percent since the war, the danger of speculative operations in silver exchange is apparent. It becomes necessary therefore for our branch managers in China, particularly in the principal markets of Hong Kong and Shanghai, to be constantly buying and selling large amounts of exchange to keep our gold position even." Attracting local deposits was "the most difficult field" for American banks, which explained why deposit levels were "strikingly disproportionate" to funds needed to finance trade. In Japan, for example, deposits secured in competition with Japanese banks are "but a fraction" of the funds needed to buy and sell foreign exchange. As a result, branch managers "must be adept in the dovetailing of their contracts so as not to be over-provided with cash which cannot be utilized from day to day and yet be sufficient to take up bills presented, and meet drawings of head office, branches and foreign correspondents." The same situation applied in the Singapore, Javanese and Indian branches as well as those in China which had the additional risks of exposure to fluctuating silver prices.

Asian branch management along purely American or European lines was meanwhile "impracticable," he added. "It is essential to conform in many particulars to long established customs. At the same time, unless a bank's local managers are experts in the intricacies of Eastern exchange and finance, their usefulness is greatly restricted."

Trading companies in China (1914–28)

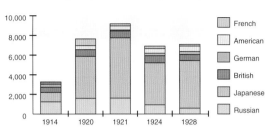

Legend:
- French
- American
- German
- British
- Japanese
- Russian

The Russians controlled more than 1,200 trading companies in China in 1914, but by 1920 were outnumbered by the Japanese. American numbers rose as Sino-American trade developed. The Germans gradually returned after World War I but French numbers declined sharply. The British presence was relatively steady

Source: People's Bank of China, America's Flower Flag Bank in China

Bachelor blues

Alexander Calhoun in Shanghai, 1927

When Alexander Calhoun joined the bank in 1919, the senior staff in Asia was mainly British, most of them Scots. There was a sprinkling of Americans in junior positions. "The hiring for overseas service was restricted to bachelors, and an officer had to reach a certain salary grade (3,000 dollars after five years) before he could apply for permission to marry. ... Tours abroad were for four years with home leave of nine months at three-quarters base salary, minus allowances." Calhoun spent 44 years with the bank including service in Hankou, Cebu, Shanghai and Manila. He retired in 1963 as senior vice president for Asia.

A typical farewell lunch in Shanghai for a National City Bank officer going on home leave in 1938

One of the Chinese calendars which IBC sent to thousands of customers every year. The photograph in the 1924 calendar shows the Pearl River waterfront in Guangzhou

The bank had opened its first Russian branch in Petrograd in January. By the end of the year, the Bolsheviks were in power and banking had been declared a state monopoly. The combined assets and branch deposits amounted to 33 million dollars—more than 40 percent of the bank's capital. After Stillman's death in 1918, William Rockefeller—a director with a large shareholding in the bank—joined forces with Stillman's son to push Vanderlip out. In 1919, Vanderlip resigned. He was succeeded by Stillman's son James, who oversaw an aggressive expansion of the bank in Cuba, where 23 branches were established by 1920, lured by booming sugar prices. When the sugar bubble burst, the younger Stillman was presiding over the bank's worst setback ever—the exposure was 79 million dollars or 80 percent of its capital. Stillman junior resigned in 1921. To clear up the mess, the bank brought in Charles E. Mitchell, who had over the previous four years built up the bank's securities affiliate, National City Company, into America's biggest distributor of securities.

In late 1926, National City Bank advised its shareholders that 17 branches of IBC in Asia would be changing their name to that of the parent company beginning in January 1927. They would form the new Far East division. The letter said that the move "signifies merely a change in name" and that the operations of IBC branches "therefore will involve no change in personnel or method." IBC branches in Manila and Cebu were not yet affected by the name change, nor were other branches in London, Madrid, Barcelona or San Francisco.

The bank opened another Chinese branch in 1928—in Shenyang, which like the rest of northeast China was under growing Japanese influence. From its humble beginnings in Shanghai in 1902, IBC/National City Bank now had eight branches across China excluding Hong Kong.

China was in chaos following the collapse of the Qing Dynasty. After briefly serving as provisional president of the new Republic of China in 1912, Sun Yat-sen resigned and

Temples of finance. Clockwise from left: Guangzhou (completed 1924), Shanghai (remodeled 1922), Manila (completed 1923), Hankou (completed 1921), Tianjin (completed 1921) and Beijing (completed 1920). The Tianjin building replicated Beijing, except for the facing of the side walls and the number of the steps leading up to the main entrance

Temples of banking

Branch buildings were one of the main ways of expressing a bank's status and solidity. In 1917, IBC chose as their architects Henry Killam Murphy and Richard Henry Dana Jr. No doubt influenced by the refurbished Old Customs House at 55 Wall Street, which became National City Bank's headquarters, IBC's Chinese branches were, in the words of the historian Jeffrey Cody, "chips off the old Wall Street block." Behind classical façades, they had to accommodate tellers, bookkeepers, managers and vaults—not to mention the comprador. Murphy and Dana designed five IBC branches in China: Hankou and Beijing; then Tianjin, Shanghai, and Guangzhou. They also did the Manila branch in the Philippines.

It was quite conventional for banks in the United States and Europe to be dressed up with some of the features of classical temples. The style was sufficiently widespread in the East to have been dubbed "compradoric." In Shanghai, architects Murphy and Dana did not build an entirely new branch, but modified the building erected by IBC around 1910. The façade and banking hall were brought into conformity with the new IBC "house style," in particular with the addition of classical features.

The branches of IBC were intended to give a consistent message, anticipating modern principles of branding. And so even branches designed for IBC by other architects, such as Harbin, Shenyang (Mukden) and Hong Kong, show a strong family resemblance.

Foreign bonds (1921–29)

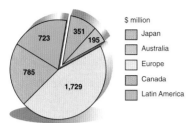

$ million
- Japan
- Australia
- Europe
- Canada
- Latin America

723 · 351 · 195 · 785 · 1,729

National City originated or participated in 11 Japanese bond issues during the period. The amount raised—252 million dollars for government or government-guaranteed borrowers and 99 million dollars for private companies—was the third-highest figure for any country, after Canada and Germany

Source: Cleveland and Huertas, Citibank 1812–1970

Interior of the Singapore branch in Ocean Building, 1923

launched an abortive second revolution against his successor, the general Yuan Shikai who sought to enthrone himself as emperor. Sun, considered the father of modern China, returned to exile in Japan where he began to reorganize his nationalist forces, eventually along Soviet lines. In 1925, he died during a visit to Beijing. Two years later, the nationalist military commander Chiang Kai-shek was to purge his communist allies, and set up a government in Nanjing, where the American, Japanese and British consulates were attacked.

In Japan, a financial panic erupted. The Bank of Japan proposed redeeming "earthquake bills" issued as part of government efforts to help companies in the aftermath of the big quake of 1923. Rumors spread that the banks holding the bills were in danger of collapse, triggering bank runs. Operations were suspended at 37 banks, including the Bank of Taiwan, which had been set up as a colonial central bank in 1899 (see p. 23). During the speculative mania of the 1920s, the Bank of Taiwan had moved aggressively into Japan itself and had been lending recklessly to the Suzuki trading company. With a near monopoly on Taiwan camphor exports, Suzuki had grown rapidly by expanding into ships, agricultural products and iron

Rigid controls at IBC

"It is doubtful if there is any other banking institution in the United States which has so many checks and balances in its operations, from the hiring of office boys to the management of individual branches. Every boy taken on is engaged with a view to his potential qualifications for special work, foreign trade banking. The men are placed in Java, Singapore, China or elsewhere with due regard to their temperaments, physical disabilities or other factors. Weekly reports are received at the head office in New York from each of its 32 branches, giving exchange rates on all centers. ... These reports also show all purchases and sales of all currencies—yen, pesos, pounds sterling, rupees. ... They show further the immediate cash position of each branch, the reserve against deposit liabilities and the position of each with respect to contracts covering purchases and sales of exchange for future delivery."

"Yankee Finance on the Seven Seas: Highlights in the Romance of International Banking and the Efforts of America's Greatest Agency in the Foreign Fields," Burroughs Clearing House Magazine

Selected accounts of foreign branches in June 1929 (millions of dollars)

	Loans	Deposits
China	36.8	53.1
Japan	28.9	8.0
Singapore	6.1	3.6
India	14.1	9.6
Java	1.3	1.5
Asia	87.1	75.8
Europe	51.6	68.6
Latin America	151.4	160.4
Total	290.1	304.8

Source: Cleveland and Huertas, Citibank 1812–1970

Total assets (1902–29)

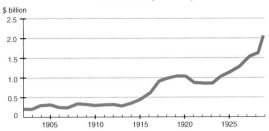

$ billion

By the time the bubble burst in 1929, National City Bank had become the biggest U.S. bank, with more than two billion dollars in assets

Source: annual reports

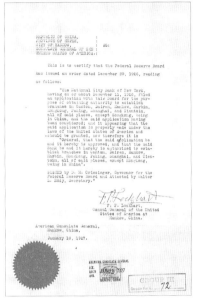

Letter from U.S. consul general in Hankou confirming Federal approval for operations in China, 1927

ore, eventually rivaling the Mitsui and Mitsubishi conglomerates. It collapsed and so did the Japanese government which had failed to get Privy Council approval for emergency central bank loans.

The new government took drastic measures, including a three-week bank moratorium and arranging central bank loans amounting to two billion yen. As a result of the collapse of many small local banks, finance was concentrated into the hands of an increasingly powerful group of conglomerates, notably the Mitsui, Mitsubishi, Sumitomo and Yasuda groups: by 1945 they would control half of Japan's banking, trust and insurance businesses.

In northeast China, the collapse of the Qing Dynasty had resulted in increased activities by Manchurian warlords. The Japanese railroad zone between Lushun (Port Arthur) and Changchun was now known as the Guandong Concession. It was being administered by two separate units under civilian and military command, with Japanese police and railroad guards protecting the trains from warlord attacks. The Guandong Army assassinated the top Manchurian warlord by blowing up his train in Shenyang in 1928, the very year that IBC opened its branch in that city. Economic development of the region meanwhile advanced under the South Manchuria Railway Company, a semi-government company founded after the war with Russia.

Known as Mantetsu, the company controlled the giant Anshan steelworks and the Fushun coal mine. In addition to railroads, it monopolized water transport, ports, warehouses, real estate, power distribution and even monetary arrangements.

On the other side of the world, the United States had enjoyed six years of unbroken prosperity. But a new storm was brewing. In his remarks to the annual meeting of shareholders in early 1927, National City Bank's president Charles Mitchell warned of the dangers of possible credit strain. "The danger to every period of prosperity lies in the development of over confidence and a consequent tendency to unwise use of credit," he said. "If this present period of prosperity is halted, it will be by the same old cause." It was.

An American sailor poses in front of a Chinese branch, probably Hankou, in 1928, a year after the bank changed its name from International Banking Corporation to The National City Bank of New York

2. The Depression and the Pacific War 1930–1945

"If it is difficult to make money in the Far East, and on this I think we are all agreed, then we should all have clearly before us the fact of how easy in times like this it is to lose it."

Marc D. Currie

Japan's financial panic of 1927 was a hint of things to come in the United States and the rest of the world. In 1929, the New York stock market collapsed. At noon on Thursday October 24, Charles E. Mitchell, elected chairman of National City Bank's board in April, joined with other bankers to form a pool to buy shares and stabilize the market. Although the Black Thursday selling was initially checked, prices resumed their downward spiral the following week. In cooperation with the Federal Reserve, the New York banks took action to keep Wall Street brokers solvent, helping to cushion the slide and prevent bankruptcies in the financial sector.

One of the immediate effects on National City Bank was the cancelation of a merger with the Corn Exchange Bank and Trust Company, which had an extensive local branch system in New York. The merger, which was being negotiated before Wall Street's collapse, would have given National City Bank the leading position in local banking. The canceled deal gave rise to international concern about the Bank's condition. Bank of England Governor Montagu Norman conveyed his concerns to the Federal Reserve Bank of New York, which ordered a special examination of National City Bank. "Mitchell had his back up against the wall, the most discredited man in New York," New York Fed Governor R.A. Young said. However, the Fed examination showed that the bank was in "first-class condition," and it ended 1929 with aggregate resources of 2.2 billion dollars,

surpassing Britain's Midland Bank and making it the largest bank in the world. The capital position was stronger than it had ever been since Mitchell took over, with liquidity running high and profits hitting new records.

Although at the outset of 1930 Mitchell believed the worst was over, he was proven incorrect. The financial and economic situation deteriorated as the year dragged on. Deflationary pressures grew following the huge blow to investor confidence. American spending, incomes and prices started to decline. And while industrial output stabilized in the first few months of the

Opposite: The Singapore branch in 1923. The bank remained in this location, the Ocean Building, until 1958, when it moved to new premises. Right: Apart from leaving millions unemployed, the Great Depression reduced foreign demand for many of Asia's exports

The building on Juan Luna Street, Manila, of which the ground and mezzanine floors were occupied by IBC, was constructed jointly with the Pacific Commercial Company, and opened formally on November 13, 1922

year, activity shrank in June and continued to drop sharply for the rest of the year. At the bank, losses on domestic and foreign loans started to swell and in Cuba alone reached nine million dollars as sugar prices plunged.

Then came what the local Superintendent of Banks warned would be "the most colossal mistake in the banking history of New York"—the failure of the Bank of United States, which had almost half a million depositors. Despite being a member of the Federal Reserve system, it was technically insolvent and therefore unable to get access to the Fed's discount window. In December, the bank closed its doors for the last time. National

Credit system overhaul

While the financial crisis highlighted the need to strengthen liquidity in New York, it was credit controls that came under scrutiny at the Asian branches. Three months after the Bank of United States failed, losses in National City Bank's Far Eastern division came to the attention of Gordon S. Rentschler. A director since 1923, Rentschler had been in the president's seat since just before the crash. He didn't like what he saw, and raised the matter at his weekly meeting with senior officers.

"He considered a very large part of these write offs due to poor credit management," wrote senior Far East division officer Marc D. Currie in a letter to all Asian managers the next day. "Apart altogether from the fact that our losses last year were excessive, such comments naturally make very unpleasant hearing in open meeting." It was time for the boys in Asia to pull their socks up. "Several branches continue to show up in the red and this is naturally having a very disastrous effect on the total earnings of the

branches as a whole," he wrote. "The whole trouble is that the volume of business is not there and consequently we cannot make any money in our exchange turnover. I refer particularly to the Japan branches, Harbin and Singapore."

For Currie, 1930 had been a "trying year in the Far East" to say the least, but this did not excuse poor judgment. "Many of these losses should not have been made," he said. "If it is difficult to make money in the Far East—and on this I think we are all agreed—then we should all have clearly before us the fact of how easy in times like this it is to lose it. Consequently ... we should be more than usually careful in scrutinizing all credit lines."

For Ralph Newell, who spent 36 years with the bank in Asia, the overhaul was overdue. In Singapore, he was well placed to appreciate the problem. "In the IBC days—and even for some time after—credit extension was done by the manager. ... Their lending activities were pretty casual.

Ralph Newell in Hong Kong, 1932

Lending was practically a managerial prerogative." While the National City Bank accounting system was implemented with the consolidation of IBC branches in 1927, credit controls weren't in place for a few more years. The world financial crisis was the catalyst for change, starting with the introduction of credit application forms in the early 1930s. "That's when the bank took over the credit arrangement, standardized it and put limits on all these things," Newell said. "Each branch was given its limits—non-reporting, discretionary and so on. But up to that point, it was pretty free wheeling. ...

"Until they actually took it over on January 1, 1927, and absorbed it, National City Bank hadn't really done a thing. In fact, it probably would have been well if they had exercised a little more credit control because the credit controls in the IBC were pretty casual. The managers had great latitude and they would commit the bank before New York started to gasp."

City Bank was appointed liquidator—and eventually got more than 80 percent of the depositors' money back. But the damage was already done and consumer confidence was eroded by the fact that the failure had been allowed to happen in the first place. Even if it was not an important national institution, the public's perception of the Bank of United States was otherwise. Public opinion was appalled by the fact that the owners had so poorly managed a bank carrying the country's name.

The contagion spread to Europe, and by May the following year, Austria's largest bank had collapsed, sending shock waves through Germany and Britain—and back to the United States.

Deflationary policies in the United States coincided with central bank determination to maintain the gold standard. Panic spread. After foreigners started pulling money out of Germany, emergency assistance was provided in June to the Reichsbank by the United States, Britain and France through the newly established Bank for International Settlements (BIS) (see p. 111).

At the same time, commercial banks including National City Bank agreed to roll over short-term credits to Germany as they matured. But it wasn't enough. After several German banks failed in July, all banks in Germany were closed for two days and the first of a series of exchange controls imposed. National

Risky business in Singapore

In the days when foreign exchange and trade financing were bread-and-butter business, Singapore was unusual.

"Singapore was the outstanding branch where earnings on ordinary lending were significant," said Newell, "Before the crash in 1929 when rubber was selling at a good price, we were lending big amounts to the local rubber companies as well as to Firestone, Goodyear, people like that. The biggest money there was in lending against overdrafts."

With such a loan portfolio, the branch inevitably faced problems when the world economy and rubber prices collapsed in the early 1930s. "We lost our shirt," Newell said. "When the slump came along, we had four million Straits dollars with one outfit and two million with another."

Newell was transferred to Singapore to clean up the mess. "We had a big bunch of machinery and a certain amount of real estate. The machinery wasn't any good to us and there wasn't anyone else to buy it. So before it deteriorated to rust in that climate, we sold it just to get something for it," he said. "Although one of them was eventually reorganized under a different name, most of this repossessed machinery that I sold down there went right back to the borrowers who had gone bankrupt. And they went right back into business. ... We lost a packet."

Rubber export coupons issued in Singapore between 1922 and 1941

Before being loaded for export, rubber and tin were stored in warehouses like this one built in the 1920s

Rubber tappers photographed in the early 20th century. Malaya accounted for 40 percent of world rubber output before World War II

Check for 200 dollars (local currency) drawn on the Shanghai branch in 1933

City Bank had 57 million dollars in assets frozen in Germany. Chile defaulted later the same month after Germany raised tariffs on nitrates, one of Chile's main exports. The default included 20 million dollars in assets held by National City Bank, almost 10 percent of its capital.

Events in Germany meanwhile led to the heavy selling of sterling. Despite the downward pressure on sterling in 1931, several of IBC's British managers "refused to believe instructions from New York," according to Ralph Newell, who was in Singapore at the time. "They were in the doghouse after the devaluation, and some of them can credit their sacking to that."

By September, Britain had abandoned the gold standard and the selling moved to the dollar, with the Federal Reserve losing 10 percent of its gold holdings in a couple of months. Bank runs soon started spreading across the United States.

Japan was also forced to abandon the gold standard at the end of 1931, only two years after it made the decision to return to it. (Unlike other countries, Japan was unable to return to the

Local recruitment drive

Boies Hart had joined IBC in 1916, and now ran National City Bank's Far East division. He favored generally substituting Americans for the British who had been a major part of IBC's staff in Asia from the outset; he sought to appoint locals as officers in the Asian branches in positions previously filled by expatriates. As he admitted, this was radical for the 1930s—especially in a region dominated by British banks.

"Without the incentives of position and the remuneration that went with official responsibility," Hart wrote, "what future could the clerical employee visualize?

"Moreover, a great wave of nationalistic pride was sweeping the world. It stood to reason that even the most backward countries would feel its urge.

"Unless the people of the country could aspire to responsible positions in foreign organizations doing business in their midst,"

Hart concluded, "an anti-foreign sentiment might cost us dear."

Localization began in 1929 when Kentaro Funatani, of the Kobe branch, became the first local officer in Asia. Then came Ho Kim Seng, who succeeded Newell in Singapore. Ho "knew more about banking than most of the managers," wrote Newell.

Within a few years, according to Hart, there was "a marked improvement in esprit de corps of our employees throughout the Orient. The friendly feeling created thereby in local government and business circles was quite apparent. It also resulted in reducing the number of American officers to less than a hundred."

Retirement party for Singapore branch manager Duncan Douglas (seated sixth from the left) at the Wing Choon Yuen restaurant on August 2, 1941. Ho Kim Seng is fifth from the right. On the right of Ho is George Magruder, who oversaw the closure of the branch six months later (see p. 72)

An embossing stamp
used by the Singapore branch

gold standard soon after World War I because of the combined impact of a financial panic and the earthquake of 1923.) China was meanwhile still on the silver standard and notes issued by commercial banks were backed by silver.

In early 1932, the United States government set up a body known as the Reconstruction Finance Corporation to help troubled banks. But as the year progressed, the Corporation came under political pressure to disclose the names of banks that had received such assistance. Despite fears that this would further destabilize the financial system, the names of the banks were publicly disclosed. And as widely feared, more runs developed, spreading from state to state. Rather than see their banks fail, governors in Iowa, Louisiana and Michigan simply closed them down. The so-called "bank holidays" only served to aggravate the panic in other states as depositors rushed to withdraw funds before similar closures were ordered.

As a result, pressure on National City Bank intensified as correspondent banks withdrew their balances to meet customer

The responsibilities of marriage

Hart admitted that it was an "unusual requirement" of the Asian district—but rules were rules. New York advised young recruits that their managers "look with disfavor on their marrying without the consent of the district vice president until they have been in our service five years and are making a certain base salary." For Hart, the regulation was justified—a young man should not take on family responsibilities until he had proved himself.

"It is in the early years of adapting themselves to new conditions and surroundings that these youngsters almost invariably cross low-pressure areas of homesickness that make them easy prey to the 'mothering females' they may encounter."

Besides, "the chances of a bachelor American making good during his training period abroad are two and a half times greater than that of a married man," he said. "There is only one personality to be fitted into a given niche. What increases the hazard on the additional personality is the fact that no matter how modest a household may be in oriental ports, servants are—or were—plentiful and cheap. The lady of the

A social gathering at the home of the Tokyo branch manager in 1936

house hasn't the customary household tasks to occupy her mind that correspond to the office work of her husband. In plain words, she hasn't enough dishes to wash! Idleness of hand and mind quickly leads to discontent and querulousness."

But when staff reach a certain rank, "there are unavoidable entertainment obligations where the graciousness of the hostess and her willingness and ability to charm have a very real effect on the success of important matters of institutional policy and business generally."

Hart paid tribute to the "tremendous role the bank wives play in the success of the bank's overseas branches. There are few careers where a wife can have such a direct influence on her husband's advancement."

The Kobe branch, located behind the Daimaru department store (see arrow), was the first Asian posting for Henry ("Hank") Sperry, who sent this postcard to his father in New York in 1933

Squeezing the competition

Like other banks in Shanghai, IBC issued its own banknotes. As the first U.S. bank in town it was known as the "Flower Flag Bank" after the stars on the American flag. Although IBC branches took the National City Bank name in 1927, the Chinese name wasn't affected and remained on the notes, which appeared on the balance sheet every year until 1945 as a liability (see graph p. 59).

"It wasn't difficult to find out the currency issue of the IBC, the Hongkong and Shanghai Bank, the Chartered Bank of India or any of the other banks operating in China and printing their own money," wrote branch inspector George Scott. "Our money was printed by American Bank Note and had nothing behind it at all except the promise to pay one silver dollar as, if and when some-

one showed up with the paper dollar.

"As a result, it was considered quite a feat to corner another bank's currency and then at the last minute to demand payment in silver. This would occasionally happen to us, or we might give it to someone else," he said. It was all very simple—just get the comprador to instruct the tellers not to give out notes of the rival bank. "When you had a sizable chunk of their total paper currency, you'd load it in a rickshaw on Saturday morning around 11:45, run around to the bank, present yourself to their manager and say: 'I've got 38 percent or 28 percent—or whatever

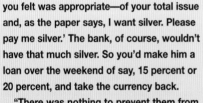

you felt was appropriate—of your total issue and, as the paper says, I want silver. Please pay me silver.' The bank, of course, wouldn't have that much silver. So you'd make him a loan over the weekend of say, 15 percent or 20 percent, and take the currency back.

"There was nothing to prevent them from doing this to you sometime later on. It was quite a common practice between managers to hopefully corner the other fellow's note issue and you always had to be on the lookout as this could happen to you."

A 50-dollar note issued by the Hankou (Wuhan) branch in 1918

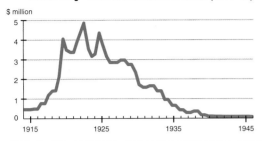

"Flower Flag" notes in circulation in China (1914–45)

$ million

The number of notes in circulation fell sharply in the early 1930s with the onset of the Great Depression and the establishment of Manchukuo, where the local currency was linked at parity to the yen. By 1945 the figure had fallen to 2,000 dollars

Source: annual and semi-annual statements of condition

---

withdrawals. In the first three weeks of February 1933, such balances with National City Bank plunged by a third, with correspondent banks pulling out 68 million dollars. During the same period, the bank's total domestic deposits tumbled by 13 percent, exerting severe strain on its liquidity ratio. America's biggest banking crisis had begun. Mitchell, who was increasingly becoming one of the key scapegoats of the crisis, was summoned to give evidence to the Senate Banking Committee.

The members of the committee largely blamed the banks in general for the speculative fever of the 1920s. As one of the nation's largest banks, National City Bank was in the firing line. The public mood was dark. And the runs on banks showed no signs of abating. The public needed a fall guy. On February 27, 1933, Mitchell resigned. "I personally have been brought under a cloud of criticism from which I conceived that the institution should not be permitted to suffer by my continuance in office." Directors met to accept his resignation and appointed City Bank Farmers' Trust Company president James H. Perkins to succeed him. In *Time* magazine's account of the drama, the caption under Mitchell's photo read: "The U.S. senators got their man."

But the banking crisis was by no means over. Correspondent banks continued to withdraw funds in order to meet customer deposits which were snowballing. By March 3, 1933, the domestic deposits of National City alone had fallen 11 percent

Silver arbitrage

As Chinese silver dollars had varying contents of actual silver, profits awaited those who knew what they were doing. One such arbitrageur was Tianjin manager Bill North. "He would have on his desk a sheet of paper which showed the silver content," recalled branch inspector Scott.

"He knew what it cost to put these into a box, what it cost to ship them to the port, what it cost to get them to San Francisco, insure them and what it would cost to melt them down into pure silver. If all these costs added together came to less than the value of pure silver in San Francisco, he'd ship 10 or 15 boxes or maybe even more, to San Francisco against a forward sale of silver.

Silver dollar minted in 1932. Shunned by the Chinese public, it was recalled and reissued in 1933—minus the rising sun and the seagulls, said to resemble Japanese planes

"If he didn't cover his forward sale by a future purchase while the shipment was en route, he could always melt the shipment down and make delivery. On the other hand, if he could cover and make a profit, he'd do so—then send his boxed silver dollars on to somewhere else where there was a bullion market for delivery in case his forward sale contract hadn't been covered."

This was a nightmare for the inspectors. In the Tianjin vault, wrote Scott, "there were about 25 boxes of these silver dollars which had left at some prior period for San Francisco, had been all the way around the world and were back in Tianjin, having never been unpacked or melted down. They were sitting there waiting for a future opportunity to be shipped overseas." There was also the branch cash—another 9,000 bags with 1,000 silver dollars in each bag. "The job took me about three days."

below their level two days earlier—down 29 percent from February 1. On that day, National City Bank's newly-appointed president and the heads of other major Americans banks met with the Federal Reserve Bank of New York to discuss the possibility of a "bank holiday" in New York. The meeting went well into the small hours of the following day, and an agreement was reached for a bank holiday on March 5. As President Franklin D. Roosevelt was being inaugurated hours later on March 4, banks across the country were closing down.

Perkins, now head of the most publicly reviled bank in the country, called on Roosevelt at the White House the same day. On March 9, the newly installed president ordered a nationwide shut-

Yokohama staff sports team, 1936

down under a new emergency banking law. Under the Emergency Banking Act, passed on March 6, Roosevelt could allow banks to reopen only when they were deemed to be in a "satisfactory condition" and capable of staying open. The National City Bank was allowed to resume business on March 13, 1933, the earliest day permitted under the emergency legislation.

On the other side of the world, the panic was only just starting. If foreigners had been unaware of the state banking closures before March, Roosevelt's actions made sure they knew now. In their zeal to stabilize the banking system at home, America's monetary authorities had forgotten about their banks operating abroad. For Boies C. Hart, who had recently arrived in Asia to head the bank's Far East division, the foreign branches of American banks were abandoned like "orphan children."

"The presidential decree that eased the worry of the domestic bankers brought intensified concern to those who were in charge of foreign bank activities," wrote Hart. "We were faced with the probability that overnight we might have a 'run' in each

of the 76 branches we were operating in 23 different countries. It was too much to expect that foreigners would unconcernedly leave their money in American banks located in their midst when the American president himself had closed the head offices of those banks for reasons that would be little understood outside the United States itself.

"Our government's order to close banks did not carry legal authority beyond the boundaries of the United States. Abroad, our branches operate under the laws of the country in which they are located. Any attempt to hide behind the skirts of our own president's authorization would have meant we were closed permanently and declared bankrupt," Hart said.

He was therefore pleasantly surprised by the foreign reaction to events back home. Local newspapers in Asia, for example, were "carrying the most alarming dispatches from America of riots among bank depositors, of bank closings, of militia being mobilized to guard the banks, of 'bank holidays' illegally ordered by state governors and finally the nationwide closing of all financial institutions by the federal government

Good friends next door ...

When the United States shut down all its banks in the financial panic of 1933, National City Bank kept its Chinese branches open.

But in the confusion surrounding the health of American banks in general, the Beijing branch experienced a run on deposits. "Our banking friends, however, like Hongkong and Shanghai and others, had much more confidence in us than the people apparently did," branch inspector Scott recalled. Arriving at work one day, he found Chinese depositors lined up for several blocks to withdraw their money, "staggering out the front door with a bag or two in silver dollars.

Lobby of the Shanghai branch in 1940, three years after war broke out between China and Japan

"They'd trot next door to the Hongkong and Shanghai Bank and put it in. We made prior arrangements with the Hongkong and Shanghai Bank. So we were taking it out of their back door into our back door, and this money was going around in circles for about two days. ... At the end of that time, I guess the Chinese were sufficiently convinced that the bank was sound and money started to flow back in again.

"I don't suppose we got it all settled. But it was an instance of how with very little money—actual currency—you can pay off an awful lot of deposits if you've got good friends next door."

itself." But "our foreign friends still maintained confidence in us—even when our own citizens were seized by panicky hysteria in which 'every man for himself' was the guiding emotion.

"During this period, when all banks in the United States were closed, the total deposits in the City Bank's 76 branches—where depositors had an unrestricted opportunity to withdraw their balances—showed a shrinkage of less than two percent," he noted. But "the realization of this foreign confidence in us and in our country did not come to use until after the crisis had passed."

Branches in the Caribbean countries, where American currency was in general circulation, received extra cash reserves before the presidential decree prohibited the export of money from the United States. "At one time, we had five special chartered planes in flight carrying one million dollars each, the maximum amount that could be insured on one plane." Building up the cash reserves in Asia, Latin America and Europe was more complicated because of the foreign exchange exposure and subsequent hedging requirements. "All these preparations kept the cables and transoceanic telephones hot," Hart said. "We were on a 24-hour schedule." In the event, the only real "runs" in Asia

Entrance to the Harbin branch during flooding, 1936

... and in Harbin

Harbin was the most difficult branch to help as cash had to be brought up from Japan, normally a three-day journey. "At the time, the railroad service had been disrupted by floods," Hart recalled. "We endeavored to charter planes in Japan to fly in the needed funds but were halted by regulations of the Japanese army. ... The situation might have been serious but for the voluntary cooperation of our competitors, all of whom were extremely helpful. ... Japanese banks arranged the transfer of funds by Japanese army planes and, without any suggestion on our part, persuaded army censors to stop the violent attacks in the press."

took place at the Harbin and Beijing branches in northern China, although these were checked fairly quickly with the cooperation of British and Japanese banks.

Manchuria was a rich farm area with soybeans as the main crop. This photograph shows soybeans in Shenyang awaiting export

The experience of depression was not limited to the western economies. At this stage, Japan too had been in the throes of depression for several years. Since 1929, foreign trade had been halved. With world demand sagging, the plunge in prices for export items such as raw silk, cotton thread and soybeans was particularly severe. For small and medium-sized businesses, bankruptcies became common. Operations were suspended, factory owners fled town and wages were not paid. Big businesses formed cartels and fired workers, triggering violent labor disputes. Agriculture was especially hard hit, prompting some desperate farmers to emigrate to Manchuria. Government measures to stimulate the economy were eventually taken at the end of 1931. By mid-1933, the economy was starting to recover, led by heavy industries such as shipbuilding and chemicals.

During this period, the Japanese-controlled Guandong Army was becoming increasingly aggressive in northeast China. It had been set up originally to protect railroads running from the Japanese concession at Dalian and Port Arthur (known today as Lushun). Extremist elements within the army had assassinated the local warlord in 1928. In September 1931, the army launched an attack on the Chinese garrison in Shenyang, using an alleged attack on the Japanese railroad by local bandits as an excuse. Although such attacks by Chinese bandits were indeed common at the time, this incident had actually been carried out by Japanese officers. With the Guandong Army increasingly ignoring the civilian government and the military high command in Tokyo, Japan's conquest of Manchuria was underway. In 1932, the Guandong Army set up a puppet state called Manchukuo. Few foreign governments recognized the state, which would remain a dependency of Japan for another 13 years. China's last emperor, Puyi, was installed by the generals as nominal ruler of the puppet state.

The bank had two branches in Manchukuo—Harbin and Shenyang—and a third in Dalian, the big port city in the old Russian concession. This was technically outside the puppet state but nevertheless controlled by the Japanese army.

The Flower Flag keeps flying

During the crisis of the late 1930s, a teller at the Tianjin branch of a European bank refused to accept one of the Flower Flag notes. In the 30-odd years that the notes had been in circulation, they had been accepted without question by all banks. "The rapidity with which rumors spread among the Chinese is astonishing. Within half an hour, there was a line blocks long in front of our branch," Hart wrote.

"The branch had ample cash reserves to pay all demands. But Ed Torrey, our manager, was annoyed at the occurrence and cleverly devised measures that soon stopped the run." Torrey sent word to Chinese exchange shops that he would pay silver for the bank's notes at a premium over their face value. "As soon as this word got around among the note holders, they left the line in front of the branch to cash their notes at the exchange shops where they could get more. ... At little expense to the bank, the manager's strategy reduced the number waiting in line by nearly two-thirds. Those who remained were depositors who wanted to withdraw their balances. ...

"Many who had withdrawn their balances had more than they could carry. Soon the lobby was filled with people huddled over piles of silver who, once they had their money, didn't know what to do with it. The sight of these heaps of silver dollars shoved across the counter and the huge stacks of boxes of them corded behind counters had a reassuring effect. Almost as quickly as it started, the 'run' was over and business was back to normal."

Banking in Manchuria

Before Manchukuo was formed, the area had been farmed out to the Japanese-backed Manchurian warlord Zhang Zuolin. When Chiang Kai-shek set up a government in Nanjing and pushed north to overthrow Zhang, Tokyo ruled against military intervention. This incensed some extremist officers, who assassinated Zhang by blowing up his train in Shenyang in 1928 to exploit the confusion. He was succeeded by his son Zhang Xueliang, the "Young Marshal," who pledged allegiance to Chiang Kai-shek, hastening Japan's actions in forming the puppet state.

The cost of running the area before 1932 was about 25 million silver Mexican dollars (eight million U.S. dollars) a year. "If that was the price, the concession was a bargain," wrote Hart. "The warlord … controlled the life and destinies of all the people. There was no appeal from his actions. He levied and collected the taxes. No possibility was overlooked. He operated the banks and issued the currency.

"The days of Zhang Xueliang were the heydays of the bandits and kidnappers and it was reliably reported that the most efficient operators were members of the Young Marshal's army who were given temporary leave to thus eke out their pay," he said. "In Harbin under the Young Marshal's administration, every person of any means—Chinese and foreigners alike—barricaded their houses. … Every home was surrounded with high walls and within the enclosure savage dogs were loosed to ward off invaders. Armed Russian guards patrolled the premises.

"After the Japanese seized Manchuria, life was very different. Bandits were rare, except in the districts remote from the cities. Taxes were equitable and fairly assessed. Free public schools and an efficient public health service—both unheard of in the Chinese regime—were widely established. A sound currency was maintained and the producer of commodities no longer had to worry about whether the value of the money would be the same when he sold his crops as when he purchased his seed."

Harbin branch manager Samuel Bitting and his deputy Milton Bates during the bandit heyday of 1930

Getting to Harbin was an ordeal. "We went up during the day as the train would not run at night," recalled George Scott. "Bandits in the area would take up the tracks and when the train went off the tracks at night, they'd loot it. So they only ran the train during the day. In front of the engine, they had a flat car with a tin roof with a bunch of Japanese soldiers on it. They usually had a tin roof over the locomotive because the trains—when they would go through passes or cuts—would be exposed to grenades or bombs or whatnot dropped on them by the bandits."

On arriving in Harbin, "one of the first things they issued to us was a revolver which they suggested we carry if we go out at night," Scott said. "We did, but it was never fired or needed. … I remember coming out of the bank one night and finding on poles across the street the heads of four bandits who had raided the post office. They were set up there as evidence that crime doesn't pay."

The Shenyang branch, the bank's third in Manchuria after Harbin and Dalian, just after the opening in December 1928

Early calculating machine

Hart explained that the Shenyang branch was closed in 1935 with the advent of Japanese market forces. "Our business there had largely been the financing of American imports which were purchased by the railroads, mines and arsenals which were all controlled and operated by the Young Marshal [see p. 63]. Most of the goods purchased could have been bought from Japanese manufacturers at cheaper prices. But fortunately for the American producers, the Young Marshal would not permit any of his enterprises to buy Japanese products. Hence the market which Americans had enjoyed in Manchuria was an artificial one which would not have existed if the Japanese were allowed to compete. When the artificial protection that created the American business disappeared, there was no excuse for a branch."

As far as the bank was concerned, life in the Shenyang branch, or Shenyang for that matter, had revolved around the Young Marshal, Zhang Xueliang. His invitations meant a "command performance," Hart recalled. "Our manager was an efficient and excellent manager for the institution—and he was also a good poker player. But on one occasion to my knowledge the bank underwrote his poker loss to the Young Marshal."

By 1935, the population of the railroad zone running from Dalian through Shenyang to Changchun further north had mushroomed to 545,000, up sharply from 80,000 in 1908 when the Japanese were starting to develop the zone. The Harbin and

Dalian branches would stay open for another six years.

Shanghai was at this stage not exposed to the conflict in the northeast. Life rolled on in Asia's biggest international financial center and the Shanghai branch of National City Bank earned considerable profits through foreign exchange trading, headed by legendary trader John T.S. "Red" Reed. Foreign exchange also remained an important activity in Hong Kong.

Reed was credited with earning huge profits for the bank in the 1930s. Between 1934 and 1938, the Chinese branches earned more than seven million dollars—almost 40 percent of the gross earnings remitted to New York from all overseas branches during the same period. Furthermore, in the difficult year when New York had to rely on the bank's Shanghai earnings in order to maintain its dividend, it was almost certainly achieved thanks to this formidable trader.

As military events spun out of control in northeast China, the political situation in Japan itself grew increasingly complex, with nationalist extremists gaining the upper hand. Following the arrest of leaders of a planned military coup in late 1931, an ultra-nationalist group known as the League of Blood murdered several politicians and businessmen, including a top Mitsui executive. A mere two months later, Prime Minister Tsyuyoshi Inukai was assassinated by a group of young naval officers.

In 1933, Japanese and Chinese forces in Manchukuo agreed to a truce while the leaders of another planned coup were arrested in Japan. Frustrated by limitations imposed on its naval capacity, Japan announced, in late 1934, that it intended to abrogate the terms of the Washington Naval Treaty of 1922. The initial five-power treaty following World War I had limited

Bandits nab naked bankers!

High walls, savage dogs and armed Russian guards were not necessarily surefire protection against the bandits roaming through Manchuria before 1932—as Hart found out on a visit to the northern frontier city.

"Prior to one of my visits to the Harbin branch, the manager had a Sunday stag picnic on his boat. ... At a suitable lonely beach, the whole party went swimming au naturel. Imagine their embarrassment when bandits chose that moment to come over the hill and capture the entire party.

"The bandits took all their clothes and valuables. But as the sunburnt nudist group slinked back into town after dark, they were elated that they had talked the bandit leader out of holding them for ransom."

The Bombay Mutual Life building, completed in 1935. National City Bank occupied the ground floor, described by Boies Hart as "a great improvement" over the previous address. A Citibank branch was still to be found here at the end of the century (see p. 118)

Boies Hart (seated front row left) and his wife on a visit to Calcutta in 1932. According to Hart, one of America's first exports to India was ice transported aboard New England clippers on their way to China. "One would think it still came that way from the constant struggles one has to get waiters to put ice in a highball," he wrote

Upgrading the Bombay branch

Boies Hart sailed to Bombay from New York on the *Empress of Britain*. He decided that managing cruises was one of the "most objectionable" jobs he'd ever come across. "It stands to reason that 400 people who could afford 2,500 dollars apiece ... must have a high percentage of selfish, spoiled, pampered fusspots." He cited a "sweet, middle-aged lady who changed her table 14 times in four weeks," and a Spanish

Marqessa "with the raging passion of her race, who used a fire axe to open the door of a cabin where she expected to find her philandering husband." Then there was the Canadian who brought a cobra to entertain the other guests in the private dining rooms. "Next morning, he took the snake to the top deck for a dress rehearsal." With a few practice bars on a flute, the cobra awoke: "Out of the basket he slithered across the deck and disappeared down the maw of a

ventilator. The Canadian summoned assistance but in the excitement forgot which ventilator held the reptile." Armed with monkey wrenches, cabin boys wearing gloves and gas masks ventured into the bowels of the ship where they found the cobra asleep. "He was promptly dispatched and the captain's face lost its purplish hue."

In Bombay, Hart was suitably impressed by the bazaar "with its jostling multitudes filling the narrow streets from curb to curb. ... The bullion exchange is one of the world's largest in volume of transactions. Here the brokers swing out on ropes over clamoring traders, not one of whom looks as if he has 10 cents to his name, executing transactions of thousands of ounces in gold or silver. The continuous clamor and turmoil makes the New York Stock Exchange a vesper service by comparison."

Foreign banks were located in the business district a mile away. "We had a terrible, miserable little office scattered over three floors and divided into a lot of rooms. We made such a poor appearance that I was surprised anyone did business with us. Before I left Bombay, I made arrangements for new quarters which were a tremendous improvement." Later he arranged for a second branch to be opened in the bazaar, close to most of the local business. "Within a year, its deposits equaled 50 percent of those of our main branch that had been established 30 years earlier."

The bank's mountain rest-house at Baguio, the Philippines, 1941

Japanese naval capacity to 60 percent of both Britain's and the United States' fleet strength. At the London Naval Conference of 1936, Japan withdrew after failing to get full parity with the British and American fleets. The same year saw yet another attempted coup, the most serious so far. Involving about 1,400 troops led by junior officers, the so-called February 26 incident resulted in the deaths of several senior government figures including Finance Minister Korekiyo Takahashi. The rebellion in Tokyo stunned Japan. Martial law was imposed and several rebels were executed after being court-martialed by a secret tribunal. Although martial law was lifted in July, the army took advantage of the incident to get bigger budgets and expand its influence. The cabinet of Prime Minister Koki Hirota tightened censorship and carried out policies favorable to the army. By 1937, Japan was ready for full-scale war with China.

It all started near Beijing on the night of July 7. Under the terms of the Boxer protocols of 1901, the Japanese had troops in the area around Lugouqiao, also known as Marco Polo Bridge. The troops were conducting routine exercises when some blank shots were fired from a Japanese position. Live shots were returned. When a soldier was later found to be missing, a Japanese officer demanded a search of a nearby town. The Chinese refused, and the Japanese responded by trying to breach the town's defenses forcibly. After a month of skirmishes around Beijing and Tianjin, the conflict spread to Shanghai in August with hundreds of thousands of Japanese and Chinese troops engaged in savage street fighting. By December, the rapidly modernizing city of Nanjing, which had been the nationalist capital after Chiang Kai-shek had achieved unified control of China in 1928, had fallen, with many thousands dead, including civilians and prisoners.

From New York, the bank sent standing instructions to all the

Master of the Universe

In the 1930s, Shanghai had the biggest foreign exchange market in Asia. And the best trader in town was Red Reed (see p. 64).

"Shanghai was a big job in exchange because there was a terrific market and most of the profit was in exchange," said Ralph Newell, who spent three years at the Shanghai branch as accountant. "Red was the exchange man. He did it right from his bathtub. He had telephones all over the damn place." In Yokohama, after the quake, Reed set up a temporary shed to replace the destroyed branch. Later he was transferred to Java and worked in the Jakarta and Surabaya branches.

From there he was sent to Guangzhou, but only briefly "because that was a waste of his time," Newell said. "It was a junk shop compared to what he could do. So they moved him up to Shanghai from there and he really went to town. He was a good trader."

The foreign officers photographed on the roof of the Shanghai branch of National City Bank, 1932. Seated second from left is Milton Bates; fourth from left is Red Reed; standing third from right is Earle Cutting (see p. 71); fifth from right is Hank Sperry (see p. 82)

Telephone used in the Singapore branch of National City Bank

branches in Asia advising managers how to run their operations in the "disturbed conditions" that were now being witnessed in China.

"Microfilm cameras were to be used to photograph in duplicate all important record books such as deposit account sheets, balance records, signature cards, powers of attorney, loan records, notes, contracts and securities," Hart recalled. In fact, the instructions from New York covered all records that would be needed to set up a new branch if its original records had been lost or destroyed. "One film was to be sent by the quickest means to head office. The other was to be placed in the custody of the United States consul."

As the war spread and hostilities between Japanese and Chinese troops intensified, the banks started implementing the emergency regulations. "Their tremendous value can be realized when one recalls that Japanese forces took possession of nine of our Oriental branches and that when they finally disposed of them, few records were left," Hart said.

In Japan the economy, and the financial system in particular, was rapidly put onto a war footing. In late 1937, a new law was passed imposing controls on the setting up of companies, capital increases, issuing of bonds and any other forms of borrowing to ensure that long-term funds were channeled into military industries. Another new law extended government controls to producing, processing, trading, holding and consuming any commodities or raw materials that were imported or exported. In 1938, the General Mobilization Law was passed, extending government controls to labor, including wages. The law also covered the production and distribution of goods and imposed controls on corporate activities such as the disposal of profits and the use of funds by financial institutions.

In 1939, full-scale controls were extended over the entire economy. The use of cotton, for example, was generally prohibited in the private sector and the rationing of steel and other metals was adopted. Black markets soon flourished, giving rise to the creation of an economic police force. With a severe drought in

Wednesday forex shutdowns

In Hong Kong during the 1930s, the foreign exchange market shut down on Wednesday afternoons. "Nobody conducted any exchange," recalled George Scott, an inspector of Asian branches at the time.

"We'd take the ferry across to Kowloon, get on the train, ride out to Fanling and play golf. The result was that on Wednesdays, business for all practical purposes in the afternoon came to a standstill insofar as the foreigners were concerned.

"Exchange trading was such an important part of your operations, and it was always done by the manager and he had sole discretion. He operated the book. And it was not unusual at night, if you were out at one or two in the morning, to have him call up the local office and get the readings on the telegraph," Scott said. "Sterling was the major currency of the Far East and you always had to know whether this opened up or down, depending on whether you were short or long.

"If it opened down and you were long, the manager would probably sign the chits and leave the nightclub. But if it opened up and you were long, the chances were that he would order another bottle of champagne and stay out until three or four in the morning."

Interior of the Hong Kong branch as it was in the 1930s

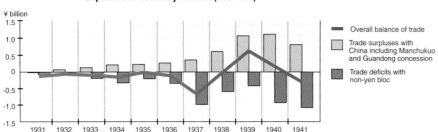

Japan's war economy deficits (1931–41)

¥ billion

Legend:
- Overall balance of trade
- Trade surpluses with China including Manchukuo and Guandong concession
- Trade deficits with non-yen bloc

The outbreak of war with China in 1937 caused Japan's trade deficit to soar due to imports for military expansion. Gold reserves plunged, forcing the Bank of Japan to buy gold from private citizens and sell foreign securities to fund imports from the non-yen bloc

Source: Takafusa Nakamura, The Postwar Japanese Economy

western Japan and Korea, rice rationing was introduced and coupons made their way into nearly all aspects of Japanese life. People were conscripted for military production and junior high school students were put to work in factories. Amid rising anti-communist fervor, Japan and Germany signed a pact opposing the Soviet Union in 1936. Italy joined the so-called Anti-Comintern Pact in 1937, followed by Hungary, Spain and Manchukuo in 1939. Despite Germany's invasion of Poland the same year, the outbreak of war in Europe was remote for most people in East Asia where Japan and China had been embroiled in war since 1937. The increasingly strong military ties among Japan, Germany and Italy nevertheless led to a military pact in 1940.

As the war with China dragged on longer than many people expected, the late 1930s also gave birth to a Japanese policy for a "New Order in East Asia." This was an attempt at making a conciliatory gesture toward China by exploiting both countries' contempt for the "old order" of western colonial powers. Chinese Nationalist leader Chiang Kai-shek rejected the overture from Prime Minister Fumimaro Konoe. However, the Japanese did have more success with Wang Jingwei, Chiang's long-time rival and eventually leader of a collaborationist government. The wider concept of a "Greater East Asia Co-prosperity Sphere" only came into vogue toward the end of 1940, around the same time as the French authorities allowed Japan to station troops and use airfields in northern Vietnam. In addition to Japan, China, Manchukuo and French Indochina, the Japanese government declared that the new sphere of prosperity would include the Dutch East Indies (today's Indonesia).

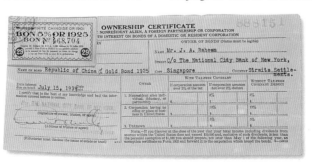

Bond ownership certificate dated 1939, Singapore

In August 1940, Hart was appointed senior credit officer in the overseas division. "By this time, relations with the Japanese were deteriorating rapidly. The State Department requested that American wives and children return," he wrote. "Within a few months, all had done so."

With the Japanese blocking the Yangtze River and the Chinese monopolizing the wood oil business, the bank decided to shut down the Hankou (today's Wuhan) branch in December. Then in February 1941, the Harbin branch was closed, followed by Osaka in April and Guangzhou in August. "American business was reduced to a trickle, and we had no further obligation to our customers or to our government to remain," said Hart.

America's freezing of Japanese funds in June and Japan's immediate retaliation against American funds removed the last remaining reason for maintaining branches in Japan. In October, the branches in Kobe, Yokohama and Dalian were all shut down, although a skeleton staff remained in Tokyo to wind up the affairs of the closed branches. Another officer stayed on in Dalian. "All were bachelors and had been chosen with the possibility that they might become prisoners of war," Hart said. "All were experienced, were liked and respected, and had many friends among the Japanese."

The bank was obliged to remain open in Shanghai, Tianjin and Beijing, as well as in Manila and Singapore—it was the official bank for the American government in those cities. American Marine Corps detachments stationed in Tianjin and Beijing were paid through the local National City Bank branches. And in Shanghai, the bank represented the United States on the local Exchange Control Board as well

Top: As the Chinese resistance withdrew from Shanghai in November 1937, they set fire to the Chapei district. This picture was taken from Red Reed's apartment on the 10th floor of Hamilton House. Second from top: Japanese victory parade in Shanghai, December 1937. Third from top: As the Sino-Japanese War progressed, Britain moved to protect its interests by bringing in troops from Addis Ababa. Inset right: The frontage of the Shanghai branch, duly protected. Main picture (right): Seen from a window of the Shanghai branch, chaos on the street during Japanese bombing in late 1937

Total assets (1930–45)

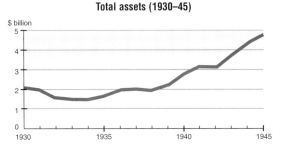

$ billion

Assets grew at an annual rate of seven percent in 1933–39. Aided by write-offs and recoveries as well as recapitalization in 1934, non-accrual assets dropped from 120 million dollars in 1933 to below 17 million dollars in 1939. During World War II, an influx of deposits from foreigners was used to fund the bank's bond portfolio

Source: annual reports

as acting as banker for army, navy and marine detachments from the United States. "Also, we were financing for clients the exportation of many war materials being feverishly purchased by our own government, and by those who later became our allies," Hart recalled. "Although Hong Kong was British territory, it was the non-official location of the Chinese Minister of Finance and the Exchange Control Board, with whom we had to keep in constant communication.

"Our Singapore branch was working day and night, financing the operations of the U.S. government in frantic last-minute purchases of tin and rubber. Manila was American territory, and for many months had been engaged in an effort to build up defenses. The wives and children of our American staff continued to live there because our State Department had never suggested they leave, as they had suggested in the case of women and children in Japan and China."

From the beginning of his trips to Asia, Hart said he had met dozens of American army, navy and marine officers and that he had always sought their opinions about the ability of the Japanese armed forces. "The consensus was that they were poor fliers, lacked initiative and would be shot down like sitting ducks if they ever came up against our own fliers. I recall that when General MacArthur was questioned as we sat around the table after a small dinner party in Manila in 1939, he too seemed to have a poor opinion of Japanese

Above left: The Osaka branch interior
Left: In 1933, National City Bank was still the only foreign bank in Osaka. Set up four years earlier, the branch financed imports of American cotton. Osaka was the center of the Japanese spinning industry. The building was designed by the Omi-based architectural firm of W.M. Vories and Co. The main contractor was Takonaka Co. The bank had another branch in nearby Kobe

Opened in 1940, the Cardinal Mercier branch was the bank's second in Shanghai and its first sub-branch in any Asian city. Among those seated in the staff picture are Gu Xingxun (fourth from left), George Greene (fifth), Earle Cutting (sixth—see also p. 66), manager William Griffiths (seventh), foreign-currency teller Yu Xiqing (eleventh) and Gui Fubao (see p. 81) from the drafts department (twelfth)

Closing the Singapore branch

While the bank's remaining branches in Japan, China, Hong Kong and the Philippines were all in Japanese hands by the end of 1941, the Singapore branch kept operating for another two months as British, Australian and Indian forces suffered a series of disastrous setbacks on the Malay peninsula and surrounding waters.

The Pacific War actually began in Malaya with the Japanese landings at the beaches in the northern town of Kota Bahru in the early hours of Monday, December 8, more than an hour before the start of the attack on Pearl Harbor (where, on the other side of the International Date Line, it was still Sunday). In the following hours, Japanese planes from Saigon bombed docks and airfields in Singapore; however, it was not until late January that Japanese troops advanced as far south as Johor to prepare for their final assault on the island.

By the time the Japanese crossed the Straits of Johor, "the bank affairs were practically all cleaned up," recalled George Magruder, who was sub-accountant at the Singapore branch. "The rest of the staff got on a boat headed for India, leaving me behind to finish up a few odds and ends."

When National City Bank decided to turn all remaining assets over to a British bank on Thursday, February 5, the siege of Singapore was five days old and long-range shelling of the Orchard Road area had just begun. By Sunday evening, the invasion of Singapore was underway with Japanese landing at Lim Chu Kang Road.

Magruder, who had been working part-time for the American military observer's office in Singapore, said he and his colleagues expected the Japanese would "get the hell beaten out of them" by the British, Australian and Indian forces. "But when they hadn't thrown them off the island by Monday night, it was obvious to people who had any idea of what was what that the place was due to fall."

For Magruder and his colleagues, "it was a sort of ticklish spot to be in" because the Americans were supposed to be attached to the British General Headquarters "which was, to say the least, far more hopeful" about defending Singapore. "We couldn't go up and tell them that we thought the game was over. Somebody, however, solved the problem very neatly by ordering us to Burma."

By Wednesday evening, the American banker and some acquaintances sailed for Sumatra aboard a yacht they jointly owned. Magruder reached Batavia (Jakarta) in late February and eventually reached Australia, where he ended up working as a lieutenant on General Douglas MacArthur's staff.

Above: Tape used for sealing correspondence, Singapore 1939
Left: Japanese planes conducted bombing missions over Singapore from their bases in Saigon as early as December 8, 1941; two months later they landed troops on the island

Left: The bank's branch in the Oriental Assurance building, Rangoon. Above: National City Bank's premises in Calcutta, 1930s. The building was still standing at the end of the 20th century, occupied by a local bank

Shanghai-Rangoon-Calcutta

On February 11, the day when Magruder was fleeing the Japanese invasion of Singapore, a sub-accountant from the bank's Shanghai branch arrived in Rangoon.

Although enemy nationals in Shanghai's international settlement and French concession were generally ignored during the early days of the Japanese occupation, Paul Hawkins didn't want to take any chances and decided to escape by pretending he was German. Leaving his colleagues behind, he went to a local riding academy where he kept a couple of horses and rode westward for a day before being forced to abandon the animals in the marshy terrain. After walking for three days, he came into contact with Chinese guerillas and with their help made it through Japanese lines, reaching the nationalist stronghold of Chongqing by plane on February 9. From there, he was ordered to report to the Rangoon branch, which he reached two days later.

Hawkins had only been in the Burmese capital for six days when Rangoon manager William Goldrick decided to close the branch. It was Tuesday, February 17—two days after the British surrender in Singapore. Japanese forces had bombed Rangoon as early as December 23 and troops advancing from the south were now within 120 kilometers of the city.

When the American army turned down Goldrick's request for a truck to evacuate the staff, Hawkins turned to his Chinese contacts, who offered as many jeeps as the bank was willing to drive and deliver to nationalist forces in the northern Burmese town of Lashio, about half-way between Mandalay and the Chinese border. However, none of the local staff could drive, so they could only accept a single jeep.

On February 19, the bank's convoy of three cars and a jeep driven by Hawkins set out with 10 staff members and three trunks of branch records and valuables along with food, water, fuel and one suitcase each. Taking a circuitous route to avoid Japanese forces near Mandalay, the convoy took four days to reach Lashio, already full of refugees trying to get to Calcutta. After waiting four days, Goldrick got a seat on a Chinese plane which flew between Kunming and Calcutta via Lashio. But he could only take the essential records and valuables, leaving the remaining items with Hawkins

and another staff member who got to Calcutta on a later flight.

Not all employees in Burma were so lucky, notably K.V. Venkateswaran who joined the Rangoon branch in 1934 after moving to Burma from southern India a few years earlier. Although his wife and three children left for India by ship before the branch closed, he had to stay behind and ended up taking the most dangerous route home. Traveling to Mandalay by rail was particularly hazardous—a special train carrying a group of British bankers fleeing Rangoon was bombed by the Japanese.

Venkateswaran was a less obvious target. He reached Mandalay on foot and then headed for the hills separating Burma from the Indian state of Manipur. He did not get to his home town in southern India until the end of 1943. "We never had any news of my father until then. ... We were all so happy to see him," recalled eldest son Venkataraman, who grew up in Rangoon and was six years old when he was evacuated in 1941. His father resumed working for the bank in Bombay in 1944, and a younger brother K.V.S. Iyer, born in 1949, was still working for Citibank's Chennai branch more than half a century later. "My father sometimes talked about that journey," the eldest son said. "He said he could see dead bodies everywhere."

Shanghai staff with Mitsubishi Bank liquidators, April 1942. Seated from left: sub-manager Milton Bates (first), managers Red Reed (third) and Elwood Mahon (fifth). Second row from left: Daniel Keating (first), Herschel Rogers (third), Gordon Ball (seventh), and William Griffiths (eighth). Back row: John Starret, John Brownley, James Aurell, Robert Russell, Woodford Fickett, Elon Olney. Not in picture is James A. MacKay

flying ability. I hasten to add, however, that the General quickly changed his mind. He was never too big to learn something new."

The only exception was an American admiral who believed the Japanese navy was "well-equipped, excellently officered and manned, and would give any navy something to worry about. Because of the ... opinions of our service officers, the buildup of our forces in the Philippines and the lack of precautionary warning from the State Department, we had a false sense of security regarding our composure in the islands."

In November, as head of the Far East division, Hart made one of his regular calls on the State Department in Washington. Rumors were flying of a deadlock in negotiations between the Japanese and the Americans. His principal call was on the department's chief adviser of Far Eastern affairs, who had always given him frank and straightforward advice on developments. "Here I am again on the same old quest," announced Hart. "Has anything happened that should affect the operations of my branches?" And, as he recalled, "It was obvious from his

Unusual conditions in Hong Kong

National City Bank's staff were well treated during the first six months of the Japanese occupation of Hong Kong. After the British surrender on December 25, 1941, "enemy" nationals, including seven from the bank, were moved to various hotels. British, American and Dutch bankers and their families were segregated from their colleagues, and put into the Sun Wah Hotel, on the outskirts of the Central district. Whereas other hotels were forced to accommodate 10 people to a room, the bankers had their own rooms and initially were given special armbands which allowed them to go to work, shop for food, and even dine at the American Club.

Jimmy Wong joined National City Bank in 1940, and continued with the bank during the occupation. Sixty years later, he recalled these events vividly. "The branch had 58 employees at the time, mainly Chinese but also Indian and Portuguese staff in addition to the seven bank officers interned." Whereas in Shanghai, Mitsubishi Bank was put in charge of liquidation proceedings, the business in Hong Kong was turned over to the Bank of Taiwan. "While all deposits were frozen at the beginning," Wong recalled, "limited withdrawals were allowed later on three separate occasions."

According to accounts published in *Number Eight* in 1942, the bankers felt humiliated at the beginning as they were ecorted to work. The guards were Japanese at first, but as demands on manpower increased, they later included Portuguese, Indians and Chinese. After a while, the walk was welcomed as a diversion—after all, it was their only form of exercise.

Under escort, Hong Kong branch manager Samuel Bitting (with dark hat) led bankers to work; they walked every day from the Sun Wah Hotel where they were interned

The vault in the Osaka branch

appearance that the adviser was not in a happy frame of mind that morning. My question evidently increased his irritation. He pounded his fist on his desk and replied: 'Hart, how many times do I have to tell you, the Japanese will never take any action that would involve major risk to their fleet.' Subsequent events would prove my informant right. The pitiful defense we put up less than two weeks later at Pearl Harbor certainly involved little risk to the Japanese fleet. But that was not the meaning the department adviser had intended."

By the beginning of 1942, the Shanghai, Tianjin and Beijing branches, as well as those in Tokyo, Hong Kong and Manila, were in the hands of Japanese administrators. After rapidly reducing its assets and liabilities, the Singapore branch handed over the remaining items on its balance sheet to a British bank on February 5. The Rangoon branch carried out a similar operation with key staff leaving on February 19. Carrying cash, bills and other assets, as well as records, they worked their way to Calcutta. The Calcutta branch was closed down in April 1942 with key staff, assets and records temporarily moved to Bombay, where operations continued on a reduced scale. Aside from Bombay, the only branches which remained open throughout the war were in Japan, where affairs were in the hands of the Yokohama Specie Bank. While 47 American staff were being held by the Japanese at the beginning of 1942, all those from Japan and Hong Kong and one from Shanghai reached New York in August after being released in an exchange of internees in neutral Portuguese waters off eastern Africa. However, 31 staff remained interned in the Philippines and China.

Hong Kong staff on the steps of Duddell Street, which ran up the right-hand side of the branch on Queens' Road Central

Evacuating Hong Kong staff

In this photograph, taken in June 1942, are manager Samuel Bitting and accountant Earle Cutting, seated third and fifth from left. On June 30, seven American staff, including Bitting and Cutting, were on board the Japanese vessel *Asama Maru* sailing for neutral Portuguese waters in Africa where they were transferred to the Swedish vessel *Gripsholm* in exchange for Japanese internees. The seven Hong Kong employees were joined by another five from Tokyo, Dalian and Shanghai. These included James MacKay, the assistant vice president for China. Sailing via Brazil, the 12 bankers returned to New York on August 25, 1942.

3. Expanding the Presence
1946–1971

"When it began to pick up, the fellas started moving aggressively in the Orient. It wasn't anything more than the utilization of resources you had where the opportunities were. It was nothing very complicated."

Walter B. Wriston

"They are back in their old haunts, greeting one another with boisterous cries at the bar," wrote *Fortune* magazine in the euphoria surrounding America's victory over Japan. It was February 1946, the Japanese surrender was six months old and one of the magazine's reporters had just spent three days and nights sitting up in a military transport aircraft eating Spam sandwiches and drinking truck-driver's coffee. His destination? Newly liberated Shanghai. The rush was on. "Mark my words, this town is in for the biggest boom you can possibly imagine," the American owner of the *Shanghai Evening Post and Mercury* told the magazine. "Anybody with wit, a little nerve and the sense to be reasonable could and will continue to make money in China." Shanghai, after all, was the "port of destiny ... nothing can stop its rise as the capital of the Orient." Well, almost nothing.

Among those back in town was Red Reed, a legend of the foreign exchange market since the 1930s (see p. 64). "In the golden age of extra-territoriality, Red kept three phones on his desk," wrote *Fortune*. "The sight of him manipulating them while leaping from Chinese fapi to Manchurian yen, from Hong Kong dollars to Bombay rupees, from gold bars to silver mex, all the while covering himself by buying or selling dollars on New York, sterling on London and gold on Bombay, was one of the memorable spectacles of the China coast."

Reed and a colleague, Mike Arnold, had apparently gotten bored sitting in their bare, unheated basement office waiting for trading to start and for the local monetary authorities to write a new banking law and fix a new exchange rate. "Well, there's always one thing we can do," Reed reportedly said. "We can always open for business." According to *Fortune*, "the austere British banking crowd was inclined to pooh-pooh the idea as a heroic but empty gesture. But the local Chase manager saw the point, the Chinese gave their blessing and the British tagged along." The opening took place in early December 1945, almost four years after the Pacific War began.

There was euphoria in Shanghai. But back in New York, management had a more somber assessment of the recent events in Asia. Twenty members of the bank's staff and their families had only just been released from internment camps in the Philippines and China. At the outbreak of

Opposite: Interior of the Yokohama branch after some modernization in the 1950s
Above: An advertisement announcing the reopening of the bank in China, January 1946

Left: The general post office in Manila in 1946, eight months after the bank reopened. Below: First day back at work at the Manila branch in 1945

the Pacific War in late 1941, the bank had 47 people interned in Japan, Hong Kong, China and the Philippines. In 1942, all of those interned in Japan and Hong Kong, plus one from Shanghai, were transferred aboard a Japanese vessel bound for Laurenco Marques (now Maputo), the main Portuguese port on the east coast of Africa, which was neutral territory. In exchanges of internees with a Swedish vessel, 26 internees were released and returned to New York. Of the remaining 20 liberated in 1945, many were in poor condition as a result of their experiences. However, all the staff were back at work by early 1946. An officer in Beijing had died in late 1942, although his illness was not in fact related to the war.

The Manila branch in the Philippines had been the first Far East branch of National City Bank to reopen after the war: this took place on June 28, 1945, and limited operations had since resumed in Singapore, Hong Kong, Shanghai and Tianjin. The Calcutta branch in India had briefly closed during the war, to reopen in November 1944. Reopening other Asian branches "will depend, first, on the needs and request of our armed forces and second, on the re-establishment of conditions under which foreign trade can be carried out safely and with profit," the bank reported to shareholders in early 1946. It added that companies could "only operate in an atmosphere of peace and justice and respect for private property."

In the report, the bank said the condition of branches in liberated areas "proved to be better than we had feared," while reserves set aside during the war "still appear to be more than adequate to cover any possible loss."

In the rented premises in Manila, the interior was a "mass of rubble," but the wall and roof were still standing, enabling rough repairs to be made in time for the reopening. "The local staff has been reassembled, with few losses, and our business has been largely for the armed forces, American business and for local business and individuals." But there were still problems regarding old loans and deposits given the transactions carried out by the Japanese liquidator in occupation currency. "Fortunately our records are good, due partly to having copies of the more important

Cause for celebration

Business in Shanghai resumed on Monday, December 10, 1945. The grand reopening, almost four years to the day after the arrival of the Japanese, was described by Charles Murphy in a report in *Fortune* magazine.

"Auspiciously, after a long spell of raw, dull weather, the sun shone and the sea sparkled. Red and Mike, each with a festive red carnation in his buttonhole, stood at the door, pumping the hands of arriving generals,

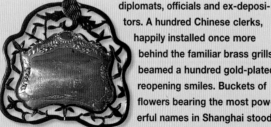

Silver plaque presented to the bank upon reopening in Shanghai

diplomats, officials and ex-depositors. A hundred Chinese clerks, happily installed once more behind the familiar brass grills, beamed a hundred gold-plated reopening smiles. Buckets of flowers bearing the most powerful names in Shanghai stood among the well-laden buffet tables. Most important in half-frozen Shanghai, a brand-new central heating system (said Red hoarsely, "It works—don't ask how we got it") bathed the hosts and guests in a warming blast."

An advertising line used by the bank in the early 1950s

records here, and partly to the loyalty of several Philippine staff members who kept track of operations of the Japanese liquidator during the occupation."

As for the other four branches, the buildings were all usable. "With the exception of straightening out the records and obtaining agreement on the effect of occupation operations of the Japanese liquidators, we anticipate few serious difficulties," the report said. Premises owned in Hong Kong, Tianjin, Guangzhou, Hankou [Wuhan], Beijing and Yokohama were "practically undamaged," but some of the staff houses owned in several countries were "damaged or in some cases almost totally destroyed."

In the late 1940s, National City Bank was contending with major economic difficulties in both China and Japan. With the civil war between communist and nationalist forces raging in China, the domestic currency situation was a mess. As more money was printed, inflation soared to unprecedented levels.

Mike Arnold had joined Red Reed in reopening the Shanghai branch at the end of 1945. "Funds were kept in banks only overnight because companies and individuals kept their balances at an absolute minimum," he recalled. "Our loans were on an overnight basis and at one time at a rate of 3.25 percent a day. ... When a Chinese worker was paid, his whole family would come down to take the pay from him. Immediately they darted off in all directions to invest it in commodities such as rice or gold or anything they could lay their hands on. The reason was obvious— by the next day, that money might

Branch at Brabourne Road, Calcutta. The bank was still there half a century later (see p. 118)

Victory bonuses in Shanghai

With America celebrating its victory over Japan, National City Bank decided to pay a "victory bonus" to its employees at the Shanghai branch, many of whom had worked for the bank before the Japanese occupation. "Every employee received a victory bonus of six months' salary," recalled Ren Zhiming in 2001. Ren had originally joined the bank in 1936.

According to several Chinese staff from the period, the post-war operation had about 150 employees in Shanghai before 1949. About 80 percent were Chinese while the rest were more or less evenly divided between Americans and other foreigners, including Portuguese and

Staff at the Shanghai branch as ping-pong champions

Russians. Liu Zhengxing, a veteran of 1940, recalled that "American bank salaries were higher than at the British banks. The atmosphere was more relaxed and easy-going."

Above: A teller prepares the monthly payroll for the Shanghai Telephone Company in 1948, a time of inflation. The branch mobilized three tellers and 10 assistants to collect the cash from the central bank. Right: The payroll for 1,200 workers on this occasion was 16 billion local dollars

have already lost 10 percent of its value. Inflation was so rampant that people stopped counting the notes when they completed transactions with us, there were just too many notes. They accepted the bank's certification as to the amount in each bundle.

"From an official exchange rate of 500 to one in late 1945, the rate skyrocketed to about a million to one in 1948," Arnold said. "In May 1949 when I was ordered to leave, the total value of Chinese deposits in our Shanghai branch—billions of yuan—were worth only about 25,000 dollars and the deposits in our vaults were only worth about 5,000 dollars. In fact, the physical property owned by the U.S. staff exceeded the value of all the Chinese cash in the branch."

In Japan, inflation was a major problem, just as it was in China; but the American occupation authorities were confronting another set of challenges. As economist Takafusa Nakamura remarked, "Japan poured all its strength into the war and in so doing was destroyed." Almost three million Japanese were dead. Total damage to the Japanese economy was estimated at 64.3 billion yen, about a third of the remaining national wealth, which had been slashed to roughly the same level as 1935. Food and energy shortages were widespread and black markets flourished with prices up to seven times the official level.

Led by General Douglas MacArthur, occupation authorities implemented labor reforms followed by land reforms in 1946. In the same year the Tokyo branch resumed limited operations for United States government agencies and personnel.

In early 1947, the bank reported "considerable progress" in reducing the number of items representing possible war-related

New York honors loyal local staff

In its report to shareholders in 1946, head office praised the courage of the staff.

"All of our people testify to their debt to loyal Philippine and Chinese staff members, friends and servants who in many cases risked their lives to procure food, medicine and other aid," the report said. Although some internees were released in mid-1942, another 20 officers, including wives and children, remained in the Philippines and China camps for a further three years.

Noting the good shape of branch records in the Philippines, the report by chairman Gordon Rentschler and other executives also highlighted "the loyalty of several Philippine staff members who kept track of the operations of the Japanese liquidator during the occupation."

Among the Americans in Manila at the time was one Walter Wriston, a young second lieutenant. Wriston joined the bank upon his return home, and ultimately became chairman. "Half the Manila branch kept all the books at home during the war," he recalled many years later. At the same time, branch manager Alexander Calhoun managed to get extra food into the Santo Tomas camp, where most of the staff and their families were interned. "He'd write on a piece of paper 'National City Bank will pay the holder 1,000 pesos for food,' and they smuggled all this food in," Wriston said. After the war, "he sat there and redeemed all those tickets, one after the other. It was amazing."

Wriston visited the Santo Tomas camp. "I went in there with the army," he said. "It was a horrible place."

Shanghai staff from the 1930s and 1940s on the roof of the Peace Hotel in 2001. From left to right: Gui Fubao, Ren Zhiming, Chen Minan, Liu Zhengxing, Qi Yiyu, Zheng Yifei

"Sign here please, Mrs. MacArthur." The wife of the commander of the occupation forces in Japan opens an account with National City Bank's Tokyo branch on July 22, 1946

losses. "Our total loss will be very much less than the amount originally estimated and reserved for," it said. "Among the questions now being raised is that of financing exports and imports beyond the period when countries are using accumulated dollars or are beneficiaries of government loans. Already in some cases, private financing is again possible. In others, the risk is so great in present unsettled world conditions that normal trade financing is not possible."

The bank continued to move cautiously in Asia, the reopening and expansion of branches largely determined by the demands of the American military. In 1947, operations resumed in Osaka on a limited basis for the U.S. army. In 1948, the Yokohama branch resumed business, again largely for military customers. In the Philippines, the Cebu branch had been reopened in 1947 and a third Philippine branch established at the Clark Field air base. In 1948 the bank also opened a second Manila branch, in its own new building near Chinatown. In China, however, the civil war claimed its first casualty—the Tianjin branch was closed and the limited remaining business transferred to Shanghai. It had been up and running again for only three years.

In early 1948, Gordon S. Rentschler, the chairman of National City Bank, died while on a visit to Cuba. His successor was William Gage Brady. Known as the "Iron Duke," Brady had been with the bank for more than 30 years, working especially on the operations and administration side of the business. As his deputy, the board chose Howard C. Sheperd, who had joined the bank in 1916 in one of the first college training classes. The succession was smooth and set an important precedent for the bank—an orderly transfer of power from one generation to the next, with the new incumbent drawn from within the ranks.

Sheperd was concerned about earnings, particularly by the end of 1948, by which time the American economy had slipped into recession. Overseas earnings in Japan, the Philippines and

Shanghai's innovation

After the Shanghai branch reopened in December 1945, business with Chinese depositors began to expand rapidly. The explanation was simple. "Before 1945, there were two obstacles," recalled Gui Fubao, who joined the bank in 1934. "You needed someone to introduce you to open a deposit and you had to sign in English. From 1946, we stopped requiring introductions and we

Gui Fubao

didn't ask customers to use English any more, and so it was okay for them to use their personal seal. That's why the business expanded so much."

Gui, who was the most senior member of the retired Shanghai Citibankers Club in 2001, later worked in the foreign exchange department for the international department of the Bank of China, a leading Chinese commercial bank with an extensive network abroad.

Military-style accommodation for the Clark Field branch in the Philippines, opened in 1947 mainly to service the banking needs of air force personnel

Chairman Howard Sheperd and his wife visiting Hong Kong in 1954 From left: Howard Sheperd, Mrs. Sheperd, branch manager Ralph Newell, Hank Sperry and Mrs. Sperry

some parts of Latin America were good but were offset by lower earnings in Brazil and Argentina along with the loss of the Tianjin branch. Sheperd set up a committee to look into these and other issues. It was initially called the "New Look Committee" and was headed by George S. Moore, a vice president in charge of out-of-town accounts in the domestic division.

The committee's biggest contribution to the bank was its recommendation that there should be a divisional profit and loss statement, a development that was apparently overdue. Moore's report noted that the bank was in fact "a composite of

a number of different types of businesses" and that more emphasis had been put on size at the expense of profits in recent years. In the words of the report, "We have never really known just where we made our net profits but have generally proceeded on the assumption that we should encourage the growth of all these businesses to the maximum, on the theory that the more they grow the more money we would make."

By early 1949, the civil war in China had reached a turning point. In May, the victorious People's Liberation Army marched into Shanghai and banking business ground largely to a halt. Most of the foreign staff left during the year, although Shanghai branch manager Red Reed and most of the Chinese employees stayed on. During this period, it was confirmed that it was not against American government policy for National City Bank to remain in China so the business continued, with the bank

Ahead of their time

When an American officer who had worked at the Shanghai branch told bank chairman Gordon Rentschler he was going to marry a Chinese girl, the reply was brief: "I know, Washington has told me."

Henry Sperry, known generally as "Hank," had met Ansie Lee when they were both interned during the war in the Philippines. When they were released by American forces on February 23, 1945, Ansie chose to go to San Francisco, not knowing where her family was. By chance, Ansie's older brother, Harold, was also in the United States and managed to locate her.

"I did not see Harold at all while in the U.S. We only spoke over the phone and I told him about Hank," Ansie recalled. At that time, Harold was advisor to Quo Tai Chi, former Ambassador to the Court of St. James,

when the latter represented China in the formation of the United Nations. They had been in San Francisco, though not while Hank and Ansie were there. "Perhaps they went on to Washington from San Francisco—Harold must have mentioned to the ambassador about me. Who else but my brother would have been so keen to find out who Hank Sperry was?"

When Hank and Ansie were married in Shanghai in 1946, "it was absolutely unheard of—we were a little ahead of our time," Ansie said. "I was rather glad to be a wedge, although the British really liked Hank's conservative ways." In due course, in Hong Kong, she was the first

Christmas Party in Shanghai in 1946. Hank and Ansie Sperry are fourth and fifth from the right in the front row. Red Reed, the manager, is clutching the dog

Chinese to belong to the Royal Hong Kong Yacht Club, the Hong Kong Club, and the Shek-O Golf Club.

Hank worked for the bank for many more years, and helped set up operations in Taiwan, Hong Kong and Vietnam.

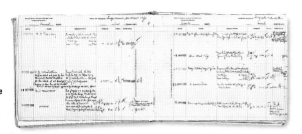

"Accounts receivable and Sundry accounts register" from the Singapore branch. Visible here are entries from 1954 to 1964; other pages go back to the 1930s

providing services to American businesses still operating there. But as the bank later told the United States Treasury, "economic conditions and business prospects following this period were not propitious." In early 1950, the balance sheet at the Shanghai branch had shrunk to only 10,000 dollars.

The continuing presence of Red Reed gave some sense of security to those employees who remained at the Shanghai branch. He had taken up residence in the Cathay Hotel, located on the Bund and known today as the Peace Hotel, and witnessed the dawn of the New China.

"We thought the bank would still function. That's what Mr. Reed told us," recalled Liu Zhengxing, a retired staff member, in 2001. "The employees were confident that we'd continue to work as before." However, this was not to be. Since Reed's return, the foreign exchange market that had brought him fame and the bank fortune, helping to pay its dividend during the 1930s, was gone. "There was a little bit of business but the current account, cash and cable departments had all closed," said Chen Minan, another veteran of the time.

In May 1950, a year after the People's Liberation Army marched into Shanghai, Reed died. "That was when we felt there was a real crisis," said Liu. "When he died, there were no funds coming from head office. When we didn't get our salaries, we stopped working but came to the office to wait for our salaries. Then the bank said they wanted to close."

After Reed's death the bank appointed a British officer named Fred Harnden to oversee the Shanghai branch. In August, he sought permission from local government authorities to liquidate the business and terminate local staff. As it turned out, the process would drag on. After lengthy negotiations, a liquidation tax of 233,000 dollars was agreed.

There was a snag, however. Harnden was still in Shanghai and the authorities would not allow him to leave until the bank paid up. On its side, the bank was reluctant to pay up until he was safely out of Shanghai. In the end, the matter was resolved and Harnden flew to Hong Kong. "His great remark to me was 'you know I never missed tiffin,'" Walter Wriston said. The future

Cotton-led recovery

With the United States sending shiploads of cotton to China after the war, the bank was in a good position to help finance the booming textile and garment businesses.

"At that time, the bank's reputation was very high," recalled Qi Yiyu, a retired staff member, in 2001. "The Americans and Chinese had just signed an agreement to import cotton. We needed to import large amounts of cotton as there was strong demand for clothing among Chinese people after the war. ... Business was excellent and in 1946 and 1947, we met a lot of the owners of Chinese spinning factories."

After 1949, Qi joined the country's new bank under the People's Bank of China, but he was later sent to work in the countryside in the remote western province of Gansu. He was there until 1980. "When I got back to Shanghai, the government said it had been a mistake," he said.

As China's post-war reconstruction accelerated, exports rebounded to 135 million dollars in the first six months of 1946—three times the value for the whole of 1939

A manual typewriter used at the bank in the 1950s

chairman said the whole exercise had been an "interesting experience" with an important lesson. "He was the only hostage we ever had. When we lost Cuba, I had everybody out of there."

The brief return to China was cut short by history. It left the bank scarred and had a profound influence on its view of Asia until well into the 1960s. As James A. MacKay, then head of Far East operations, commented: "We had great plans. But then we realized when we went back out there that there was no hope."

After the communist victory in China, the American occupation authorities lost interest in reforming Japan. Containing the perceived communist threat became the top priority in Asia.

In the early days of the occupation of Japan, the Americans had implemented land and labor reforms while making a half-hearted attempt to dismantle huge conglomerates such as Mitsui, Mitsubishi, Sumitomo and the Fuyo group centered around Fuji Bank. In trying to stabilize the financial system and control rampant inflation, little progress was made until Detroit banker William Dodge arrived in Japan in 1949 to serve as financial adviser to General MacArthur. Under a series of measures, the national budget was balanced, international trade was returned to the private sector and the yen was fixed at an extremely low rate of 360 to the dollar despite opposition from some American economists who felt that this rate was excessively generous to Japanese exporters. It was, but Japan's export industries would take years to recover and the exchange rate wouldn't become a big issue for another 25 years.

Black money

After the Pacific War, the United States financed aid shipments to China. But corruption among nationalist government officials led to huge fortunes being made through artificially high exchange rates.

"China was exporting so little in value that the imports were almost all paid for by the U.S. government through the aid program. This was where a great deal of corruption of the Chinese government came in because the exchange rate was never realistic," recalled Ray Kathe, who was working at the Tianjin branch at the time.

With inflation out of control, a new currency called the gold yuan was introduced in 1948. At first, the official exchange rate was four units to the dollar. But "the gold yuan was no more gold than the paper it was written on, and the last quoted rate for that was 240 million to the dollar so you can see the great blowup of the currency.

"The government would try to hold the exchange rate at an unrealistic level. So if the black market rate was 10,000 but the official rate was 3,000, the government would import at 3,000 to one with aid dollars and sell it on to the market at 10,000 to one. They were also buying up gold and sending it out of the country. So they had a beautiful game going. Many of the Chinese officials made huge amounts of money on the aid shipments."

Above: The gold yuan, a short-lived attempt to achieve a stable currency.
Right: As inflation skyrocketed in 1948 with the reckless printing of money, Shanghai citizens rushed to buy dollars or gold

Above: Victory parade in Shanghai in July 1949. The banner reads: "Celebrate Liberation." Right above: "The Chinese people have stood up!" Mao Zedong proclaims the People's Republic of China from Beijing's Tiananmen Square on October 1, 1949

New shutdown in Tianjin

With civil war raging around Tianjin, the bank closed the branch there in December 1948 and moved operations to Shanghai, the only other branch in China still operating.

The clients in Tianjin had been mainly trading companies or foreign manufacturers producing small export items and commodities such as carpets, hides, skins, wool, hog casings and bristles, and dried egg yolks.

Other exports included works of art made in the "antique factory" in Beijing, recalled Ray Kathe, who had helped to reopen the branch three years earlier. "There were huge volumes of that going to Europe as well as the United States. They didn't try to sell their products as other than reproductions but they were very good pieces."

Other clients included the oil companies Shell and Caltex as well as Standard Vacuum (later split into Exxon and Mobil). "Those three companies were very big in our picture, and we lent them most of our lendable funds that we didn't use for the trading company activities."

When fighting spread north, Kathe was sent to the old Beijing branch, still closed since World War II. "We had records there going back to World War I days," he said.

"My job was to see that all records, except a very few which I was to personally take to Tianjin, were destroyed. I set out on my final trip." The train trip took eight hours—four times longer than normal. In Beijing, Kathe spent days "doing nothing but shoveling records into an old coal stove and making sure they burned. Then I hurried back."

Back in Tianjin, it was much the same. "For several days we didn't have to use any coal for heat as we threw records, travelers checks and pre-war IBC currency into the furnace. Shoveling materials into the fire was slowed down by the routine of first cutting the items and recording what we were destroying." Records were put in crates and loaded onto an American ship evacuating United States government personnel and other citizens. Although the branch closed on December 4, Kathe and the manager had to wait another three weeks before leaving for Shanghai. "The old airport was closed," he said. "We finally got a plane out on a special runway that was made inside the racecourse in the city." The building was left in the hands of a Russian employee who made the decision to stay—he had lived in Tianjin since fleeing the Bolshevik revolution 30 years earlier.

Down and out in Shanghai

It was springtime in Shanghai when Chairman Mao's victorious troops started marching into the city. "Before they came, a major part of my job was to liquidate records and protect shipment and the bank's house," recalled Ray Kathe, who had been in the city for barely four months after closing the Tianjin branch in December. The house was meant for the manager but he had moved his bed into the bank itself as the fighting moved closer.

Kathe said the first inkling he had of the turn of events was one morning at 3 a.m. when he was awoken by the sound of shooting and howling. "I made my own version of a bullet-proof suit by rolling myself up in a thick carpet and lying on the floor for about an hour," he recalled. "I later learned that first nationalist troops had come dashing past followed by columns of communist troops. With the latter came a solitary tank which let loose with a few blasts and moved on." Although the branch closed its doors the next day, Kathe remained in Shanghai until October 1949.

The People's Liberation Army parades down Nanjing Road, Shanghai, 1949

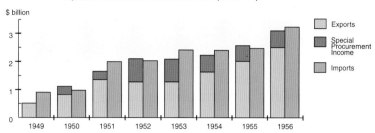

Japanese trade and the Korean War (1949–56)

$ billion

	Exports
	Special Procurement Income
	Imports

Special procurements by the U.S. military during the Korean War allowed Japan to double imports without adversely affecting its balance of payments. Industries relying on imports for raw materials could suddenly expand production significantly

Source: Takafusa Nakamura, The Postwar Japanese Economy

The economy of Japan was slowly emerging from the devastation of war but it was still only staggering. In 1950, it received a powerful shot in the arm with the outbreak of the Korean War. Special procurements of goods and services to support the war effort were a significant boost to the economy, allowing Japan's industrial output to surpass pre-war levels. As Takafusa Nakamura noted, "the influence of the Korean War was nothing short of prodigious" given the huge amount of foreign exchange income derived from American military spending. Foreign currency from this source reached 590 million dollars in 1951 and more than 800 million dollars in 1952 and 1953. These were gigantic sums for those times. "To the Japanese economy, which had been doing its best just to import something less than one billion dollar's worth of goods in 1949 and 1950, two billion dollars in imports meant that the key industries which depended on imports of raw materials could virtually double their scale of production," Nakamura said. "Freed of balance-of-payments limitations, firms which were extremely anxious to increase

production could obtain the imports needed to support a much larger scale of activity."

With the Korean War in full swing, National City Bank reported to shareholders in early 1951 that the volume of foreign trade financed the previous year had been the highest since World War II. Moreover, as the pickup in industrial activity strengthened in Japan, the bank opened a new branch in March in the central city of Nagoya, close to the headquarters and major plants of Toyota Motor Corporation. The expanding Japan network was further reinforced in 1952 with the establishment of limited banking facilities for the American military at Camp Otsu and Camp Zama, two of the major bases in Japan.

But that is where it stopped for several years, as the bank's overseas division began to focus on Latin America and Europe rather than Asia. In the years up to 1955, the bank had concentrated its Asian operations in the two countries with the biggest

A day in the life of the commercial credit department

In early 1951, the bank took the unusual step of publishing in the annual report for 1950 a selection of transactions from a "typical day" in the commercial credit department in the New York office. The move was prompted by the surge in trade during the previous year, and the fact that the volume of international trade financed by the bank had hit a post-war record.

"The business of the overseas branches was extremely active, and the number of business travelers to whom the bank was able to render aid was greatly increased," the bank's annual report said.

Copra from the Philippines to America	$126,000
Crude rubber from Malaya to America	$53,000
Marine engine parts from America to French Indochina	$48,000
Raw cotton from America to Japan	$41,108
Crushing equipment from America to the Philippines	$40,000
Aluminium from Japan to America	$7,600
Penicillin from America to India	$5,500
Alarm clocks from Germany to the Philippines	$1,340
Dyed silk from Japan to Mexico	$924

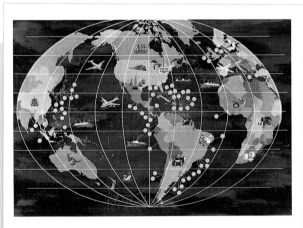

How bankers "on the scene" make the difference overseas

The FIRST
NATIONAL CITY BANK
of New York

N.C.B. PORT AREA BRANCH CHRISTMAS PARTY
DECEMBER 22, 1953

The staff at the Port Area branch, Manila, hold a Christmas Party on December 22, 1953

American military presence—Japan and the Philippines. In these countries old branches had been reopened and new branches set up, mostly to serve the military. The Nagoya branch was an exception, but even this branch was an indirect outcome of the Korean War.

With the military taken care of, the secondary priority for reopening branches came into full play—the need to be able to trade safely and profitably. The effect of the guidelines reported to shareholders in 1946 was to restrict severely the Asian expansion of National City Bank. Apart from the big presence in Japan and the Philippines, the only other operations in Asia were branches in the British colonial trading outposts of Hong Kong and Singapore along with the Indian branches in Bombay and Calcutta. To sum up, National City Bank's operation in the region was now limited to two Cold War allies and four ports.

Walter Wriston explained that with the Marshall Plan for rebuilding Europe eventually followed by the Treaty of Rome, expanding the bank's presence on the European continent became the top priority for the overseas division. Latin America also figured prominently in the

global strategy. But with the end of the civil war in China followed by new wars in Korea and Vietnam, and instability and eventually "konfrontasi" in Indonesia, the head office strategy toward Asia was cautious. It would remain so until the mid-1960s.

"After the Second World War, the place was in a shambles," Wriston said. "The bank was quite small. When I joined the bank the assets were four billion dollars and we earned 17 million dollars that year. We had 20 branches overseas, and the reason we went to Europe was that the Treaty of Rome was signed. The only people who believed in it were the Americans so we had an opportunity to put branches in every common market country and do what no European bank did—Deutsche Bank didn't even have a branch in Paris. So how did you do that? Well, there was blocked currency all over Latin America,

The last of the compradors

The branches in Japan were the first to phase out the comprador system; the legacy survived the longest in Hong Kong—until the 1960s.

When Ray Kathe reopened the Tianjin branch in 1945, the son of the previous comprador was still working there although his role was starting to fade. "In Shanghai, we had pretty much gotten rid of the system altogether. The old comprador died but we did have a number-one Chinese officer who acted a bit like a comprador without guaranteeing anything.

"In Hong Kong, we had a Chinese who was the comprador who was merely a front and no longer brought in business. But he still guaranteed the cash and

tellers department. Consequently most of his relatives, even when I was there in 1961, were in the teller positions. He was still active but only with regard to the tellers. He had a little office in our building. ... Because of the unusual law governing exchange business, we used his name to do open-market transactions instead of the name of the bank."

Left: Hong Kong branch's first comprador Iu Ku Un (see p. 32), with his son, Iu Tak Cheuk, in 1933. Above: Iu Tak Cheuk when he retired, with Hong Kong manager Samuel Eastabrooks, 1969. Iu joined the bank in 1927

Above: Ground-breaking ceremony according to Shinto rites, for the new Nagoya branch in 1951. Leo W. Chamberlain, resident vice president, digs in front of a temporary altar bearing trays of "fruits of the field" (the boxes on the stands). Right above: Exterior of Camp Zama branch near Yokohama. Right below: American soldiers changing money at Camp Zama branch

principally in Brazil and Argentina. So all we did was we sent all our trainees down there. They got paid in local currency, we got a bunch of really well-trained people and they went to Europe and opened all these branches.

"In the meantime, right after the war, the Orient was kind of a disaster. Things were basically destroyed. Hong Kong was in bad shape and Singapore was nothing. It was not as robust and didn't have the potential at that point that Europe did. And you had limited resources. When it began to pick up, the fellas started moving aggressively in the Orient. It wasn't anything more than the utilization of the resources you had where the opportunities were. It was nothing very complicated."

It is true that the bank's resumption of activities in Asia in the 10–15 years after World War II was less dynamic than what followed. Commercial opportunities were initially limited. However, the seeds were being sown for an extraordinary

transformation of the bank which reflected, and promoted, that of Asia's national economies. Some of the first signs of an "economic miracle" were beginning to appear in Japan. The post-war period saw the emergence of Tokyo as Japan's undisputed center of finance as it drew business away from the western cities of Osaka and Kobe. Much of National City Bank's early post-war business in Japan had been with the occupation authorities, opening letters of credit for imports of commodities such as grain and cotton. Japanese companies later took over the imports and until the San Francisco Peace Treaty was signed in 1951, most of the bank's income was derived from commissions on commercial credits through Japanese banks.

Ray Kathe recalled: "During all this time, of course, we were lending yen to our foreign clients, primarily the oil companies which could use almost any amount that we could provide." But lending was limited due to the low level of deposits. "The system

"When you have to leave your desk to get information ... let the customer know how long you'll be gone and offer to call him back. He'll appreciate it!"—a tip from *Number Eight*, March 1954

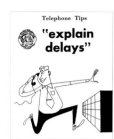

in Asia in all our branches—including the Philippines, Singapore and the rest—was always never to lend more money locally than we could dredge up as deposits. Deposits were the all-important thing and we didn't lend foreign currency." But an important captive source of yen deposits did emerge in Japan—the American movie companies bringing in films from the United States for screening in Japan. Due to controls in force at the time, they had to build up substantial deposits before being allowed to remit funds to the United States. Notwithstanding the movie companies, however, the deposit

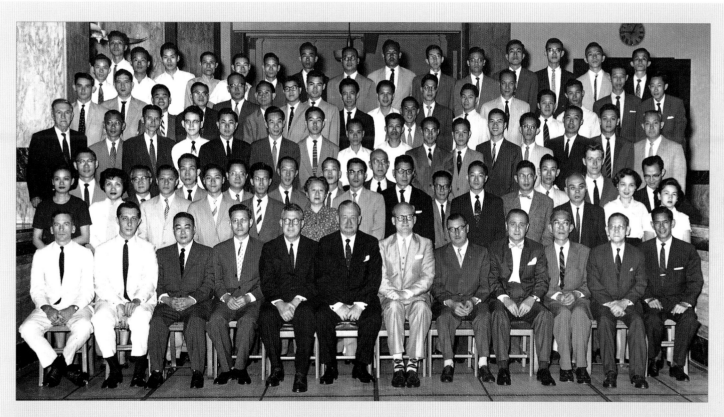

Hong Kong staff

A typical group photograph taken during the 1950s. Seated in front are: Hank Sperry (fifth from left), Leonard Johnson (sixth), Ray Kathe (seventh), Fred Harnden (eighth) and comprador Iu Tak Cheuk (tenth). Jimmy Wong Kwok Hing joined the bank in 1940 and continued to work there with Bank of Taiwan liquidator Oi Junji throughout most of the war. Here he is standing behind Harnden in the second row to the right. Also shown here are other staff members Ho Man Chiu (back row, fourth from the right) and Lau On (second last row, extreme right). The elderly gentleman on the extreme left in the dark suit is "Mr. Manton," a British doorman who lived above the bank with his wife. "To have an Englishman standing outside was unique," Sperry's wife Ansie said. "Mr. Manton was always properly dressed with jacket and tie and spoke quietly with a slight cockney accent. He obliged the bank wives by getting movie tickets from two nearby theaters."

THE NATIONAL CITY BANK OF NEW YORK

NO LEFT TURN
竹向不
號左准

FIRST NATIONAL CITY BANK

Far left: The main Hong Kong branch on the corner of Ice House Street and Queen's Road Central
Left: The Kowloon branch, opened on June 4,1962
Below: The opening ceremony for the Causeway Bay branch on October 5, 1964. The branch was located between two hairdressing salons. "I remember one woman came in and asked if she still had enough time for a shampoo," recalled one employee

FIRST NATIONAL CITY BANK

萬國寶通

Different skills

The people who rebuilt the bank in Asia in the 1950s and 1960s had a different set of skills from today's bankers. But for Walter Wriston, the differences weren't simply between the banking generalists of yesterday and the specialists of today. History itself played a defining role in attracting different types of people to the bank.

"In 1933, the balloon went up and people were afraid to go home to their children if they worked in a bank," the retired chairman recalled in 2001. "From about 1937, the arsenal of democracy was beginning to crank up and everybody got drafted so in

1945 there was nobody home. That's how we all got our promotions so quickly because there was nothing ahead of us.

"The generation that came out of the war were very different guys from the people that were there," Wriston said. By the time he joined the bank, the future chairman had already served as a soldier in the Philippines and many other new recruits had served in the Pacific.

"On my right was the first man across the Remagen Bridge. On my left was a guy who flew P38s in the Pacific. My best friend saw 360 days of continuous combat," he recalled. "So when Mother Bank said 'We'll

never be able to rebuild it,' they said 'Baloney, we're in business.' They were adventurous souls. These guys would go someplace, literally, with a general ledger and hire the staff and hang out a sign and get people and start a business—they were amazing people.

"The bank was always a meritocracy. There was damn little politics—there were too many smart people who wouldn't buy it. It's still that way today but it's a different set of skills required. I wouldn't say they were better or worse than some guy with a Ph.D. in math who can figure out a derivative. I'm sure none of us could have even touched that."

base remained relatively small. "We never put much out to clients," Kathe said. "Even when we did ... we always kept a lot of money in the interbank market so that if one of our clients drew on us quickly, we would have to get the money from another bank to cover the withdrawal. So we were lenders to the interbank market."

From the mid-1950s onward, the bank started offering acceptances to Japanese banks for paper drawn on New York. The commissions were huge—1.5 percent—and the market grew to be worth hundreds of millions of dollars, and a major source of earnings for the branches in Japan. And from the late 1950s, the bank began foreign currency lending to Japanese companies, known as "impact loans." Such foreign currency lending was another major source of earnings in Japan and would remain so for 20 years until Japanese banks were finally allowed to undertake similar activities.

By the end of the 1950s, credit procedures had been strengthened and the corporate lending department reorganized. In 1959, the bank started tapping a new source of funds in the emerging Eurodollar market, a child of the Cold War which began with Soviet banks depositing

Staff of the Manila branch at work, 1960s

their dollars in London rather than in New York. By 1961, the bank was able to announce a major innovation—the negotiable certificate of deposit (CD). While such instruments were hardly new in themselves, negotiability was and a secondary market soon developed, competing with government securities and commercial paper for corporate funds.

Bank president James Stillman Rockefeller visiting the Port Area branch in Manila in 1958

On the switchboard

When Dolores Brown joined the bank in Hong Kong in 1961, each department shared three or four telephones; the main Hong Kong office had only a few dozen lines. "When I first started on the switchboard, we had to recognize people's voices and we had to have our own directory," she recalled 40 years later. "All the long-distance calls were channeled though the switchboard. I'd have to consolidate the calls and the bill would come to me at the end of every month." Management guidelines on telephone etiquette were strict. "You never said 'okay' to anybody—it was considered rude and not acceptable to everyone." While receiving a fair share of nuisance calls over the years, Brown said the advent of credit cards had resulted in

some particularly unusual requests. "Some people ring up and ask how to stop their sons from using their credit cards," she said. Being a Cantonese speaker, Brown has also been exposed to some of the more colorful aspects of the southern Chinese dialect. "Then I pretend I don't understand the language." After years of speaking to her over the phone, local staff were sometimes astonished to find she was not Chinese when meeting her in person. While Brown was born in Hong Kong, her father was born in China to a Danish father and Chinese mother (and was also the proud owner of the 1924 Hillman featured in "Love is a Many Splendored Thing"). Her mother's parents were both Russian, emigrating from Vladivostok to San Francisco before moving to Shanghai and eventually Hong Kong.

Training in New York

In the 1950s, the bank was a pioneer in developing the careers of its local staff. Branches began to send promising young employees to New York for career development assignments—and many of them ended up in very senior positions. Among the first was Tatsuo Umezono, a young Japanese hired in 1948 following in the footsteps of his father who had joined the Kobe branch shortly after it opened in 1904. On Wall Street in those days, Umezono recalled, there were separate toilets for white and "colored" people. On a visit to Kentucky, he discovered that segregation extended to public transport as well. "I got on a bus and the driver said: 'You sit in the middle.' I was not sure what he meant until I realized that only white people could sit in the front of the bus while the black people had to sit down the back. I suppose I was considered somewhere in between," Umezono recalled. "I felt very uneasy."

While bringing Asians to New York may have been rare in the 1950s, it was not so in the 1960s, when the head office training of local staff gathered pace and the bank started hiring MBA graduates. Among them was a young Filipino named Rafael Buenaventura who, after a long career with the bank, would eventually become central bank governor in the Philippines. And among those getting head office experience in the 1970s were a young Chinese, Antony Leung, who ended up as Hong Kong's Financial Secretary in 2001, and an Indian named Victor Menezes who was destined to become chairman of Citibank.

As for Umezono, he went on to become the first Japanese senior vice president and the bank's first Japanese country head for Japan. Walter Wriston, who ran the overseas division in the 1960s, typically didn't care what other Americans thought. The bank had a principle and stuck to it. "We hired brains, and we didn't care what color you were, or the color of your passport or your gender," he said. "Talent has no borders. There's smart people all over the world. We went from 20 branches overseas to a thousand. That's fairly substantial and you had different languages, different customs, different cultures and different currencies. When you had some native of some country who was outstanding, the word was out—see whether you could get him or her on the international staff.

"That's how Victor Menezes came out and all of these people. I don't think anybody woke up one morning and said 'Let's hire Orientals.' What we did was hire brains—whoever, whatever they are."

Greenhorns in New York

By 1967, the bank was sending a number of its promising Asian employees to New York for hands-on experience of American banking practices. Among them was Wong Nang Jang, who had been working with the bank for five years. "I'm not sure if you'd call it training in today's terms but in those days it was a big deal as I was allowed to be away for a year," Wong said.

The future executive vice president, and then deputy president, of Singapore's Oversea-Chinese Banking Corporation recalled that First National City Bank's human resources department at head office was thrown in "total turmoil" as a result. "They knew how to pay expatriate allowances to Americans living overseas but they didn't know how to handle us greenhorns from Asia in New York," he said.

Walter Wriston (center) with U.S. Ambassador to Malaysia James Bell (left) during Bell's visit to the overseas division. On the right is Carleton M. Stewart, a veteran of the bank's Asian operations both in the branches and in New York. He joined the bank in 1947

The 1960s was a time of expansion and development. Worldwide, the decade was marked by a new strategic vision for the bank, defined by George Moore and his close associate Walter Wriston. When James Stillman Rockefeller, the bank's president in 1959, moved up to become chairman after Howard Sheperd's retirement, Moore succeeded him as president. Wriston was put in charge of the bank's overseas division. The strategy now devised by Moore and Wriston focused on product diversification and branch expansion at home and abroad in order to deepen the relationships with existing customers and find new ones as well.

As explained by Wriston, the first phase of the overseas division's plan was to put a branch "in every commercially important country in the world. The second phase was to tap the local deposit market by establishing satellite branches or

Located near the central market in Medan Pasar, the bank's first branch in Kuala Lumpur, Malaysia, began operations in 1959. Shown here is the branch after an extra floor had been added

The Grindlays connection

In the late 1960s, Britain's National and Grindlays Bank had 293 offices in South Asia as well as the Middle East, Africa and Britain. Its chairman Lord Aldington visited First National City Bank chairman George Moore. According to Moore, Aldington said: "I'm on my way to Chase. I want a godfather. Lloyds Bank won't give me any capital and I need more capital." Moore came up with his own deal.

Moore argued that they didn't really compete as National and Grindlays had 25 percent of all rupee deposits while the American bank had only one percent. "Your customers in India are Shell, Dunlop, Imperial Chemical. Ours are Exxon, Firestone, Du Pont and your customers want dollars while ours want rupees. We've got different customers and different

businesses. Stay right here!" The deal was struck the same day with Wriston joining the two for lunch. In 1969, First National City paid 37.8 million dollars for 40 percent of the British bank and Lord Aldington joined the board in New York.

Bank president George Moore and his wife in Taiwan in 1964. With them are (far left) Hong Kong manager Hank Sperry and (far right) Taipei manager Bob Morehouse

The match was uneasy. In India, distinct American and British banking cultures had developed over the years. "At Grindlays, if you wanted to get married, you had to present your fiancée to the branch manager," recalled Nanoo Pamnani, later country head for India and the Philippines. "It took at least 18 months to pull together as one," he said. "There were lots of overlap, lots of excess staffing." In Calcutta, Pamnani had to hold meetings with his Grindlays counterpart. "I don't know why all you Americans do all this planning," the British banker sniffed. "We just get on with the business of making money."

After Citibank and Grindlays parted, Lloyds became Grindlays' major partner. Australian and New Zealand Banking Corporation (ANZ) acquired Grindlays in the early 1980s. Later still, it was sold again—to Britain's Standard Chartered Bank.

Golden eggs

Ray Kathe worked out a system for handling acceptances in Japan in the mid-1950s with Chet Leaber, who was in charge of credit policy in the overseas division. "Others thought it would never work but it became one of our biggest businesses—handling acceptances for Japanese banks, primarily. They would make their imports and bring us eligible paper and we would send the eligible paper to New York for discounting.

"They never used acceptances in the Far East until that time," Kathe recalled. "So that business built up to hundreds of millions of dollars in Japan. And while the Japanese banks weren't using us any longer for the opening, confirmation or advising of credits, they were using us for acceptances. That gave us very large earnings. We also handled a lot of their export bills, mainly because we could pay them at sight then send the bills abroad for collection."

Kathe said the foreign-currency lending to Japanese companies started in the late 1950s, first for three years then for five and eventually seven years. "These loans were to companies without any particular purpose specified but they were in foreign currency. The reason they were called impact loans was because they impacted on the local currency money supply when they were converted," he explained. Kathe said the bank had impact loans of up to a hundred million dollars to a single company and that total exposure in impact loans and acceptances rose to four billion dollars.

According to Tatsuo Umezono (see p. 92), the bank was the biggest handler of acceptances until about 1975. "Up to then this was a major contributor to the bank's earnings. ... No other country used this gimmick. Other foreign banks became quite keen but in the early days we were getting commissions of 1.5 percent per annum."

Door of the old Yokohama branch, incorporated in the later building

Rick Roesch, at the Nagoya branch, once received documents for a shipment imported years earlier. "We weren't sure what to do but were told that it had the endorsement of a Japanese bank and the backing of the Japanese government so go ahead. It was a no-brainer business. You didn't have to think twice about commissions of 1.5 percent."

The Yokohama branch in 1950. Before it reopened, the building was used by the 179th finance disbursing section of the United States army

Revolving facilities

New fashions in the 1960s weren't limited to clothing and business—the world of architecture was also affected. And among some of the most ubiquitous additions to office buildings was the revolving door.

Rick Roesch was working at the Nagoya branch when new premises were secured. "The revolving door was the current rage in the U.S. and the people who designed the branches in New York were pretty insensitive," he recalled, noting that counters were always too high for the Japanese while the huge desks designed to be spaciously laid out would often end up migrating to the center of the Japanese office floor.

The Nagoya branch was fitted with a revolving door, the first in Nagoya and possibly even in Japan. During a visit by a senior officer from New York, an important Japanese customer was invited to the bank. As the meeting ended, the group of guests was ushered into the lobby. Everyone bowed before taking their leave. As they moved through the door, they continued bowing and eventually disappeared into the street— and came back into the lobby backwards.

The revolving door proved such a big hit in Japan that revolving restaurants soon started to appear on top of buildings. Roesch was at the opening of one of these restaurants in a new building that had been partly financed by the bank. "We all approached the revolving part of the restaurant and removed our shoes before walking onto the revolving tatami floor," he said. "But there was this huge chaos after the meal as nobody could find their shoes, which were all on the other side of the building. After that, they quickly carpeted the restaurant so people could keep their shoes on."

Nagoya branch—with revolving door

Tokyo Citibankers with the Ginza in the background.

In Tokyo–the right bank in the right place

These Citibankers are shown in Tokyo's famous business and shopping district. Normally, you'll find them at our busy branch, where they offer a full range of banking services to meet both the complex requirements of international business and the personal banking needs of people in Japan. In this country, where opportunities keep growing at a fast pace, there are other Citibankers to help your enterprise at our branches in Yokohama, Nagoya, and Osaka. Wherever your interests lie, Citibank... with fully-staffed branches, subsidiaries and affiliates in 64 countries...is the right bank in the right place to serve you.

FIRST NATIONAL CITY BANK
PARTNERS IN PROGRESS AROUND THE WORLD

First National City Bank's corporate
seal after the 1962 name change

The opening ceremony of the second Bombay branch, in Jeevan Deep building, 1967

mini-branches in-country. The third phase was to export retail services and know-how from New York. All of these phases ran concurrently or overlapped."

This strategy of expansion was fully reflected in the bank's attitude to Asia in the 1960s. Apart from a branch in the newly independent Federation of Malaya in 1959, the bank hadn't opened any new non-military banking facilities in Asia for a decade. Things soon started to change with an inaugural branch in Pakistan in 1961 and a second branch in Hong Kong in 1962. Savings accounts were introduced to Japan in 1963 and new branches opened: Madras in 1962, New Delhi in 1963, Taiwan in 1965, South Korea in 1967 and Indonesia in 1968. Taiwan and South Korea were emerging as important economies, and in Asia as a whole the first glimmerings of an economic

Ding!

When Nanoo Pamnani joined the bank in 1967, the Fort branch in Bombay seemed frozen in time. "It was very much in the colonial style," recalled Pamnani. In the banking chamber itself was the "platform," where the corporate bankers sat. "That was the plush part of the bank. It was carpeted and had big art-deco desks. Beyond that was the office of the branch manager, effectively the number two for India."

Life on the platform had its own pace. Each person had his own messenger just a few feet away. "You had this bell. Ding! And then a man in a white uniform and a turban would appear," Pamnani said. "We were a much more formal organization in those days. You could only wear a white shirt, although on Saturdays you could wear blue. You could never take your jacket off, even when the air conditioning went off. But we

weren't quite as bad as the British banks. So we felt kind of emancipated."

Some of the women were emancipated too. Pamnani's future wife, Chitra Gholap, joined the bank a year later, becoming India's first female foreign exchange dealer and later the first woman treasurer in the bank's overseas operations.

Pamnani, who graduated from the London School of Economics, experienced the platform first-hand when he worked in Calcutta. "For a year in Calcutta, I was the platform wallah. We'd leave at two or three on a Saturday afternoon and have a few drinks," he said. "At this stage we used to have a lot of staff agitations. Most of the junior officers including me ended up spending long hours every night, balancing the ledgers, while the staff refused to work overtime. I couldn't believe it—why did I go to the LSE? I could have been a clerk all my life!"

Citibankers at "The Gateway of India"

In Bombay—the right bank in the right place

In the background, "The Gateway of India." Up front, some of the Bombay Citibankers who provide a banking gateway to India for businessmen with interests there. In Bombay, Madras, New Delhi, and in two branches in Calcutta, 376 resident Citibankers offer broad experience in international banking—plus a grasp of Indian trade and economic conditions that dates back to our first branch in India in 1903. Complete banks-on-the-scene in 45 countries on 5 continents make Citibank the right bank in the right place to serve you.

FIRST NATIONAL CITY BANK
PARTNERS IN PROGRESS AROUND THE WORLD

War finance

Wars in Korea and Vietnam in the 1950s and 1960s provided a major boost to many economies in Asia. When demand for rubber for military use increased, the bank's Singapore branch was ideally placed to serve the trade from rubber plantations in neighboring Malaya. Singapore was also an important center for regional trade, and this status was enhanced as manufacturing developed in the newly independent state.

"The rubber companies were very actively buying rubber from Singapore," recalled Wong Nang Jang, who joined the bank in 1962. At the time, the bank's main activity in Asia was to serve American companies overseas, such as Firestone and Goodyear. Other companies included Standard Vacuum, which later became Exxon and Mobil, as well as Caltex, which had significant crude production in Sumatra. "My major task in the bills department was to process letters of credit exporting not only rubber but also batteries," he said, noting that Union Carbide had started producing batteries in Singapore and exporting them to places such as Saudi Arabia.

Although rubber was also exported to Latin America, the boom in prices was short-lived. "After the Vietnam War, rubber prices came tumbling down and companies were switching to a blend of synthetic and natural. That began the demise of the importance of rubber."

Other companies such as Eastman Kodak used Singapore as a warehouse for shipments to other countries in the region. "Kodak had a fairly large wholesale business here in Singapore and they were distributing products out of Singapore to places as far afield as Burma, Thailand and Indonesia," said Wong, who left the bank in the late 1970s to join Singapore's Oversea-Chinese Banking Corporation.

A year before the bank published this booklet in 1951, Singapore was handling two-thirds of Malaya's exports of four billion Straits dollars, of which about 25 percent was destined for the United States

Above: Staff award presentations in Singapore, 1954. Manager Ken Emerson is on the far left, next to regional vice president Alexander Calhoun. Right: After occupying a single branch at Denmark House from 1958, the bank established a second in Orchard Road in 1959 and a third in Jurong in 1965. In 1969, the operations staff of all three branches were shifted to the Maritime Building (shown here) at Collyer Quay

Electrically driven mechanical
calculating machine

renaissance had been detected. New branches were set up by multi-national teams made up not predominantly of head office staff, but of local staff from other Asian branches.

Hamilton Meserve was acting country head in Taiwan in 1967. Head office had planned that First National City Bank should be the first foreign bank to open up in South Korea, and discovered they were about to be beaten to the mark by Chase Manhattan, headed by David Rockefeller. The order came to "open soonest at all costs!" As Meserve recalls, "I signed out 10,000 dollars in travelers' checks to myself, flew up with my eight-months-pregnant wife, and lived out of the old Chosun Hotel (we and vice-president Humphrey were the last guests before it was torn down). We found premises, recruited staff and opened in four months, just a couple of weeks after Chase."

The importance of the bank's attitude to recruitment from the late 1960s onwards was enormous. In the IBC days, many of the bank's staff had been British, recruited from other banks operating in a colonial environment. The 1930s had seen a greater preponderance of Americans, but the ethos of the bank had remained somewhat traditional. With the 1960s and 1970s came a different spirit.

Billboard advertising the opening of the branch in Seoul in 1967

Participants in a supervisors' conference in Bombay, 1968

In the words of Victor J. Menezes, a recruit from India who rose to become Citibank's chairman, the new generation were an international group of "really bright guys who could have made a name for themselves in New York or London, wanting to build a career in Asia." "Instead of sons of missionaries or the sort of folks who would be interested in the foreign service, you started having MBAs with some Asian experience through the navy, army and air force," said Rick Roesch, who was initially posted to the Nagoya branch in Japan.

In interviewing prospective candidates for postings abroad, Roesch recalled that the bank was also interested in the wives—or in his case, the fiancée. "They flew us both to New York," he said. "Everybody at Berkeley was astounded." Over time, the MBA program would start feeding itself—when returning to America on leave, Roesch and other officers working abroad would be expected to go back to their old universities to help recruit more fresh graduates. "The injection of MBAs changed forever the way the whole bank was

Left: Invitation to the reception at the Chilin Pavilion of the Grand Hotel, to mark the official opening of the Taipei branch on February 15, 1965. Above: The ribbon-cutting ceremony

Studying Chinese

When Ray Kathe was sent to help reopen the Tianjin branch in late 1945, he was one of the few American bankers to have studied Chinese. "After college I went into the military service in 1943 and was attached to the Chinese Air Force," he recalled late in his career. "So after the war I wanted to join the bank or some organization that would send me to China," he said. "I had read a book called 'Four Hundred Million Customers in China' and that's what made me study Chinese and want to make a career in China." Kathe said it was not unlike the stampede many years later with foreigners eyeing the potential market of a billion customers. Except "I'm still waiting for the 400 million. ..."

"There were no Americans in the bank who went out when I did who knew Chinese." Still, Kathe recalled that he used his language skills more with the Chinese military during the war than he did with clients of the bank in Tianjin and Shanghai. "Most of the Chinese would come to my office and talk Chinese and be polite and social," he said. "But when we started to do the actual business transaction, they would switch to English. That was very annoying to me as a young man but I've long since gotten over that."

Both Kathe and Walter Wriston served in the military during the war; both joined New York head office in 1946; and both retired in 1984, when Kathe was senior corporate officer for the Asia-Pacific region. In 1946 they worked briefly together in the comptrollers department on domestic branch inspections. "We stuffed some envelopes together late at night occasionally," Kathe said. "After that, I went to China."

Wriston credited Kathe with being the driving force in the group of young bankers who rebuilt the Asian operation after the war. "These guys built the bank. They went out with nothing but a general ledger," he said. "It took a long time with a lot of very able people such as George Vojta and Rick Wheeler and all those people to turn it into the bank which they now have."

From left, Taipei manager Robert Morehouse, Hong Kong resident vice president Hank Sperry and his wife Ansie, and vice president Ray Kathe with his wife Jacqueline, at the reception marking the opening of the Taipei branch

What's in a name?

While the bank's English name changed over the years (see p. 13), the Chinese name used in China remained. Huaqi Yinhang, which literally means "Flower Flag Bank" (after the stars on the American flag), was the name used on the banknotes issued during the period. Also retained was the different Chinese name used in Singapore and in Cantonese-speaking Hong Kong: Mankwok Potong Nganhong, which roughly translates as "Global Treasure Bank." In general, however, the "Flower Flag Bank" was more widely used.

The Chinese characters for bank (yinhang in Mandarin or nganhong in Cantonese) mean "silver merchant" and are also used in Japanese (ginko).

Check-writing machine

どちらも世界中でお買物・お支払い
に使えますが，紛失したり盗まれた時に
払いもどしをしてくれるのは
旅行小切手のみです。

世界中どこへ行っても，ファースト・ナショ
ナル・シティー・トラベラーズ・チェックは替
んで受け入れられます。現金と同じ使うこと
はありません。

どこへ行っても，ファースト・ナショナル・
シティー・トラベラーズ・チェックは万一紛失，
または盗難にあった時，即座に払いもどしても
らえます。これは現金の場合には望めないこと
です。

ファースト・ナショナル・シティー・トラベ
ラーズ・チェックは，現在に払いもどせる権限
を持つエージェントを 35,000 以上世界中に
有しており，購入契約に基づいてお払いもどし
を致します。

次の御旅行には，どこへお出になるにして
も，安全な方をお選び下さい。本少の現金と，
沢山のファースト・ナショナル・シティー・ト
ラベラーズ・チェックをお持ち下さい。トラベ
ラーズ・チェックには期限はありません。

どこへ行かれても，トラベラーズ・チェック
は現金と同様に即使用になれます。そしてもし
事故にあった場合は，ファースト・ナショナル・
シティートラベラーズ・チェックは払いもど
しをしてもらえます。

次の御旅行には，最寄りの銀行で是非トラベ
ラーズ・チェックをお求め下さい。そして，安
心して御旅行をお楽しみ下さい・・・。

First National City Travelers Checks

Advertisements for the bank's travelers checks in Japanese magazines (top) and on pocket calendars

Good relations

In Singapore towards the end of the colonial era, left-wing trade unions were very influential. As Charles Stockholm recalled, "Strikes or 'go-slows' at month-end closing had the officers working until three or four in the morning to close the books and report earnings to New York. More than once, pins and paper clips were put into the old NCR bookkeeping machines. Once even water! Fortunately, Citibank had far better labor relations with their staff than most banks. Once I had to go to court to testify against a staff-union member during a labor negotiation. The union's lawyer had me on the stand for over two hours and was very intimidating. The overhead fans in the old Singapore courtroom didn't keep you cool, and my white linen suit, which we wore in those days, was wet through. The lawyer went on to become the Prime Minister of Singapore, and one of the leading statesmen in Asia. I would not want to be cross-examined again by him!"

run," Roesch said, noting that it also contributed to the development of investment banking activities.

With the expansion that started under George Moore came a generational change. Staff were given more leeway and entrusted with authority. And, in time, their hands were to be strengthened by the tools of modern management. The effect was to place the bank at the vanguard of the changes that were transforming many of the countries of Asia into developed modern societies. Very soon came the recruitment of some of the brightest people from the region, who were brought into the bank's training programs and in many cases groomed to run the bank at very senior levels in years to come.

By the end of the 1960s, First National City Bank's holding company had ventured into several major acquisitions. Following the purchase of a 50 percent stake in an Australian retail financing outfit in 1966, the bank acquired 40 percent of Britain's National and Grindlays Bank Ltd. in 1969 for 37.8 million dollars. Grindlays had more than a billion dollars in deposits in the Middle East, Africa and Asia including India, Pakistan and Sri Lanka (Ceylon). Another major acquisition was made that year, with the purchase of 76 percent of Hong Kong's Far East Bank, which had 13 branches in the British colony and 19.4 million dollars in assets at the end of 1969. By the beginning of the 1970s, a number of leasing and management consulting ventures had also been formed with Japan's Fuyo group of companies centered round Fuji Bank.

The 1960s also saw a major reorganization of the bank in the wake of a report by management consultants

Dancing sixties-style at a staff party in Japan

Staff at the Manila branch in the 1960s taking a break

McKinsey and Company. In 1967, by which time Walter Wriston was president, a preliminary report from McKinsey asked two important questions. The first was whether the bank was organized soundly for optimum profits against the separate markets it served. The second was whether it was organized in such a way as to provide sufficient top-management direction to its evolution as a financial conglomerate. The answer to both was "no."

As far as foreign activities were concerned, McKinsey noted that relationships with big multinational customers were often fragmented—divided among two different divisions in New York as well as in the foreign branches where the companies operated. McKinsey found that it was not unusual to have up to 40 officers working in different locations at different times on a single account. "Therefore it is critical that the actions of these officers be coordinated and directed," McKinsey said. As a result, the bank decided to designate to each customer a

single officer who would be responsible for coordinating activities across the whole bank. A transition team was established and the "new" First National City Bank opened for business in January 1969.

The bank also took steps to improve management information, back office procedures and risk management practices during this period (foreign exchange trading had already reached almost 150 billion dollars in 1964). And in the face of

The building occupied by the bank in Surabaya before the Pacific War

Living dangerously

In 1918, IBC opened up branches in Batavia (today's Jakarta) and Surabaya. Both were closed during the Pacific War, and remained so for more than 20 years.

In 1968 the bank reopened the Jakarta branch, sending a couple of officers there, including Charles Stockholm. "We were waiting for our license and most foreign businessmen were staying at the Hotel Indonesia. So we'd sit in the bar and talk to the guests who were coming in to find out which ones we could finance," he said. Once the license was granted, however, raising deposits proved to be a serious

George Scott and Charles Stockholm with a local official in Jakarta in 1968

challenge. "We managed to get the American and Canadian embassies but then we realized that the people with the most money were the Eastern bloc embassies," Stockholm said. He added that the bank soon had Soviet, Polish, Czech and Hungarian account holders. "We had everyone there except Albania, East Germany and Yugoslavia."

Later, retired Citibanker William Taylor visited the old Surabaya branch building, which was still standing. He proposed the vault door be opened—no one knew what might lie inside. He was advised not to try it. To do so might bring down the building.

Denis Dovey, who worked for the bank in Asia throughout the 1970s, lecturing in 1974 on credit analysis to bank staff in Jakarta

regulatory restrictions on certain activities, the bank decided on a novel approach to comply with the Bank Holding Company Act of 1956. The law applied to holding companies that owned "two or more" banks. Accordingly, management decided to set up a "one-bank" holding company which it did with a share swap in October 1968. Shareholders exchanged their First National City Bank stock for shares in a new holding company, First National City Corporation. Walter Wriston succeeded George Moore as chairman of the new holding company in 1970.

In early 1971, First National City was in a position to boast that it had tripled its offices around the world over the previous decade and now had 18,000 staff abroad. First National City "entered the seventies as the world's leading commercial bank," said Al Costanzo, executive vice president in charge of international operations. In a new-look annual report in English, French and Spanish, Costanzo noted that through finance companies in Asia and Latin America, the bank was now providing new opportunities to lower-income people who had previously

Grooming local talent

For Philippe Delhaise, who founded Asia's first regional bank rating agency, "It was not until major American banks became active in the region that local bankers received proper training," he wrote in 1998. "The best bankers in Asia have usually spent some time with a major American name." And Citibank was an "excellent school for commercial bank management."

When Mehli Mistri joined in 1960, his training consisted of a 12-month schedule, spent on-the-job. "I spent time in every part of the bank, observing and handling all functions, including the most routine, such as sticking envelopes in the mail department, processing dividend warrants, posting statements on the NCR Class 32 accounting machines, opening letters of credit and so on." Later, training centers were set up in Manila and Beirut, to which trainees from the region were sent for formal classroom and case-study-based training. More specialized function training programs of varying duration were also introduced

during the 1960s. These included credit, treasury, marketing, operations, and so on. The Overseas Division Credit Analysis Division (ODCAD) was set up in New York in 1965, followed by a number of CADs in Asian locations, such as INDCAD in India, and PHILCAD in the Philippines. Denis Dovey, who worked for Citibank in Asia in the 1970s, recalled spending his first nine months on the PHILCAD course.

One outcome was that staff were often poached by other banks in the Philippines. By the late 1990s, most local bank heads and even the heads of the central bank and deposit insurance agency were former Citibankers.

"Citibank provided the leadership in banking," said Rafael Buenaventura, named Philippine central bank governor in 1999. His career included a stint in Milan as the first Asian country and regional head in Europe. After leaving, he headed a local commercial bank, sitting on the 15-member board of the Philippine bankers' association. "At one point, there were 12 of us who were

Governor Rafael Buenaventura, named Central Banker for the Year in Asia, 2001

ex-Citibankers," he recalled. At one meeting, an older board member interrupted: "Hold it! You guys are talking in gibberish." Indeed, they were. As Buenaventura said, "We were all using Citibank acronyms."

Richard W. Wheeler, who oversaw many of these early developments, felt that the long-term benefits outweighed the problem of losing staff. "We weren't going to keep everybody," he said. "We sent an extraordinary message to the whole region that the bank could be run by individuals from the country. ... There was upward mobility for anybody coming into the bank; it was not just simply the province of those people coming out of New York."

In 1971, the bank set up its Asia-Pacific Banking Institute in Manila, also home to the Asian Development Bank. Programs included training for central banks, government-owned banks and regulatory agencies in Asia. By 2000, it had trained 200,000 customers and partners as well as almost 100,000 officers from within.

Total assets (1946-71)

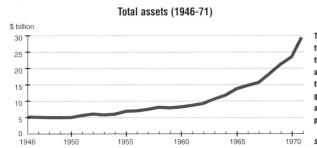

$ billion

The merger with First National Bank of the City of New York in 1955 expanded the balance sheet by 700 million dollars, although it was in the next decade that the bank's post-war expansion seriously got under way. Between 1961 and 1967, assets grew at an annual rate of 11 percent—the highest rate in 40 years

Source: annual reports

been virtually excluded from the consumer economy. At the same time, the bank's training courses were fulfilling educational needs linked to the development of emerging nations—notably in the Philippines where the bank's credit analysis department was providing young Asians and Africans with advanced training in financial analysis and the extension of credit.

By this stage, the bank was slowly coming to realize the importance of consumer banking, an area long neglected by the bank outside its home territory of New York. In October 1971, Manila was chosen as the venue for a meeting of the First National City Bank board. In Australia, the bank's finance company affiliate was expanding into consumer finance. And in Hong Kong, deposits of the new Far East Bank subsidiary were growing at an annual rate of 22 percent, faster than the rest of the British colony's banking system.

But two events in 1971 would have far-reaching effects on the bank's international operations in the years to come. The first of these came in July when President Richard Nixon announced plans to visit Beijing and meet Chairman Mao Zedong the following year. The second came a month later when Nixon announced a new economic program which included abandoning the gold standard for the dollar and replacing it by a system of floating exchange rates.

In Japan, these two events became known as the *Nikuson shoku* ("Nixon shocks"). They were the turning point in post-war relations that Wriston had called for in 1965.

Seventies fashion

If the early 1970s was a time for bizarre fashions in clothing, they were also a time for new fashions in American business. The bank wasn't spared; in this case, the fashion was for an international advisory board.

"There was heat on my back," recalled Wriston. "Why don't you have one?" His reply was characteristic. "I said 'they don't have any more authority than Billy the Kid outside the three-mile limit but the guys that should know are our board.' So every 12 months, we took the board abroad, saying 'We want you guys to see the quality of our people—so when we come to change the troops, you won't be reading memos, you'll know the people.'"

Starting with Tokyo, the bank's board members and their spouses started flying overseas every year. In one of the more memorable excursions, Prime Minister Lee Kuan Yew hosted a dinner for the visiting board in Singapore. "These men and women on the board got to know those people as human beings. It worked terrifically. It was expensive but it paid for itself 10 times," Wriston said.

"If you go around and talk to the guys in the branch you get a sense. A good captain can walk on a ship and in 20 minutes tell you whether it's a happy ship or a disaster. I don't know quite how you do that but it works. You can do the same if you walk into a Citibank branch. Since the international bank was so important to the bank, I felt that was the thing to do."

Wriston was under no illusion as to how much strain the logistics of organizing these international jamborees put on the staff. "In Tokyo, I remember when the plane took off, we all looked

The Juan Luna building in Manila, occupied since the early 1920s, shortly before the bank left it in favor of new premises in Makati City

out the window and they were dancing ... since they'd gotten rid of us."

4. A New Style of Banking
1972–1985

"The relationships that had been built up over time supported the achievements of a younger, often more specialized, generation of managers. This combination, together with a new emphasis on customer needs, enabled us to grow as rapidly as we did."

Victor Menezes

With the American war in Vietnam becoming a serious drain on its balance of payments, the United States announced, in August 1971, that the dollar would no longer be convertible into gold, thus sounding the death knell of the system of fixed exchange rates. This dated back to 1944, when the world's leading powers met in Bretton Woods, New Hampshire, to draw up a post-war framework for the international financial system. The shock move by President Richard Nixon meant that other countries could no longer exchange the dollars accumulating in their reserves for diminishing American holdings of gold. Its repercussions were to have a huge impact on the development of First National City Bank in the 1970s, a decade which also saw the bank change its name, in 1976, to Citibank, N.A.

The upshot to the closing of the "gold window" was the dollar's devaluation against other major currencies. As a result, the yen shot up 16.9 percent to 308 to the dollar, up from the rate of 360 to the dollar that had prevailed for more than 20 years. According to the agreement reached by the Group of Ten countries at the Smithsonian Institution, Washington, in 1971, the dollar could rise or fall by as much as 2.25 percent from the new level of 308 yen. But the agreement was doomed, and a brave new world of floating exchange rates was just round the corner.

At about the same time, Japan was rapidly being drawn into international diplomatic developments in Asia. Despite the absence of diplomatic ties, Japan and China had been trading

unofficially through private trade agreements going back to 1952. But the existence of the nationalist government in Taipei had proven an obstacle to trade links. In the early 1960s, for example, the Taiwan authorities opposed an attempt by the Export Import Bank of Japan to finance a Chinese synthetic fiber plant. China was admitted to the United Nations in 1971, and President Nixon

Opposite: Name change in Hong Kong, 1976. Two years earlier the bank's parent holding company, First National City Corporation, had changed its name to Citicorp. Right: Chairman Walter Wriston (standing), and president William Spencer (far right) review the new name and logo

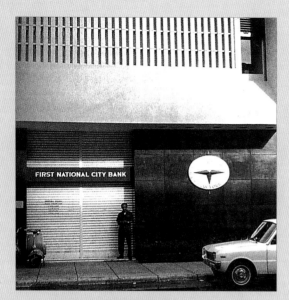

Saigon branch. After the evacuation, the board congratulated all members of management and staff for safeguarding the interests of the bank, its employees and their families in the "extremely difficult and often life-threatening circumstances"

Down and out in Saigon

Having an officer stranded in Shanghai for several years (see pp. 83–4) had taught Walter Wriston a lesson. When withdrawal from Vietnam seemed certain, he ensured that nobody was left behind. By early 1975, the Saigon branch, opened in 1972, had three expatriate and a few dozen local staff.

"I was worried about a hostage situation," Wriston later recalled. "We got a cable saying that the CIA had arranged a deal where the fellows in the branch and their families would go to some particular spot and they would get out of the country. I really didn't

believe that. I had a few friends in the CIA in Washington and I called them up. They checked it out and said it was a trap to kill the staff. So we chartered a plane and sent it to Saigon."

In Saigon itself, John Riordan was filling in for the branch manager, who was on vacation. Head of operations was Bill Walker, who had his wife and five-year-old son with him. Walker later recalled: "We received a coded cable from New York saying we'd been 'promoted to Hong Kong.' So we all flew to Hong Kong via Manila. Like everyone else, we lost our belongings."

In Hong Kong, the two met with Richard Freytag, who was coordinating the operation. Despite concern about the Vietnamese staff, Freytag relayed instructions from New York that neither man should return. But, Freytag recalled, "as the end drew nigh, all of our rules and neatly laid out plans and strategies were broken."

On a Sunday morning in Hong Kong, Riordan came to Walker's hotel room, asking for all the cash he could spare. "I gave him my dollars and off he went," said Walker.

Riordan went back to Saigon, and got 44 mostly female staff members and their families on a flight to Guam. "There were 105 Vietnamese, including spouses, children and one grandmother," Walker said. During a stopover at Clark Field in the Philippines, the plane let off one passenger and his pregnant wife who was about to give birth. The baby was later named Clark.

The plane flew on to Guam, where Walker had flown in from Hong Kong. One of the employees, Mrs. Khanh, handed him a bag of gold bars for safekeeping while the most-senior Vietnamese staff member, Uong Chuyen, gave him a briefcase. "It was full of unissued travelers checks worth more than 100,000 dollars."

Among the evacuees was a driver who used to deliver 500,000 dollars' worth of local currency to the United States defense attaché's office in Saigon every month. He decided to stay in Guam, becoming the first refugee to be "placed." The rest went to the United States and many of the staff got new

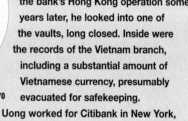

John Riordan, acting branch manager in 1970

jobs with the bank. "They received financial support and counseling. But it wasn't the staff who had difficulties getting accustomed to the American way of life—it was the spouses, mostly men. They tended to be well-educated, but they didn't speak a word of English," said Walker.

When Victor Menezes was running the bank's Hong Kong operation some years later, he looked into one of the vaults, long closed. Inside were the records of the Vietnam branch, including a substantial amount of Vietnamese currency, presumably evacuated for safekeeping.

Uong worked for Citibank in New York, becoming a vice president. He returned to Vietnam in 1994 after the bank opened its office in Hanoi, which was upgraded to full branch status in 1995. In 1998, he was named manager of the new Ho Chi Minh City branch—his life had gone full circle.

Living in America: former Saigon branch employees and their families visit an amusement park in New Jersey

Gathering silk cocoons in Haining county, Zhejiang province, in 1980, two years after China launched its initial agricultural reforms

Chairman Mao greets President Nixon in Beijing on February 22, 1972. Nixon urged China to join the United States in a "long march together" on different roads to world peace

made his historic trip to Beijing in early 1972. This prompted Japan's Prime Minister Kakuei Tanaka to make a similar trip six months later. Japan annulled its peace treaty with Taiwan and diplomatic ties were established between Japan and China. With Taiwan no longer regarded as an impediment, Japan and China moved quickly to conclude trade, air, navigation and fishery agreements before turning to the more-difficult issue of a peace treaty, China and Taiwan having been excluded from the San Francisco treaty signed by Japan and 48 other nations in 1951.

Singapore and the Asiadollar

Singapore's Wong Nang Jang and Japan's Tatsuo Umezono were the first two Asians to be put in charge of entire countries. And both helped to develop the Asiadollar market, Singapore's answer to the burgeoning market for offshore funds in London.

"Umezono and I were the 'first wave,'" recalled Wong. "We were the first Asians to be given any kind of scope to disprove or prove ourselves. So Umezono and I had a kinship because of that. They were all watching us."

Although Bank of America was the first bank licensed to carry out offshore trading in the Asiadollar market, Wong picked up the second license in 1969. Wong attributed much of the market's development to senior executive Ray Kathe, noting that he "had a way with Asian bureaucrats which nobody else had. He believed that after the Eurodollar market, the Asiadollar market would come on as well. So he spent a lot of time helping me spread this word, that Singapore could be an Asiadollar center."

Initial demand for offshore funds came mainly from Japanese, South Korean and Philippine companies. Banks in Singapore borrowed the funds from the London interbank market through their branch networks. Umezono was "very reluctant" because the London branches were earning a spread on each deal. "But Ray Kathe leaned on him to do it," Wong said, adding that he promised his Japanese colleague that he would provide the funds at the same rate he got them from London. The first few deals with Tokyo were like that— not a great way to make money, but at least it got the market going.

Apart from banks in London, another important provider of funds to the new market was the Singapore government itself. The market was given a further boost in 1984 when the Singapore International

Asiadollar market's total assets

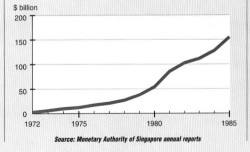

Source: Monetary Authority of Singapore annual reports

Monetary Exchange (Simex) launched a Eurodollar futures contract, the first in the the Asian time zone. It was during this time that the region's foreign exchange markets began to flourish. Singapore "really came into its own in the 1980s," although Tokyo was the center. "Hong Kong was trying but not really succeeding very well," Wong said.

Citibank was soon presenting Wong as the foremost expert on the Asiadollar market. After an International Monetary Fund meeting in Washington in the late 1970s, he was asked by Al Costanzo, a former IMF man himself, to fly to Caracas and brief the Venezuelan central bank on his experience. "Venezuela had oil money and didn't know what to do with its excess money.

"So Al had this idea, 'you put it back in your jurisdiction, but denominated in dollars. Then you lend to all the other Caribbean and Latin American countries denominated in dollars, but under the sovereignty of the Republic of Venezuela.' I had to brief the central bank governor," Wong said. "After that, Al liked it so much he sent me to Barbados for more discussions. Nothing happened, of course, but I won points for Citibank."

T. Morinaga, president of the Tokyo Stock Exchange, presents First National City Bank vice president Robert Davidson with a certificate marking the listing of the bank's shares on December 18, 1973

The former branch building in Harbin, China (see p. 37), photographed in 1979

After Nixon's landmark visit to Beijing in 1972, First National City Bank wasted little time in spotting the business potential in China. In early 1973, it published a trade guide to the country and predicted, if somewhat optimistically, that trade between the United States and China would reach "major dimensions" by 1975. Mao died in 1976 and within two years a rehabilitated Deng Xiaoping would be endorsing Hungarian-style agricultural reforms and limited market activity.

While Nixon and Tanaka were establishing their relationships with Mao, the international financial system was in serious trouble. Nixon's Treasury Secretary, John Connally, architect of the Smithsonian Agreement, had been succeeded by George Shultz, who thought the whole agreement had been a mistake. America's new exchange rate with European countries and Japan had not addressed international trade imbalances, and Washington was forced to yield with a further devaluation of the dollar in February 1973. The final nail was driven into the Bretton Woods coffin in March 1973, when Shultz flew off to Europe and the new era of floating exchange rates was born. The dollar lost further ground against the Japanese currency, falling to the 271-yen level.

In the view of Walter B. Wriston, chairman of First National City Corporation and a close friend of George Shultz, the overhaul of the international financial system was long overdue. "The old discipline of the gold standard has been replaced, in fact, by the discipline of the information standard," Wriston asserted. He warned that government efforts to apply reserve requirements or other controls would only mute the market's response to different economic policies in each country. "Such moves carry with them grave risks for global financial responsibility," he said. "If governments and central banks now intervene more actively to control international credit markets, it cannot be doubted that another fruitful source of political conflict among governments will

Banking in the information age

Walter Wriston sensed that the financial revolution sweeping the world was not limited to international trade flows.

"Whether we are ready or not," he said, "mankind now has a completely integrated international financial and informational marketplace capable of moving money and ideas to any place on this planet in minutes. ... This intermixing of data makes it even harder to pass laws restricting the transmission of one kind of information without impinging on others. Streams of electrons are either free to move across national borders or they are not. ... The fact is that banking is a branch of the information industry."

The upshot of the brave new world of almost instant information was clear. This new phenomenon "exerts global pressure on all governments to pursue sounder economic policies because it is becoming increasingly obvious that it is now impossible to hide in our new electronic world."

Wriston agreed that the unwanted side effects were disconcerting. "Markets can and do overreact until fact can be sorted from fiction, often at great cost," he conceded. "Maybe life was easier in the age of the homing pigeons, but the hard truth is that the genies will not go back into the bottle and the scientific advances are irreversible. Modern gold—or the liquid capital of our citizens—will flow in and out of countries in response to inflation, as did gold itself in other times."

Walter B. Wriston, chairman 1970–84, steered the bank into the information age

Ministers attending a meeting of OPEC (Organization of Petroleum Exporting Countries) in 1976. Security was heavier than usual, following a terrorist attack on the organization's Vienna headquarters in late 1975

thereby be opened up—along with the negative effects of such interventions on the economic efficiency of those markets."

If information had replaced gold as the standard for setting exchange rates, communications technology would be the key in the future. In response, the bank soon bought two satellite transponders and set up earth stations in more than a dozen American cities to handle domestic data flows.

This different world had an immediate impact on earnings, as profits repatriated back to head office were suddenly worth more in dollar terms. In 1972, First National City Corporation reported that overseas earnings amounted to 54 percent of net income of 202 million dollars, up 55 percent from a year earlier and the first time that foreign operations had accounted for more than half the total. At 34 million dollars, Asia-Pacific's earnings were up almost 80 percent and accounted for almost a third of all profits outside the United States. By 1973, the foreign share of net earnings had climbed even higher, to 60 percent. The foreign contribution of 153 million dollars exceeded the bank's entire profit of three years earlier. For much of the 1970s and the 1980s, Citibank was to be the dominant player in foreign-exchange dealing.

A new series of challenges emerged with the first OPEC oil crisis of 1973. It had profound international implications. In Asia the booming Japanese economy fell into recession for the first time since World War II. Similar developments in South Korea resulted in the bank's arranging a 200-million-dollar loan to help the country get through the crisis.

Around this time, the bank radically reviewed the way it was financing clients, particularly in Japan. A trend had emerged in Europe whereby consortium banks were making Eurocurrency cross-border medium-term loans, often on a syndicated basis. This prompted Citibank to enter a joint venture with Fuji Bank called Asia Pacific Capital Corporation (APCO), to establish a regional syndicated loan business. Philip D. Sherman was managing director, and offices opened in Singapore and Hong

Communications

When John Reed joined the bank in the 1960s, the telex machine was still the main way of communicating between the New York head office and the overseas branches. "In the late 1960s, that changed," he said, "Telephones were beginning to work. In the old days, you couldn't call any place that easily because the phones were radio and you couldn't get any lines."

At the same time, bank officers posted overseas were starting to have home leave annually instead of once every three years. "When I joined the bank, we were beginning to have 707 flights. This idea that

Late-model telex machine used by the bank in Singapore

to go to Hong Kong was a three-and-a-half-week boat trip out of San Francisco—which it had been—was beginning to break down." The improvement in communications and transport greatly affected the foreign branches, especially in the distant Asian locations. "By 1972 or 1973, the overseas guys suspected—quite correctly—that the guys from head office were going to develop a point of view of how they should be running the business and what they should be doing," Reed said. "I was seen as the front end of the wedge that was going to bring that change about so I was not widely welcomed."

Japan's Prime Minister Kakuei Tanaka with the bank's president William Spencer in Tokyo, 1973. Local staff were embarrassed when Tanaka addressed Spencer as "Rockefeller-san"—after the head of Chase Bank, First National City's biggest rival

Commemorative stamps were issued for the 70th year of the First National City Bank in the Philippines

Kong. By the time of the first oil shocks in the 1970s, APCO was a leader in Asian syndicated loans, which allowed Citibank to be the first to arrange loans for countries such as Korea who bore the brunt of the shock. The joint venture was ended in the 1980s, when Citibank and Fuji Bank decided to pursue different strategies. But the foundation had been laid for Citibank's continuing leadership in syndicated loans.

Syndicated loans were identified by Victor Menezes as one of several business areas where specialists within Citibank, often in different territories, formed very effective networks of expertise. Others were the treasury business, cash management and project finance. The bank incubated a generation of talented individuals in these areas, who went on to play key roles within Citibank, in other banks, or in the community. One recalled by Menezes was David Leong, who became investment bank and treasury head in South Asia. Dennis Martin was corporate bank head for the area at the time. As Martin recalled, Leong was "one of the main people to attract and retain vast amounts of local talent for the treasury business, and expand the business."

For Wriston, recycling of capital by means of loans made economic sense. "When the first oil crisis occurred in 1973, there was immense anxiety over a shortage of domestic oil and a surplus of money flowing to the Middle East oil-producing states. What happened, of course, is that the OPEC countries deposited their cash surplus in American and European banks, which re-lent them to borrowers in other countries, especially developing countries that had no other means of meeting their increased oil bills.

"Along with these funds, members of the international banking community became the recipients of much gratuitous advice, usually from the same people who were devising new ways to regulate the oil markets, urging us to follow their example.

Korea's aversion to debt

In Asia, South Korea was among those countries worst hit by the 1973 oil price hike and soon suffered severe balance-of-payments difficulties. In New York, the bank's senior vice president Richard Wheeler, working with Philip Sherman in Seoul, put together a loan of 200 million dollars to help the South Korean government through the crisis. The Koreans originally wanted 400 million dollars but had to settle for half.

When South Korea asked for a clause stipulating no penalties if the loan were repaid early, Wheeler obliged—after all, the bank already had adequate up-front fees and commissions, and the likelihood of prepayment on a loan for seven or eight years seemed remote. "Everybody thought Korea was going down the drain," he said.

In 1977, Wheeler got a call from Al Costanzo, who was in charge of the international operations. "Rick, I think you better come down here." Wheeler rushed off and found a delegation of South Korean government officials with his boss. They had, contrary to expectations, paid off the loan. "Rick," he said, "Couldn't you have made a loan that lasted a few more years?"

Above: Rick Wheeler and Kim Bong Eun, President of the Korea Exchange Bank at the signing. Left: Order of merit presented to Korea manager Philip Sherman in 1978. The presidential order said Sherman had "rendered distinguished service to promoting economic cooperation" between Korea and the United States and had "greatly contributed toward further strengthening the ties of friendship between the two countries"

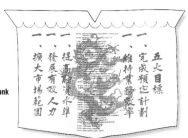

A pennant listing five goals for the bank in the 1970s: accomplish plans, maintain competence, improve financial standards, develop people, and expand market boundaries

Had we done so, the world's financial markets would have become as chaotic as the world's oil markets, and it is entirely possible everyone's worst fears might have been realized. Instead, we adhered to what we knew were traditional principles of sound banking."

As the economic dramas of the 1970s unfolded, the bank renewed its interest in the Bank for International Settlements (BIS). By a quirk of history, First National City Bank was the American shareholder in the BIS, a multilateral financial institution based in Switzerland and otherwise known as the "central bankers' bank" (see below).

John S. Reed: chairman 1984–2000

In the early 1970s, a young executive vice president by the name of John S. Reed came to prominence in New York. Reed had been raised in Argentina and Brazil and served in the army corps of engineers in South Korea. He started work for the bank in the overseas division, then headed by Wriston. "The first job I had working for Wriston was to write a report for the board on Japan. The board was concerned about whether Japan was a good credit risk," he recalled. "There was concern about our exposure to Japan and whether it was too much."

The "Central Bankers' Bank"

Swissair's first flight from Geneva to Basel left at seven in the morning. It took only 20 minutes. And for the discerning Swiss business traveler, the service in first class was impeccable. "They'd be drinking whisky straight up at seven in the morning," recalled Rick Wheeler, the Asian banking veteran whose new mission in life included calling on the Bank for International Settlements (BIS).

The world's leading central banks set up the BIS as a public company in 1930 to deal with the issue of German reparation payments from World War I. At the time, the United States had a regulation that the government could not invest in public companies, so the Federal Reserve got First National Bank of the City of New York (acquired by National City Bank in 1955) to serve as its proxy shareholder. As a result, correspondence such as invitations to meetings in Basel was sent to the bank's headquarters in New York, although the United States was represented at the

meetings themselves by officials from the Federal Reserve. The BIS had arranged special credits to support the French franc, the Italian lira and the British pound in the 1960s. Although its public profile had diminished, it continued to act as a forum for central bank cooperation.

In the new environment of floating exchange rates and the internationalization of financial markets, Wheeler recommended it was time to exchange views with the world's leading central banks. "In the 1970s, there were problems emerging," he recalled. "We'd been the pre-eminent U.S. bank. Everybody started looking at our balance sheet, and the Asia-Pacific region was the largest profit center for the bank. Other people started going abroad, and then people started doing foolish things in developing countries. We were getting into a situation abroad where loans were cratering. The Fed was uneasy, without really having any knowledge of what was going on, and the German banks were sending signals, so the BIS got reactivated."

Wheeler added that relations with the Washington-based International Monetary Fund (IMF) were not particularly close in those days. "We were all struggling for some means to get the emerging countries into the international financial system. The BIS was a natural," he said. "It sort of came out of the closet."

Wheeler said overseas division chief Al Costanzo was "enormously supportive" in the moves to forge cooperative ties with the central banks. "As a former IMF official, he had a feeling for its importance."

The influence of the core group within the so-called Group of Ten countries grew to unforeseen levels by 1985, when the Group of Five met at New York's Plaza Hotel (see p. 136). In a move that would change Asia's financial and economic landscape forever, they agreed that other currencies should appreciate against the dollar, setting the stage for the yen's phenomenal ascent over the next 10 years and, arguably, sowing the seeds of Asia's financial crisis in the late 1990s.

Singapore in the mid-1970s. The waterfront was the bank's home for many years after its arrival on the island. In this photo can be seen (1) the approximate site of the first premises on Prince Street, which no longer exists; (2) the location of Ocean Building (see p. 52), later replaced by the tower block visible here; (3) Denmark House, occupied from 1958; (4) Maritime Building, which housed the bank's operations from 1969; (5) Robina House, home to consumer banking activities from 1982. The UIC Building, which housed the bank from 1973, is not visible in this picture

The vastness of China

In 1978, the senior Asian management team went to Beijing for a conference. Tokyo was then the main gateway to Beijing and flights were operated by the Civil Aviation Administration of China (CAAC). "We took the same plane that some of the delegates of Nixon had used," recalled Rafael Buenaventura. "The seats were still military seats, bucket seats along the side. One question asked was what would happen if the plane went down. We said we would have happy guys being promoted."

William Ferguson and Ray Kathe (right) at Kathe's retirement party in Hong Kong. The dress theme was "Shanghai in the 1930s"

The timing was fortuitous. "This was when China finally opened up. We were, I think, the first commercial firm to have a conference in China, and we stayed at the State Guest House." After visiting the Great Wall, some of the bankers went exploring. "I remember a few of us sneaking out and

taking the subway. We figured we wouldn't get lost … it was only one line." Later, some of the group went to Shanghai. "We got a sense of the vastness of China."

When corporate head for Hong Kong, Victor Menezes was able to visit some of the former branch buildings in China. Robert Grant, who had worked for Citibank since going to Shanghai in 1946, and was in Hong Kong from 1979 to 1982, had done a lot of the preparatory groundwork for a return to China. From Hong Kong, Menezes drove the process energetically forward. He opened Macau as a full branch, and set up a representative office in Shenzhen in 1983. As he said, "To reopen in China took quite a lot of negotiation." After Shenzhen, a second office followed in Beijing in 1984, and a third in Shanghai in 1985.

The old Beijing branch remained closed after World War II and was abandoned in 1948. Later it became a police museum

Reed was "comfortable" working in the overseas division. Growing up in Latin America had already brought him into contact with people from the bank. "Those of us who had spent our lives overseas were really expatriates. It wasn't one of those deals flying in an airplane. You took ships. It took three weeks to get any place, we came back to the States for home leave once every third year, and most of us expected to live our lives overseas," he said. "It was a culture that I was comfortable with. The people I got to know in the bank saw me as a real overseas guy, and it was made really clear to me that I should identify with the overseas guys and not the New York head-office types."

When he started in the overseas division, Reed said, Asia was "very much there as a big piece of our culture" along with Latin America. "We had a substantial business in Asia, and Japan was an important country in our minds." But the bank was still largely a "traditional" foreign bank. "We tended to have as our customers international companies who were doing business and local companies who had international activities. It was a good business. It grew with the economy, grew with trade, and we were very much involved in letters of credit."

Reed recalled that when he joined the bank there was little planning or budgeting. The bank "knew what the earnings were about a month after they happened." In 1967, he was moved to the comptroller's department where he worked on budget and planning systems. "I was much engaged with the overseas people during this time. One of the great dilemmas of the company was how you compared the performance of, say, Germany and Hong Kong. ... [The overseas branches] didn't really know how much they earned. They sent whatever earnings they had home and you sort of counted how much."

In the late 1960s, even getting customers to provide the right financial information was not easy; many customers did not have the skills or the experience to produce it. Often, bank staff had to teach customers how to do business forecasts. This learning process benefited Citibank too—by the early 1970s, it had formulated a systematic approach to credit assessment. One practice introduced by Citibank ahead of the competition was lending on a cash-flow basis, rather than on the traditional asset-backed model. Banks had generally regarded asset backing as the best assurance that they would get their money back. Citibank started lending against cash-flow projections, because this provided a more reliable profile of the customer and the appropriate exposure. However, it also required access to in-depth financial data, and business forecasts as far ahead as five years.

Hip place to bank: 1970s style at the Taman Jurong branch in Singapore, opened in the mid-1960s under Wong Nang Jang as manager

Launching a joint venture in Singapore. From left: regional vice president Charles Stockholm, Tan Chin Tuan (chairman of Oversea-Chinese Banking Corporation), and N.N. Handa (general manager of Great Eastern Life)

Technology in the 1970s: Citiflash was an early form of electronic banking, involving the use of IBM computers such as the one shown here

In 1972, John Reed went to William Spencer, president of the bank at the time, and said, "'Bill, I don't think we know what we're doing in the consumer business.' It had gone through a phase of what was called 'congeneric acquisitions,' which basically meant buy anything that had anything to do with money." Begun in the late 1960s, the "congenerics" strategy was an extension of the earlier strategy of Wriston and Moore, of expanding the bank's footprint wherever and in whatever manner possible. It resulted in the establishment of dozens of joint ventures. The bank also acquired minority and majority interests in existing companies, and sometimes even outright acquisitions were made. The policy was energetically pursued in Asia.

In the 1970s for example, Singapore was actively promoting the establishment of manufacturing companies, so industrial finance looked promising to one of the major local banks, Oversea-Chinese Banking Corporation (OCBC). "OCBC knew how to lend against a car, lend against a house, provide installment finance for pianos, or whatever. But how do you finance a lathe machine? How do you finance a color separator? That became a bit of a quandary for them," recalled Wong Nang Jang, a former Citibank country head for Singapore who had joined OCBC, and eventually became its deputy president. The two banks set up a joint venture called First Oversea Credit Ltd, which Wong described as a "significant but not extremely profitable business." Ultimately the joint venture fell victim to Wriston's decision in the late 1970s to check the proliferation of unprofitable joint ventures.

Part of the problem with "congeneric" investments seemed to be defining what actually constituted one. According to long-time Citibanker Peter Howell, the requirement was that it should be finance, but not banking per se. With such broad criteria, almost anything to do with money seemed a legitimate investment.

"Anything went. If it moved, you grabbed it," recalled Sam Eastabrooks, who was working for the bank in Hong Kong at the time. "We bought an airfreight company in Hong Kong. ... We used to fill the empty planes that took soldiers out to Vietnam with garments on the return journey to New York. That was good business while it lasted."

Traditional bamboo scaffolding in evidence as the bank moved into the UIC building in Shenton Way, Singapore, in 1973. Here customers were channeled into a single line for the first time, rather than forming individual lines for each teller

The bank's receptionists in Manila, dressed for a formal occasion

In Hong Kong, the bank promoted its travelers checks with portable mahjong sets for travelers

Other congeneric investments were more clearly not successful, for example in Australia, where an initial investment was made in the Waltons retail finance company, in the form of FNCB-Waltons Corporation. In these early years, volatility in the real-estate market hurt the business. Despite this, the bank continued to invest in Australia, and later entered into another Australian venture, acquiring 40 percent of Industrial Acceptance Corporation (IAC), a leading local finance company. "IAC got into real problems with real-estate," recalled Peter Howell.

Glen Moreno was country officer in Australia in the later 1970s, with a brief to manage the institution and its joint ventures through these difficult times. In retrospect, Moreno felt the bank turned a difficult situation to its advantage. "It was the very fact of that crisis that gave us our very significant base in Australia, because these were large companies," he observed. "Citibank was a name everybody was terribly familiar with. So when we rebranded the consumer franchise and our upmarket

corporate franchise on that base we gained a lot of respect. We became prominent, became known and became politically important. It gave us a very high profile, and as the business turned, and became profitable, it really gave us a leading foreign financial institution position in the country." Citibank was among the first group of foreign banks to be granted a full license in Australia.

In the more-traditional financial sphere, the bank also set up a joint venture with Thailand's Bangkok Bank, which was known as Bangkok First Investment Trust. Rick Roesch was seconded to the new affiliate. "It was one of the first investment banks in Thailand," he said. "It was very successful and very profitable."

Eventually the congenerics strategy was abandoned. As John Reed put it later, "We bought all sorts of things, but there was no rhyme or reason to it. We had a division in the company that ran the congenerics, but the only common thread was that they weren't the bank and they had something

Preaching the new gospel

Rana Talwar, who was later to become chief executive of Standard Chartered Bank in London, joined in New Delhi in 1969. "I probably just snuck in," he said. By the late 1970s, Talwar was running Citibank's treasury operations in India and then he was asked to transfer to Saudi Arabia.

While he was there, John Reed dropped by, preaching his new consumer banking gospel. Talwar was impressed by the new vision. Later he wrote to Reed: "I said I'm not a consumer guy but is there a role for someone like me?" By 1981, he was bound for Hong Kong to gain experience in this new world of consumer banking, at the time

Rana Talwar, head of consumer banking, Asia

despised by some corporate bankers as little more than a cheap source of funds.

Hong Kong and Australia were the first major components of the consumer operation in the Asia-Pacific region, although the bank was also quite active in the Philippines. In Hong Kong, the main activities were car loans and mortgages, especially to the middle class. Talwar focused on Hong Kong and the Philippines.

In 1982, Talwar was transferred to Singapore. The consumer business then had about 20 people in Singapore and about a dozen in Malaysia. It made no money. "Over the next few years, we started building up in Singapore and Malaysia," he said. "Then we started in

Indonesia and bought the Mercantile Bank in Thailand." By 1985, Talwar had set his sights on India. "You wouldn't believe the problems—I couldn't get any people from the corporate side." Frustrated, he called on an old Indian colleague, Jerry Rao, who was working as a financial comptroller at Citibank in Venezuela. "I said 'Jerry, do you want to be a bean counter all your life?'" Rao came home to India.

The bank also transferred a group of consumer people from Hong Kong to Tokyo, which became the new consumer headquarters for Northeast Asia. From the two regional centers in Singapore and Tokyo, the seeds of something major were being sown. Nobody realized how large the plant would grow, or how big the harvest would be.

A tale of two branches

In the 1970s, two small branches showed Citibank's determination to offer the full range of banking services to the residents of Hong Kong.

On the south side of the main island of Hong Kong, Repulse Bay was better known for its beach, overshadowed by expensive housing, than it was for its banking services. And on the other side of the territory, the tiny island of Cheung Chau was inhabited mainly by fishermen. There were affordable places to stay, and the island was a favorite weekend destination for many young people.

Citibank was the first bank ever to open a branch in Repulse Bay, drawn by the large expatriate population which lived nearby. The branch rapidly grew into a convenient stopping-off point on the way back from the beach. There was always sand on the floor, public transport was abysmal, and there were no restaurants nearby, so the employees had to cook their own lunch in the back.

Staff at the Cheung Chau island branch, Hong Kong

Noodles and Chinese sausages were the staple fare, and a pleasant aroma of cooking would waft through the branch as caucasian ladies in bikinis dropped by to withdraw cash before lunch. The branch was ultimately closed, but it is still fondly remembered by the staff who worked there.

Over on the island of Cheung Chau, where fresh seafood was more likely to be on the lunch menu, the bank had inherited a branch through its purchase, in 1969, of a majority holding in Far East Bank from Deacon Chiu, a local television mogul. Cheung Chau was such a novelty in the international network that it got a mention in the annual report.

But global reach clearly had its limits and the branch eventually shut down in the late 1990s, when the local manager retired.

"In terms of clientele, it did not fit into our strategy," said Danny Liu, manager for the global consumer business in Hong Kong and Macau.

Chopstick Brothers

Four years after Y.S. Wong started work in the bank's import and export bills department in Hong Kong in 1969, Antony Leung joined as a management trainee. By 1975, they were both working in the dealing room. "We were more or less the same height and we were both slim, although we didn't look alike," Wong recalled. "We joined the dealing room as trainee dealers in the same year. We were real buddies. There was this band with two girls called the Chopstick Sisters. So people called us the Chopstick Brothers."

Twenty-seven years later, Wong was executive vice president and global head for

Antony Leung (left) as treasurer in 1979 before leaving for New York. Y.S. Wong (right) as chief dealer the same year

Citibank's emerging markets sales and trading, the top-ranking Chinese officer at Citibank. And Leung was Financial Secretary of Hong Kong, one of the most senior government positions in the Hong Kong Special Administrative Region.

Mrs. Wong's holdups

In her 40-year career with Citibank and its Hong Kong subsidiary Far East Bank, teller Wong Kwan Ling was a first-hand witness to no fewer than four bank robberies at the Jordan Road and Tsuen Wan branches. "In two of the holdups, the robbers actually handed the note to me," she recalled. On another occasion, a teller at the counter next to Wong received a note demanding 50,000 Hong Kong dollars. "The teller didn't believe it so he handed the note to me and walked away. The robber got really angry and threw a firecracker behind the counter and fled." The most memorable incident was a holdup involving two brothers who were both students. "They were from a very good family," Wong said, explaining that the father was a company manager while the mother worked for the Hong Kong government. "One of the brothers stood outside while the other jumped over the counter and took about 100,000 Hong Kong dollars from three cashiers. He was brandishing some kind of toy gun and it turned out that it was a birthday present from his father."

By the early 1990s, holdups and occasional shoot-outs at banks and jewelry stores had become so common that most banks began installing bullet-proof glass.

At the corner of Ice House Street, Hong Kong, Citibank Tower was occupied from 1974 to 1983: it replaced the building used by the bank for more than 40 years (see p. 90)

Money box in the form of Citibank
Tower, Hong Kong

The bank's directors and senior
management from New York meeting
with the influential Japan Federation of
Economic Organizations (Keidanren) at
the Keidanren Hall in Tokyo

to do with money. I just couldn't understand why this made sense. So I was asked to develop that idea."

Reed later approached George Vojta, who was running the international business, and said he wanted to "travel around overseas and get some idea of what you guys are doing." The idea was not popular. Until then, "the guys in the field would ignore head office for long periods of time. There was no question that this was the foreign legion. ... Of course, the people in Asia took the position that if you hadn't spent time out there, forget about Asia—everything was different and nothing in New York counted," Reed said. "We fought those battles." Vojta instructed one of his assistants to accompany Reed, and in 1973 the two left for a six-week tour of the bank's overseas operations.

For John Reed, rapid improvements in transport and communications made it increasingly inappropriate to organize a global business solely on the old-style geographical basis. "Communications almost forced you to organize that way historically, but the changes in communications made it more difficult to justify," he said. The alternatives were to organize by product or by customer. Wriston chose the latter. The upshot to all this was a shift in the way the bank was managed, which was to shape its operations in Asia over the next 30 years, and led to the establishment of a global consumer business.

"The logic was that you could focus on customer needs, and then deal with them across geographies and product lines," Reed said. "It resulted in fragmentation, so if you were corporate head in Hong Kong, you had a guy in Hong Kong who was responsible for the world corporate bank, you had another guy in Hong Kong who was responsible for

local banking, and you had another guy in Hong Kong who was responsible for the consumer business. And it didn't matter if they didn't like each other one bit and they were all line-managed from New York." This new pattern of reporting relationships came to be known as "matrix management."

One of the first signs that a new era had come was the establishment of the "world corporate group." Wriston saw that major multinational companies had particular needs which transcended national boundaries, and which therefore required some reallocation of resources on the ground. Twenty-four country heads were summoned to New York in 1973, and the new business unit was born, under the leadership of Tom Theobald. As David Gibson put it, "That began the real focus of the customer being the real determinant of organization, structure and resource allocation." Mehli Mistri was the bank's country head in Indonesia in the early 1980s, and recalled the

New stuff

When John Reed asked to travel abroad to review the bank's foreign operations, George Vojta, international banking chief from 1973, agreed: but Vojta also instructed one of his assistants to accompany Reed. The problem was that the assistant was a woman and this was the early 1970s.

"I had never traveled with a woman, and in 1973 the idea of a woman traveling around the world was unheard of," Reed said. In no time, the head of personnel was on the case, telling Reed that it was not possible, as the woman was married and that he too was married.

"I said, 'Well, you talk to Vojta. I don't know how to travel with a woman either—do you carry her bags, don't you carry her bags?'

"This was new stuff. It was not done."

Left: The ground floor of the Bombay Mutual Life building was leased to the bank after the building was completed in 1935. It was still the Fort branch, Mumbai, in 2001. Above: Branch at Brabourne Road, Kolkata. Below: The bank's 75th anniversary in India celebrated in Calcutta (Kolkata)

Consumer banking grows offshore

In the early 1980s, Singapore was gaining kudos as an offshore banking center with the development of the Asiadollar market (see p. 107). Citibank quickly saw another opportunity and set up a new offshore banking arm, the Asian Banking Center, in 1983.

"We were holding a sizeable portfolio for around 2,500 foreigners living and working in Singapore at that time," recalled Amy Tan. "Customers had chosen to bank with us because of our established brand name and satisfied customers' referrals. We wondered what we could achieve if we put in more effort." Offices in Hong Kong and San Francisco quickly followed. Services broad-ened from simple U.S. dollar savings accounts to include other foreign-exchange accounts and eventually investment and insurance products. "We said that if we could grow the business to a billion U.S. dollars we would hold our next staff conference in Hawaii. We achieved that within three years." In 1990 the Asian Banking Center was renamed International Personal Banking, and by 2001 its 20 centers worldwide had around 130,000 customers.

In 1985, Citibank India launched another offshore business focused on the large and growing international Indian community. At the time the Indian government was seeking ways to service its foreign currency needs.

By offering rates above the market it hoped to draw foreign currency deposits from some of the world's several million non-resident Indians. Citibank set up offices in Asia, the Middle East, Africa, Europe, Canada, the United States and West Indies. In 1995, when the Indian government stopped offering the service, Citibank's clients had deposited two billion U.S. dollars in India in foreign currency and Citibank had created a highly valued offshore customer segment to which it could offer a new product range.

By 2001, it had more than 50,000 customers in 90 countries being served from 18 locations and increasingly via the internet.

The original vault on the ground floor of the branch at Brabourne Road, Calcutta. The vault is still used on a contingency basis today

usefulness of the new organization: "For example, by working closely with Toyota's subsidiary in Indonesia, we were able to forge closer relationships with Toyota's head office in Japan, competing more effectively with Japanese and other heavy-weight banks." The world corporate group enabled the bank to operate more effectively also in relation to large industries with specific needs. In Australia, as Glen Moreno recalled, Citibank became the bank of choice for the finance of major infrastructure such as mining and energy projects. The new structure gave the bank extra focus, and made it possible to bring in heavy-weight industry expertise. "There is no way you are going to do one of these deals locally without a lot of technical assistance. So it wasn't just the multinational focus, it was the industry focus that helped."

According to James Collins, who was in turn country head in Korea, India and Indonesia during the 1970s, the world corporate group had a more general impact. "It helped spread the bank's franchise to the local corporate groups. People understood that you had to listen to what the customer wants. The whole marketing attitude changed. Maybe because of competition, the bank got more in the way of going out and seeing customers, bringing new business in, bringing new products on

line: it was quite a change. The bank became considerably more proactive." The account officers got the message that "to bring in a new customer was good."

The role of the SENOF (senior officer in the field), as the country head was called until that time, had to evolve substantially, as staff in the individual businesses acquired new lines of

Geographic flexibility

It was one thing to hire lots of local staff as managers, train them and promote them up through the ranks. It was also important to encourage a willingness to move around.

Under Walter Wriston and John Reed, the bank lost much of its "white American" face starting with Wriston's appointment of the first black member of the board.

"We couldn't have cared less," said Reed. "People were people, it didn't matter whether you were Indian or Pakistani or whatever. But you can't get to the top of this place without being geographically flexible," he said. "You can't just run Japan and all of a sudden become chairman. We had a hell of a time over the years trying to get Japanese or Chinese or Koreans to move, and the reason was they're so embedded in their local family culture." It was a similar case with Singapore. "We've had wonderful Singaporeans, but as soon as you try to get them out of Singapore they quit," he said.

"We always said hire everybody you can and promote them and train them. So you find we've got a lot of Pakistanis, a fair number of Palestinians and a lot of Latin Americans"—especially Argentinians, but not Brazilians, who were reluctant to move.

When Reed joined the bank, there was an understanding that senior officers would

never get to run their own country. "So if you were Indian, you'd never run India, although you might run Japan or something. The feeling was that you'd become too vulnerable to the local community and behave in ways that weren't appropriate. That died. We found, particularly during the debt crisis in the 1980s, that people knew the difference between where they worked and what community they were in.

"Victor Menezes was one of our first big tests. He became head of Citibank India at age 28 and he was Indian. Then we took him from India to Hong Kong, where everybody said you can't possibly have an Indian running a bank." The doubters were wrong.

Colombo branch opening, December 1979: Jack Clark, first Sri Lanka country head Chong Quan Khoo, and Phil Markert, with Victor Menezes

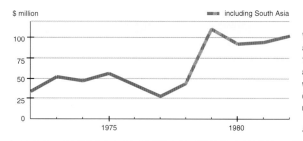

$ million — including South Asia

When the region's operating earnings after tax fell to 28 million dollars in 1977, the Asia-Pacific operations accounted for only seven percent of worldwide earnings. Within five years, earnings had almost quadrupled and the regional share was almost 14 percent

Source: annual reports

reporting within those businesses. As John Reed recalled, "It was in some ways traumatic for the culture of the overseas staff, because they felt disenfranchised and because there was too much head-office involvement." But, according to David Gibson, the changes were worthwhile. "Yes, it took a long time; yes it was effective; the results clearly demonstrated the value of the concept. ... A lot of stuff which is blamed on matrix management is nothing more than internal politics and competition."

The company's presence in Asia was much impacted by the cultural change. Between 1902 and 1972, it had enjoyed the sort of linear growth that was fairly predictable for an overseas, geographically organized bank staffed by the sons of missionaries or people who would otherwise have become diplomats. In those days, Reed said, "We'd hire somebody, send them overseas and say 'do good things.' They would tend to ape what they thought were best practices around the world. And our customers were the people who gravitated to our door."

While chairman George Moore oversaw a rapid expansion of the bank's overseas activities in the 1960s, it was his successor Walter Wriston who from the 1970s on made sure that the international bankers serving abroad were more professional. "George Moore was really the guy who expanded the international side of our bank. He was the flag planter," recalled Stephen H. Long, a real-estate workout specialist who helped to steer the bank through the Asian financial crisis in the late 1990s. "What Wriston did was change the paradigm of the way we did business internationally and the degree of professionalism in the

people we had ... we started to see a lot more people who were professional managers or who had certain expertise. Asia benefited a lot from that." As William Ferguson put it, "there was a very strong group of people of all nationalities, from all market places, who worked together very closely, who had an intense sense of pride in their work, were very bright, very eager, and really carved out some tremendous businesses."

During the 1960s and even more so the 1970s the corporate customer base expanded and changed in character. Expansion was not a matter of following United States trade interests, as it had largely been in earlier days, but was based on the marshaling of capital and the harnessing of management skills and technology, in support of the development of local companies. These companies included many national airlines, power companies, and other customers developing infrastructure. Many of the houses prominent at the end of the century got their seed capital with the aid of First National City Bank, and later Citibank. In this period Australia and Indonesia were particularly important markets for the corporate bank. As Moreno recalled, in Indonesia "the private bank and treasury were huge. There were lots of multinationals and interesting local companies which made for a frontier market. If you got your risk management profile right, which we did, you could do extremely well. We had remarkably sophisticated people working with clients to build a business." In his meetings with country heads, Moreno would stress the importance of target marketing. "Let's focus on the winners—the companies that are going to be important national

A Philippine customer of worldwide Citibank owns 42 of these giant dump trucks. Cost for tires alone: $1.2 million a year.

Citibank's customer is one of the world's largest copper-mining companies—as the equipment it uses attests. This electric rear dump truck, for example, has a capacity of 120 tons, and costs about half a million dollars. Its six 9½-foot-diameter tires cost $5,000 each.

The $1.2 million electric shovel is the first of its size outside the United States. Its 23-cubic-yard bucket can lift 40 tons of ore at a single "bite."

Operating on this scale calls for financing to match. Besides participating in syndicated term loans for specific expansion projects, Citibank provides this customer a continuing multimillion dollar line of

credit—thus helping one of the Philippines' top dollar earners extend its operations, and provide jobs for 8,000 people.

As a leading international bank, with branches, subsidiaries and affiliates worldwide, Citibank supplies effective, innovative "growth banking" to customers, large and small. At the same time, we work consciously and constructively to contribute, in every way we can, to the economic betterment of every community we serve.

CITIBANK⊕

Heinz Riehl

Left: Hong Kong's first Bourse Course, Sept 1974. Staff and customers learnt about the foreign-exchange market, the roles of commercial and central banks, and what it took to be a trader through theory and role-playing exercises. Right: George Vojta addressing BIMSCAD in Singapore, March 1976

companies with a chance of going beyond their national boundaries." This focus not only on the multinationals but on local corporate customers with real potential turned Citibank, to use Moreno's term, into a "blue-chip corporate bank." It was a formula which turned several of the bank's Asian markets from problems into profitable franchises.

The bank had a powerful weapon in its diversity of expertise. Many senior people, such as Ray Kathe and Robert Grant, had Asian experience going back many years. In the view of Victor Menezes, the bank's long experience in Asia made for valuable continuity. "The Old Asia Hands knew the corporate customers, the major families, the government figures. The relationships that had been built up over time supported the achievements of a younger, often more specialized, generation of managers. This combination, together with a new emphasis on customer needs, enabled us to grow as rapidly as we did." Glen Moreno was one of many who remembered the particular contribution of Ray Kathe. "The fact that he'd been in Asia for so long, with a predominantly Asian client base, meant that he was a huge help in terms of client contact. Ray and I would do 14 calls a day, and then sit down to an 18-course banquet. He was an iron man. I was exhausted after a few weeks of that, and he just rolled on."

Training played a key part in this success, for example in treasury management. Heinz Riehl set up a treasury training course, which then was extended to customers. Initially centered in Manila, it moved around. Those trained by Riehl, such as John Thom, who built up a treasury team in Asia, held seminars on treasury, money management, and derivatives, not only for Citibank staff but, crucially, for corporate customers. These two- or-three-day sessions were packed, and made a big contribution to the reputation of Citibank as a leading corporate and investment bank. Customers became familiar with Citibank techniques, which often became the standards for the industry. The result in 1979–80 was a great growth in regional earnings, partly from the turnaround in Australia, but also from growth in India, Indonesia, Singapore and Malaysia.

Nowhere was the cultural change in the bank more evident than in the new emphasis to be put on banking for the private individual. For Reed the consumer business changed the way

After you've given your check to be cashed, do they make you wait and wait and wait and...

Not at Citibank. With the Citicard.

Citicard

Card advertising in the Philippines, 1980

None of the above

"When we perceived, some years ago, that if consumers were paid a fair return on their savings there was no way a bricks-and-mortar branch could earn any money for bank stockholders, we invested heavily in technology for our Citicard automatic teller machines.

"We were told by experts in other financial institutions, by financial analysts and, of course, the media, that:

(a) older people would not use them
(b) younger people would not use them
(c) men would not use them
(d) women would not use them

"As it turned out, none of the above was true. ... We created a customer and built a profitable consumer business when others were getting out of the market."

Walter Wriston, Risk and Other Four-Letter Words

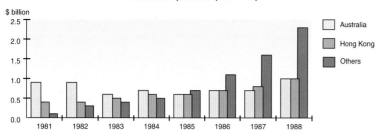

Asia-Pacific consumer portfolio (1981–88)

$ billion

- Australia
- Hong Kong
- Others

In the early 1980s, the consumer portfolio in Australia dwarfed that of the rest of the Asia-Pacific region. By the middle of the decade, average loans in Hong Kong were at the same level. By the end of the decade, average loans in the other countries surpassed Hong Kong and Australia, which together accounted for 11 percent of the total

Source: annual reports

the bank had been operating in Asia for 70 years. The new philosophy was articulated by Reed in a seven-page document written while he was on vacation in 1976. Addressed to senior vice-presidents and other key managers and officers in the consumer-services group, the document became immortalized as the "Memo from the Beach." Reed envisaged that consumer services would be a core business, and not a sideline in the years ahead. "We are creating something new," he wrote. "I am not referring to these new technologies or new delivery systems. Rather I refer to a fundamentally new business starting with a dedication to the consumer, and to the proposition that we can offer a set of services that will substantially satisfy a family's financial needs under terms and conditions that will earn the shareholders an adequate profit while creating a healthy, positive and straightforward relationship with the customer."

As Reed reflected some 25 years later, the consumer business became a "driving force" of the bank in Asia. "If you look at the size of the footprint in Asia and the number of employees, it grew dramatically as our consumer business took hold and went

into new businesses. We hired new people and, of course the leadership of the company started coming from the consumer." Within a few years, the regional consumer business had been transferred to Singapore and was being run by Rana Talwar.

The company's initial expansion into consumer finance in the Asia-Pacific region largely focused on Australia, Hong Kong and the Philippines. By 1976, there were significant consumer banking and finance operations in all three markets. At the same time Japan emerged as one of Citibank's key markets, accounting for five percent of all operating earnings after-tax, the same as Germany and slightly less than Britain. Within five years, new banking and financial services were being offered in Australia, Hong Kong, Japan and South Korea. Australia and Hong Kong were the first two markets showing major consumer loan growth in Asia, followed by Taiwan and the Philippines.

The growth of the consumer bank required a long-term perspective. James Collins was running the consumer business in the Philippines in the early 1970s. "In many cases it required an investment in things that didn't pay off right away. … The

Citibanking

The early 1980s saw the arrival of the desktop computer. The bank's senior officers were given personal computers, and also access to an electronic mail package using dedicated satellite lines, called Citimail.

It operated exactly like the email that came later, but was remarkably ahead of its time, and was the main means of long-distance communication within the bank by 1981.

Citibank began to install PCs at corporate customers' offices to allow them to "connect" to the bank's operations, mainly to view their account balances and monitor transactions. Initially

"The process of initiating, producing and delivering all of our services electronically": a display of Citibank technology in Manila in the 1970s

it was a matter of providing information rather than transferring funds online, but the system soon became the basis for electronic banking proper, and gave rise to the cash management service known as "Citibanking." Venky Krishnakumar recalled the pioneering days: "The PC was still a novelty in some Asian markets and in many cases we were introducing customers to their first PC. It was such an event that some CEOs insisted the terminal be set up in their office. In Asia, we were using a Japanese PC called the Sord. We ran some spectacular ads showing monks in Sri Lanka connecting to Citibank through their PC."

The Reuters "monitor" foreign-exchange service used in dealing rooms in the early 1980s. Apart from rates, it also provided market reports and news from around the world

Teller tips such as the one shown here were a common feature of internal newsletters in the 1970s

fact that you had to make your lobbies look attractive to people coming in, the heavy expenditure on marketing, advertising and so on—all those things cost money. At the same time the return was not all that apparent. The amount of money that had to be spent just to bring in a few customers, the outlay on equipment, the computer systems, customer service—all those things involved heavy front-end expenses and seemingly little immediate return. That certainly caused questions to be raised." Collins credited the growth of the consumer business mainly to the highly focused approach of John Reed, who created an organization for it, distinct from the prevailing corporate-banking culture; and to the support Reed received from key managers such as Rick Wheeler.

Japan, the biggest potential market, remained problematic. In 1983, Reed acknowledged "difficulties penetrating the Japanese market in a satisfactory way," even though other consumer operations in Asia were doing well. Japan was still "a marketplace offering substantial long-term opportunities for the development of the individual banking business," he said. Reed

The Singapore branch holds its annual adding-machine contest in 1979. The winner was Kwan Koh Tai from the data-processing center, who completed 10 mathematical problems in 11 minutes 59 seconds

was right—but it would take more than a decade for those opportunities to be realized.

By the 1980s not only was Asia an extremely important part of Citibank's global operations, but management responsibility

Demonstration to the media of the CitiPhone 24-hour "hotline" in Singapore, 1983

once again moved away from New York back into the region. Wriston introduced a new role, that of "senior corporate officer," designed to devolve some of the chairman's responsibility into the region which now represented a sizable business. In the words of William Ferguson, a long-time veteran of Citibank's Asian operations: "It was never a line job, but because the individuals assigned to the roles were always respected, well-liked and seasoned, they carried quite a bit of influence, especially in arbitrating issues between the different business managers." Ray Kathe took this role in 1980, and among his successors were David Van Pelt, Larry Glenn. Another who served in the post was William R. Rhodes, who later rose to become senior vice chairman of Citigroup.

Country officers reported to the senior corporate officer in respect of matters concerning the local franchise in general; however, other reporting lines continued in force regarding specific operational areas. People could have a variety of bosses, according to geographical area, customer, or product. The country corporate officer's job was, according to Rhodes, that of a co-ordinator, ensuring that representatives of all the business groups operating in a country were pulling in the same direction. This remained an important role, even after the senior corporate officer position disappeared in the early 1990s.

NCR terminals were used in the branches in the late 1970s. With these terminals, the processing of customer accounts was fully computerized

In the mid-1980s, following the bank's global and regional success in foreign-exchange dealing, it was decided that a new focus on investment banking would be a logical strategy. An investment bank was spun off from the corporate-banking operation as a separate entity, and in 1986 its headquarters was moved to Tokyo by the then-head Peter Schuring. It handled the profitable treasury business and related capital market products. In 1984 it acquired a stake in British stockbroking firm Vickers da Costa, giving it access to several securities markets in the region. The same year saw the company extend the distribution of U.S. securities to Tokyo. Securities trading and distribution were launched in Australia. And in an important strategic move, the company acquired existing securities companies in both Japan and Australia. By 1985 a

私たちには、ハッキリ見えます。

CITICORP◆VICKERS DA COSTA

Vickers da Costa was in the first group of foreign securities firms rushing to get a seat on the Tokyo Stock Exchange

full banking license was acquired in Australia, where Citicorp also established a venture capital company. Stockbroking businesses were now operating in Japan, Hong Kong and Singapore as well as Australia. In Tokyo alone, the Vickers da Costa affiliate traded 25 billion dollars in debt securities during the year and was also among the first six foreign securities companies to acquire a seat on the Tokyo Stock Exchange during the first round of negotiations that year. The bank itself obtained a Japanese trust banking license, giving it access for the first time to the vast market for investment management in Japan. Following mixed results, the investment bank was recombined with the rest of the corporate operation in 1989.

However, earnings in Asia were still largely determined by profits from foreign-exchange trading. The bank was now the

Cycle lessons

When Y.S. Wong became a trainee dealer with First National City Bank in Hong Kong in 1975, the U.S. dollar was going through a period of extreme weakness.

"It went all the way down until 1980, when Paul Volcker increased interest rates and rates jumped to over 20 percent. Then the dollar went all the way up until 1985, when the G-5 had the Plaza Accord, and then the dollar came all the way down again," he said. "I've always had the idea that a good trader is someone, who, besides other qualifications, must have the experience of down cycles and up cycles.

"It's a problem when people haven't gone through cycles. Normally they have a one-track mind," Wong said, pointing to

some of the big traders in Europe before the early 1980s when the dollar started to rebound. "In the 1970s, the dominant

Hong Kong dealing room in 1979. At the time, the Citibank Hong Kong foreign-exchange page on Reuters was being accessed by other banks and institutions about 1,500 times a week, making it the second most popular page in Asia

foreign-exchange centers were Frankfurt and Zurich—combined, they were bigger than London. When we wanted to get a price on dollar against deutschmark, we went to Frankfurt. We didn't go to London.

"Since the dollar was floated in 1973, those guys made all their money by shorting the dollar. The dollar dropped like a stone, so when it turned, it was very difficult for them to accept the fact that the dollar could become so strong.

"Those centers later weakened, apart from having too many regulations vis-à-vis London, because quite a number of those banks and traders in continental Europe, especially Switzerland and Germany, lost quite a bit of money as many of them only knew how to sell dollars."

Dealing room in Sydney where the merchant-banking subsidiary Citicorp Australia was a leading force in local financial markets. A full banking license was granted in 1985

Panic in Hong Kong

In 1983, the Hong Kong dollar went into a tailspin amid concern about the future of the British colony. The Hong Kong dollar, which was then free-floating, plummeted from 6.50 to the U.S. dollar at the beginning of the year to 9.60 in the interbank market on September 24, before the government introduced drastic measures to halt the slide.

Y.S. Wong was the treasurer in charge of Citibank Hong Kong's dealing room at the time. "It was a Saturday. I sat in the dealing room and managed the FX position personally. The Hong Kong dollar started at 8.80 and weakened all the way. We were the only bank that kept on selling U.S. dollars all the way up to all the banks that called us."

Wong, who later became the New York-based executive vice president in charge of sales and trading in emerging markets, said

he nevertheless had mixed feelings. "It's odd. It was a day I made good money. But I felt so unhappy because I was from Hong Kong and the currency went down the tubes."

Chinese leader Deng Xiaoping and British Prime Minister Margaret Thatcher in Beijing in September 1982. Under an agreement reached in 1984, Britain agreed to return Hong Kong to China on July 1, 1997

Wong said rumors later surfaced that the currency would be pegged under a "currency board" system. These were just rumors that measures would be introduced, so the market was extremely nervous and very uncertain after the weekend.

"I still remember brokers asked us for a price but nobody was quoting any prices. So I quoted the widest price of my life! I had sold good amounts of U.S. dollars on Saturday, therefore I had ammunition. I said, it must be lower than 9.60, but I don't know where, so I just quoted 8.00–9.00, and I bought dollars right away at 8.00!"

On October 17, 1983, the currency was pegged at 7.80, the government essentially leaving the conduct of monetary policy to the United States. Despite occasional pressures, Hong Kong has been able to maintain that rate ever since.

City Bank Club Inaugural Party - Sept. 22, 1946

CITIBANK
TROPICAL BEACH NIGHT

Out of office hours

1: The Far East Bank in Hong Kong was acquired by First National City Bank in 1969. Shown here is a friendly basketball match among the Far East Bank staff

2: The Far East Bank staff club on an outing in June 1978

3: Members of the City Bank Club in the Philippines at the inaugural party on September 22, 1946

4: The City Bank football team from Singapore in the late 1990s

5: A staff fashion show in Singapore in the 1970s

6: Bombay branch City Bank Club celebrates the Annual Cricket Festival with cricket matches among staff, 1955

7: Winners of a fancy-dress competition in Bombay, 1949

8: City Bank Club members from Osaka, Japan, gather for popular hobbies such as reciting poetry, 1953

9: Staff from the Philippines all dressed up for a Halloween party in the late 1990s

10: A game of limbo on Tropical Beach Night in Singapore

11: Halloween party in the Philippines, 1960s

12: Staff celebrate Indian Independence Day with a flag-raising ceremony in front of the Calcutta branch, 1955

13: The first annual Cherry Blossom picnic by City Bank Club members in Japan, held on the banks of Nishiki River with the famous Kintai Bridge in the background

14: Hong Kong staff after a dinner

15: A dinner for the Quarter Century Club members in Singapore at the Hunan Restaurant, Apollo Hotel on June 18, 1974. They had collectively contributed a total of 419 years of service

16: A staff performance on the occasion of Sanford Weill's visit to China, 2001

17: A Citibank Quarter Century Club dinner in Hong Kong, 1993

18: Agnes Chu from Hong Kong, one of the relatively few female QCC members during the 1970s, receives a souvenir at her retirement

19: Quarter Century Club members in the Philippines at a dance

1		6	8				
	5	7	9	14			
2							
3	10	11	15	16		18	
4	12	13	17			19	

CITIBANK QUARTER CENTURY CLUB DINNER
1993

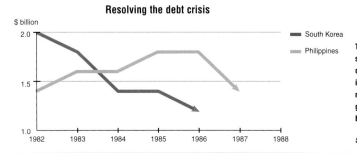

Resolving the debt crisis

$ billion

South Korea
Philippines

The bank's exposure to South Korea fell steadily after the onset of the debt crisis. Problems took longer to resolve in the Philippines. But an accord was reached with the new Philippine government in 1986, and exposure began to fall the following year

Source: annual reports

world's biggest foreign-exchange trader and had major dealing rooms in Tokyo, Singapore, Hong Kong and Sydney. In 1983, net income from Asia rose from 180 million dollars the previous year to 191 million dollars, partly reflecting gains on the sale of real estate in Hong Kong. Net income fell to 175 million dollars in 1984 due to lower foreign-exchange earnings.

Consumer banking had begun in Malaysia (1980), Indonesia (1984) and India (1985). The acquisition of the Mercantile Bank (founded in 1853 as the Mercantile Bank of India, London and China), from Hongkong and Shanghai Banking Corporation in 1984 gave Citibank a full-service bank in Thailand, where there was a ceiling on foreign bank licenses. A branch in Bangkok was opened in 1985. In the same year, Citibank was the first foreign bank to receive a consumer banking license in Taiwan, and it has remained a leader in the field ever since. However, despite benefits from the bank's expanding consumer business and a rebound in foreign-exchange earnings in 1985, net income from Asia fell further that year due to narrowing interest rate spreads and increased write-offs.

An important working relationship was established with the International Monetary Fund (IMF) as a second oil crisis occurred in 1979 and a crippling debt crisis hit some less-developed countries, largely triggered by rising interest rates in the United States in the early 1980s.

For Walter Wriston, the debt problem that emerged in developing countries from 1982 had two major causes, and they were both highly relevant to the situation in many Asian countries. The first involved developments in the rest of the world—a global recession from 1979, a quantum jump in oil prices from two dollars a barrel in 1972 to 30 dollars a barrel in 1982, and an unprecedented decline in world exports which led to the lowest commodity prices in years. The second cause was more technical—the lack of private investment. "Too much was financed by debt and too little by equity," Wriston said. "In many countries the state of affairs was as much a political decision as an economic one, brought on by national policies that tended to

Wriston's secret weapon

Wong Nang Jang, the former country head for Singapore, was transferred to New York for two years in 1976. It was there that he encountered chairman Walter Wriston, who could be disarmingly charming but also exceedingly blunt.

Being one of the bank's first two senior Asian managers, Wong played a useful role at the Washington meetings of the International Monetary Fund (IMF) when commercial bankers such as Wriston would descend upon the annual financial jamboree and meet with the world's finance ministers and central bank governors. "I was very good to have around with all the Asian finance ministers," he recalled. "I was a slant-eyed boy with all the 'round eyes.'" During one IMF meeting, he was summoned to see the chairman. "I walked into the briefing room, and

Wong Nang Jang in the 1970s

Wriston looked at me and said: 'Come on in, Tiny. I know your reputation. Now you sit down and you listen.'"

Wong was stunned by Wriston's knowledge of Asia. "He knew every relationship, every central bank governor and every finance minister. He was a formidable guy." But Wong appears to have been quite formidable too. He believes he earned his spurs with head office when an official of the New York Federal Reserve came to visit Singapore while he was country head in the late 1970s. The official "admitted he did not quite know what to expect, meeting a young native of Singapore," especially one who had only graduated from a local university. "I see you didn't go to graduate school in America." He then asked Wong how he got to speak such good American English. "I told him I had the best textbooks—*Time* and *Fortune*."

equate foreign capital with exploitation. Those countries that attracted foreign capital and let it flow in and out without hindrance did not have problems of the magnitude of those with restrictive investment policies."

Although he was criticized by many for alleged financial heresy, Wriston stood by his remark that countries could not go bankrupt. In 1987, three years after his retirement, he elaborated further. He explained to *Institutional Investor* that "the infrastructure doesn't go away, the productivity of the people doesn't go away, the natural resources don't go away. And so their assets always exceed their liabilities, which is the technical reason for bankruptcy. And that's very different from a company."

The company's greatest exposure was to Brazil, Mexico, and Argentina, with important amounts to several other countries. In Asia, the company's biggest exposure to a developing country involved South Korea, although its military leaders proved to be quite adept at keeping their house in order. The biggest problem in Asia was the Philippines, which ranked alongside Latin America.

Faced with foreign-exchange liquidity problems in 1983,

Clockwise from top right: After opening offices in Shenzhen in 1983 and Beijing in 1984, Citibank published a 24-page investment guide to China; Victor Menezes dotting the eye of the dragon, on the opening of new premises in 1984; banner presented to the bank, bearing good wishes for the Macau branch opening in 1983

the Philippines restricted imports, devalued the peso and declared a moratorium on external debt, affecting repayments of principal. Debt rescheduling negotiations were launched along with IMF discussions on a comprehensive program for 1984 aimed at narrowing the country's balance of payments deficit while ensuring the external payments could be met on schedule. In 1984, the Philippine government reached an

CitiGold

Citibank introduced a new service in 1982 called CitiGold. First launched in Hong Kong, and extended throughout the region, it was pitched to the "middle affluent"—not quite the clientele of the private bank (see p. 149), but those with more than 100,000 U.S. dollars (or the equivalent) to invest. The exact figure depended on the country.

It started with a humble "customer center," a small area set aside from the rest of the branch, with two staff members to deal with priority customers. "Then, all the banks had high counters with bars on top," recalled Allen Tan, business manager for

Luxurious surroundings at CitiGold Center, Robina House, Singapore

consumer banking in Malaysia. "We took the bars off, and reduced the height of the counters, so that customers could look at us face to face. We changed the look and feel so much we had competitors coming in to take measurements. The local architect became famous." By 2001, CitiGold offered a wide range of banking and wealth management services, including wealth planning, portfolio tracking, and other savings and investment products. The counters had gone, replaced by online analysis brought to customers sitting in comfortable armchairs. CitiGold premises were developed entirely around client conference rooms.

Total assets (1972–85)

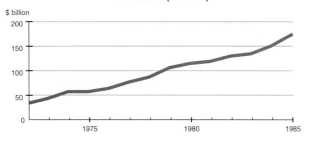

$ billion

Assets worldwide grew steadily, although much of the lending in the 1970s was rescheduled after the international debt crisis of the early 1980s. By 1985, outstandings with refinancing countries were 15 billion dollars, almost 10 percent of total assets

Source: annual reports

agreement in principle with a 12-member bank advisory committee on rescheduling the existing debt and new medium-term financing. At the same time, the IMF agreed to provide a standby credit after approving a letter of intent from the Philippine government. In its 1984 annual report, Citicorp said the rescheduling would affect "substantially all" of its public and private sector outstandings to the Philippines. Total outstandings to the country were 1.6 billion dollars after adjustment for net local-currency outstandings, external guarantees and collateral. Of the unadjusted figure of 1.4 billion dollars, almost 60 percent was owed by the private sector and almost 30 percent by the public sector. The rest was owed by Philippine commercial banks.

Amid growing concern about the debt crisis, the company instituted a practice of disclosing details of all outstandings.

In 1985, the Philippine government and the bank advisory committee announced a rescheduling agreement for 5.8 billion dollars of existing debt, including 371 million dollars owed to Citicorp. The IMF agreed to provide standby credits as long as the government met specific targets and conditions. Separately, the banks signed a nine-year loan to the Philippines for 925 million dollars, with Citicorp providing 126 million dollars. As an additional lifeline, the banks agreed to maintain 2.9 billion dollars in short-term trade credits to the end of 1986. The Citicorp share was 751 million dollars. By the end of 1985, the company's total outstandings to the Philippines had risen to 1.8 billion dollars.

In 1998, a merger took place which would combine Citibank with investment bankers Salomon Smith Barney as part of a new structure named Citigroup Inc.

Striking the right note

"Trunks hoisted in salute, richly caparisoned elephants trumpeted a welcome, as garlands of marigold and lilies perfumed the air." It was September 1984; Citibank was hosting a tour by the New York Philharmonic Orchestra under the baton of Indian-born Zubin Mehta.

Myrna Chaves, Citibank's coordinator for the tour, recalled: "The bank had never organized a cultural event of this stature. It was a challenge to look after 121 musicians of varied talents and temperament—and their instruments, so that humidity didn't dampen the orchestra's ability to stay in tune.

"Bureaucracy threatened to derail our planning at many stages. A local senior bureaucrat, a personal friend of Mehta, took a keen interest in the visit, resulting in an

Sponsored by
CITIBANK●

Tour logo based on a peacock, India's national bird

official welcome in the capital. The official arrangements also prompted a welcome by the insects resident in the hotel rooms. Amid howls of consternation the entire orchestra beat a hasty retreat to the lobby in an emotional crescendo— the cue for the bank to move out of the wings and on to center stage from there on.

"In those days, companies were not officially permitted to indulge in publicity on audiovisual media. However, careful planning behind the scenes resulted in a curtain-raiser we hoped to get broadcast before the orchestra arrived. To our delight, the program got the official nod from the cabinet of Mrs. Indira Gandhi, and Citibank became the first foreign institution to air a sponsored program on Indian television."

Zubin Mehta, as seen by Indian cartoonist Mario de Miranda. The orchestra's 32-day tour covered eight Asian countries

An Independence Minded Country Needs An Independent Minded Bank

Brunei's varied and dramatic history will soon culminate in full independence. With it will come new challenges, new opportunities, new demands. Including in the world of international finance.

Brunei has been preparing for independence for many years, and so have the people of Citibank. Citibank has been in Brunei for over a decade learning the markets and bringing to clients here the kind of independent and dynamic banking that characterize it in Asia and around the world.

Citibank's independent approach is exemplified by staff training programs. Training opportunities for Brunei staff are superior, with the result that Citibank has more Brunei citizens and permanent residents in senior positions than any other bank in the country.

Citibank's exceptional training programs are also made available to government agencies, our customers and even other banks. We truly think that Brunei deserves the best in modern banking.

The people of Citibank have established a tradition of moving ahead, aggressively and independently in meeting the banking needs of Brunei over the last decade. For example, Citibank is a major bank to the oil service industry and maintains a branch in Kuala Belait to facilitate quality banking for this vital industry.

Now, with the advent of independence, a new tradition of service is being forged.

CITIBANK

When Brunei achieved independence in 1984, the bank had already been operating in the sultanate for more than a decade

Salomon Smith Barney and its precursors had significant histories in their own right. Before its merger with Charles D. Barney in 1938, the underwriting firm Edward B. Smith and Co. had ties to the Guaranty Company of New York. In 1924, it acted as lead manager for the first Japanese bond issues in the United States. The companies were Tokyo Electric Light and Toho Electric Power, which would later form Tokyo Electric Power Company, the world's biggest privately owned power company. Between 1924 and 1929, the firm raised 130 million dollars through five issues for the two companies.

Three decades later, the American depositary receipt (ADR) market was just getting under way. In 1961, Smith Barney helped arrange the first issue for a Japanese company in the New York market. This client was a relative newcomer—it had set up its first showroom in the Ginza shopping district of Tokyo only the previous year. Its name was Sony Corporation, and the issue was so successful that Ernest Schwartzenbach, the Austrian banker at Smith Barney who headed the team of underwriters, would later become president of Sony's American subsidiary.

During the late 1950s and early 1960s, Smith Barney managed 11 offerings of dollar-denominated bonds by the government-owned Japan Development Bank and Nippon Telegraph and Telephone Corporation (NTT), which was also owned by the government at the time. Smith Barney also lead-managed several private placements for Japanese companies including the Mitsui trading house, electrical machinery

manufacturer Toshiba and agricultural machinery maker Kubota. In 1964, Smith Barney's Burnett Walker was duly decorated by the Japanese government.

In the early 1970s, the Japanese government allowed foreign securities companies to open representative offices in Tokyo. Until then, the only United States securities firm in Japan was Merrill Lynch, which had come into Japan during the occupation. In 1972, Smith Barney, First Boston, Morgan Stanley and Goldman Sachs all opened offices within a few months of each other. In 1973, Smith Barney and Goldman Sachs arranged a private placement for Mitsui that was rated by Standard and Poor's, becoming the first Japanese corporate

Staff kept up with company news through Citibank newsletters such as these. Top, left to right: Singapore, Hong Kong, and Korea. Below, left to right: the Philippines, India, and Indonesia

Translation of characters on honor scroll conferred on Burnett Walker May 7th, 1964.
Presentation was made by Prime Minister Ikeda in his office at the Prime Ministry, Tokyo.

The Emperor of Japan confers upon Burnett Walker, American National, The order of the Sacred Treasure Second class. The Imperial Seal has been duly affixed at the Imperial Palace on this Seventh Day Fifth Month Thirty-nineth Year of Showa.

Chief of Bureau of Decorations,
Signed, Iwakura Norio.

Prime Minister,
Signed, Ikeda Hayato.

Number 7770 TH.

In recognition of the firm's role in bringing Japanese borrowers to international markets, Prime Minister Hayato Ikeda presented this imperial scroll to Smith Barney's Burnett Walker on May 7, 1964

bond issue ever to be rated by an international rating agency.

In 1975, the Japanese government, through a Japan Development Bank issue co-managed by Smith Barney, received its first sovereign rating. At the time there was international concern about the Japanese economy in the wake of the first oil crisis. Richard Janiak, who was Smith Barney's representative in Tokyo then, remembers a *New York Times* article on Japan shortly after he arrived in Tokyo in 1974. "The headline said Japan was an island nation sinking into the sea," he recalled. The government-owned bank's triple-A rating was especially welcome.

By 1980, Smith Barney decided to set up a full branch in Tokyo. "People thought we were nuts, but we wanted to deal directly with the Japanese investment community," Janiak recalled. At the time, Merrill Lynch and Bache had branches in Japan, the former dealing in securities and the latter primarily in commodities. "Because no one had gone through the process of applying for a full securities license for many years, if ever, the Ministry of Finance didn't know what to ask us for, so they requested everything," said Janiak, who ended up submitting three

or four piles of documents about two meters high to support the application. Smith Barney crossed another landmark in 1982 by arranging the first corporate issue of samurai bonds (yen-denominated debt issued in Japan by foreigner borrowers). The 20-billion-yen issue was for Dow Chemical, which had a substantial presence in Japan.

It was around this time that Salomon Brothers was developing a serious interest in Asia. Founded in New York in 1910, Salomon Brothers had set up an office in London in 1971. By 1976, Salomon Brothers International was underwriting and trading securities in London and decided to send three salesmen to Hong Kong to look for business opportunities around Asia. By the end of the 1970s, the attractions of Japan, where the big institutional investors were located, and offering a bigger market than Hong Kong, were becoming clear. By 1980, Salomon Brothers had moved to Tokyo and begun hiring a small Japanese sales team. "It really focused on selling U.S. bonds to Asian investors, typically central banks, commercial banks and institutional investors," recalled Deryck Maughan, a former British Treasury official who joined Salomon, and moved to Tokyo in the mid-1980s to run the business in Japan. He was to receive a knighthood in Britain's 2002 New Year Honours.

Although the Hong Kong office closed in 1981, Salomon Brothers extended its presence in the region with the opening of a new office in Sydney in 1983. Australia had just elected a new government, and became an important client for sovereign issues which until then had been exclusively arranged by

News conference

When the Prime Minister of India, Mrs. Indira Gandhi, died in October 1984, Nanoo Pamnani (see p. 96) was on a visit to Kathmandu at the time.

"My boss from Singapore was there and we were planning to host a reception that evening for our clients in Nepal as well as for the central bank governor and the finance minister," he recalled.

Pamnani, who would later become the bank's country head in the Philippines and ultimately in India itself for the second time, said the bank had called a news conference and was demonstrating new technology to the assembled journalists.

"The press was absolutely goggle-eyed at this technology," he said. During the demonstration, the screen turned to a page with a news flash from India announcing Mrs. Gandhi's assassination.

"The whole press corps disappeared. They were out of there. They even forgot to have lunch."

Morgan Stanley. "It was fortuitous timing as the currency was floated and the banking system was being deregulated," recalled Trevor Rowe who had, before moving to Sydney, handled the Australian business out of New York. Within a couple of years, however, competition was fierce as international investment banks fell over themselves to arrange bond issues for Australian borrowers in the burgeoning Euro-Australian dollar market.

The collapse of the Australian dollar in the mid-1980s burned many European investors, highlighting the fact that sharp currency devaluations were not limited to developing countries.

As Citicorp chairman Walter Wriston pointed out, "National governments in all countries have been debasing their currencies for more than 2,000 years, and so there is very little mystery left about how they do this, or even how to stop it. We know what measures must be taken to right an economy over time. We know that the IMF has overseen dozens of successful programs, and we know that the nature of these programs is similar no matter what language is spoken. They are all based on the fact that no one can do for a borrower the things it must do for itself."

Accounting lesson

Sony's co-founder Akio Morita said that the work on the ADR issue "may have been the hardest I ever had to do" because of all the official approvals required. "Fortunately, Prime Minister Hayato Ikeda was pleased with the idea, because he was an internationalist and this would be a first for Japan," Morita wrote in his memoirs. "His positive attitude had a lot to do with convincing the conservative, traditional thinkers at the Finance Ministry that they should approve our request."

Morita said they had a "difficult time" meeting Securities and Exchange Commission (SEC) requirements for consolidated accounts. However, there were benefits. "We are much better off for learning to consolidate, and after our experience consolidation became the standard reporting method in Japan."

After three months of preparation, the team moved to New York, staying up every night until two in the morning to check the closing price of Sony's shares in Tokyo. This went on for several weeks. On the big day,

everyone was ready for the 2 a.m. closing price and the final approval from Smith Barney's Ernie Schwartzenbach. Only then could the price be inserted into the prospectus which was ready to be rushed off to the printers. A lawyer was poised to take the 6 a.m. train to Washington to file it with the SEC, calling back on the public phone once it was approved.

Schwartzenbach was dead on his feet. "He decided to go home and get some rest. But when we called him, he was sleeping so soundly we couldn't wake him up. We rang

Schwartzenbach and Morita in New York

and rang and rang. No answer. Time was running out." As Schwartzenbach was also the town mayor of Great Neck, the local police were asked to go to his house and wake him up. "But it happened that only the week before, some nut in Great Neck had been harassing the mayor and the police chief with crank phone calls," Morita wrote. The request met with a cool reception followed by laughs from the police. After a long explanation by the desperate bankers, a patrol car was finally sent.

A Sony TR-610 transistor radio from the 1960s

Morita said he was "pleasantly shocked" by the result—a check for four million dollars, the biggest he had ever seen.

"When Schwartzenbach retired from Smith Barney in 1966, I jumped at the chance to hire him as Sony America's president, replacing me while I moved up to chairman. He knew as much about Sony as I did after going through our stock offering experience, and he held the post until he died in 1968."

5. An Asian Brand
1986–2001

"Citibank was a talent machine. … There were no bars on origin or nationality, performance was the only criterion."

Shaukat Aziz

Masamoto Yashiro was an oil man with no prior experience in banking. So, shortly after joining Citibank in 1989, when he saw an article which compared bank branches with gas stations, he felt it had been written expressly for him.

Yashiro took over the job of running Citibank's Japanese operations in 1992. He had spent the past 30 years working for American oil companies in Japan and in the United States, ultimately as president of Esso Sekiyu Japan. He had lived through the oil crisis of 1973, the Iranian revolution, and the Exxon Valdez oil spill off the Alaskan coast. And now he was running a bank.

In 1986, the dozens of foreign banks in Japan accounted for barely one percent of the country's entire banking system. With progressive deregulation since 1979, foreign banks such as Citibank had lost the lead they had once enjoyed in such businesses as providing acceptances or foreign-currency loans to Japanese companies. As Japanese banks progressively offered more-competitive products, many foreign banks concentrated on the areas they knew best, such as foreign exchange trading or securities and investment banking, especially in such areas as financial futures and options, where Japanese financial institutions had little experience.

However, even before Yashiro's appointment, Citibank had been nurturing its presence in the Japanese consumer market—this was, after all, the world's second-biggest economy. It now considered the possibility of acquiring a Japanese bank. However, given the complications posed by the network of interlocking share holdings and the sheer expense of such an acquisition at the time, Yashiro thought it would be better to build up Citibank's own business. In New York, chairman John Reed agreed, and the bank started mapping out a new strategy for the Japanese market.

One innovation was the introduction of foreign-currency deposits, which had been hugely successful in Hong Kong. As Yashiro later found out, innovations that had worked well in one market did not necessarily succeed immediately when transplanted to Japan. The higher interest rates on Italian lira deposits were, for example, essentially offset by the commission charged on changing the lira back into yen—the commissions were so high because there were so few deposits in the Italian currency. However, deposits in other currencies posed fewer challenges, and overall the initiative yielded results similar to those that had been achieved in Hong Kong.

Opposite: Branch at the bank's headquarters in Bangkok, where the acquisition of Mercantile Bank in 1984 gave Citibank a full-banking license in a country where ceilings on foreign banks applied.
Above: Sponsoring an international golf tournament in Japan in 1985

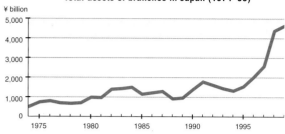

Total assets of branches in Japan (1974–99)

¥ billion

Assets at Citibank's Japanese branches grew to over a trillion yen in the early 1980s, but did not expand greatly thereafter until the later 1990s, when consumer banking operations began to take off in a big way

Source: annual reports

Another great idea was the Global Cash Card. Given the millions of Japanese traveling abroad every year, why not offer yen accounts allowing Japanese customers to withdraw local currency overseas? This service became one of Citibank's flagship products in Japan.

The transformation of the company's fortunes in Japan was in part the outcome of an effective strategy. But it would not have happened had the bank not responded cautiously to the various shocks that had hit the Japanese financial system since the mid-1980s.

In September 1985, the finance ministers and central bank governors of the Group of Five (the United States, Japan, Germany, France and Britain)—the five countries whose currencies formed the basis for the special drawing rights of the International Monetary Fund (IMF)—met at the Plaza Hotel in New York. Signaling for the first time their intention to carry out coordinated intervention in the foreign-exchange markets, they agreed that "further orderly

Mountain of gold

Exchange arrangements in Northeast Asia varied during the first half of the 20th century: Japan and its dependencies in Taiwan, Korea and Manchuria adopted a gold standard for most of the period while China and Hong Kong stuck with silver. When the yen depreciated sharply against the dollar during the 1930s, National City Bank began to ship gold abroad. Kentaro Funatani, who joined the Kobe branch in 1928, recalled packing boxes full of 20-yen gold coins and transporting them to the local port on a truck guarded by police. Hank Sperry, who transferred from Kobe to Shanghai in 1934, recalled shipping huge quantities of silver following a surge in silver prices around the same period. As cashier, his job was to supervise shipments to mints in San Francisco and London. While sitting on crates of silver at the wharf in Shanghai, Sperry said he could not help thinking that the value of the shipment was worth more than a million dollars.

Fifty years later, Tatsuo Umezono was sitting on a mountain of gold worth three billion dollars. It was 1986 and the massive order had come from Japan's Ministry of Finance, which appointed Citibank to acquire some 223 tonnes of gold for special

Tatsuo Umezono

coins commemorating the 60th anniversary of Emperor Hirohito's reign. After becoming the first local country head in Japan, Umezono was now heading the Asian global business division in New York, which was put in charge of the deal for reasons of confidentiality. To show the bank's full commitment, Umezono and vice chairman Hans Angermueller flew to Tokyo to meet Finance Minister Noboru Takeshita, the powerful ruling party politician who became prime minister in 1987.

Amid much secrecy, Citibank quietly purchased the gold through its trading company in New York. "The bank's role was acquiring the gold at the cheapest possible price," recalled Umezono. As it was impossible to insure the cargo beyond a certain amount on commercial flights from New York, the bank chartered its own aircraft to deliver the gold to Osaka where the finance ministry's mint was to produce the 100,000 yen coins. In discreetly arranging for the huge purchase and shipment, Umezono was assisted by several Japanese finance ministry officials including Eisuke Sakakibara, who would later become vice minister for international affairs and ultimately a member of the international advisory board of Salomon Smith Barney.

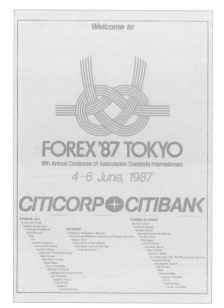

High profile at the annual congress of the international association of foreign exchange dealers in Tokyo in 1987

Branch near the south exit of Shinjuku station in Tokyo. Used by roughly three million commuters a day, Shinjuku has long ranked as the busiest railroad station in the world

appreciation of the main non-dollar currencies against the dollar is desirable." The yen's dramatic ascent after the Plaza Accord led to intense foreign interest in Japan, especially in the equity market, where prices started to rise substantially.

The impact on the currency was dramatic, and the long-term consequences were devastating for both Japan and the rest of Asia. Between 1985 and 1987, the yen more than doubled, from 260 yen to the dollar to around 120 yen. However, with the

Revolutionary restructuring

In 1986, the Philippine people took to the streets and brought down President Marcos. In its annual report, Citicorp said "progress" was finally being made in efforts to resolve the debt crisis in developing countries.

When the global debt crisis blew up in 1982, the Philippines was the only Asian country seriously involved. Citicorp had since welcomed an initiative by U.S. Treasury Secretary James Baker to address the crisis, noting that it was "based on the success of such economies as South Korea, Taiwan and Hong Kong which have continued their economic growth and avoided the debt problem." But Marcos had left the economy in a shambles.

CITI⊕BALITA
Issue One   1986

CITIP⊕WER

Supplement to Manila staff magazine prepared, although never distributed, when Marcos fell

Under the first phase of restructuring after 1982, short-term balance-of-payments deficits were addressed by such measures as devaluations and reduced government spending. The second phase involved rescheduling debts of three years or more.

The third, now welcomed by Citicorp, focused on structural adjustment, with reforms to encourage savings and investment, reduce government intervention and improve competition in the private sector.

After Marcos was toppled, the IMF agreed to a new standby facility as well as a compensatory financing facility. At the end of 1986, creditor banks agreed to a 90-day extension on Philippine debt maturing in the first three months of 1987, and extended to mid-1987 a 2.9-billion-dollar trade facility due to expire in a few days. This was followed by a debt-rescheduling by the Paris Club of creditor nations, and a restructuring and repricing of public sector debt by creditor banks at the end of 1987. With total outstandings of 1.8 billion dollars (after adjustments), Citicorp had the biggest exposure to the Philippines of all the creditor banks in 1986. Accordingly, it was the biggest contributor of new money and to the trade facility, encouraging support for the

Above: Gabriel Singson, the first governor of the restructured Philippine central bank (center), with his successor, long-time Citibanker Rafael Buenaventura (left) and vice chairman William R. Rhodes (right)
Left: Citation presented by President Fidel Ramos to Bill Rhodes for Citibank's "invaluable contribution to Philippine economic development" and for consistently contributing the highest amount of new money during refinancing negotiations throughout the 1980s

restructuring among other banks. However, it would take another five years of difficult negotiations before a definitive resolution of the Philippine debt problem was achieved under the Brady Initiative, which succeeded the Baker Plan and was signed in 1992.

Close ties with the central bank were later reinforced by Citibank's assistance in setting up compliance systems and paving the way for the country's return to the international capital markets.

His Majesty King Bhumibol Adulyadej receives John Reed during a visit to Thailand

Japan eased monetary policy, leading to an unprecedented era of low interest rates. Armed with cheap money and an extremely favorable exchange rate, Japanese investors then started flocking abroad to buy everything from impressionist paintings in Europe to real estate in the United States.

The bubble had begun. It started to burst when Japanese share prices peaked at the end of 1989, falling precipitously over the following year. By 1991, people were already talking of the "post-bubble era" and a "hollowing out" of the Japanese economy.

Meanwhile, the yen maintained its relatively high value, and there was an accelerated move of investment by Japanese companies to cheaper manufacturing locations in Southeast Asia. The Japanese banks followed with financial backing and were soon joined by other foreign banks, especially European financial institutions. With the sudden influx of tens of billions of dollars, it was not long before new bubbles were springing up all across Asia.

increased volatility in currency markets, Citibank emerged as the leader in foreign and interest-rate risk management across the region. As the yen strengthened, Japanese asset values shot up, and price–earnings ratios skyrocketed as the traditional ways of evaluating share prices were cast aside. By the second half of the 1980s, the market capitalization of the Tokyo Stock Exchange exceeded that of the New York Stock Exchange. To relieve the intense pressure on Japanese exporters, the Bank of

Getting out

How does a foreign-exchange dealer react if he doesn't feel comfortable with that very different beast, the stock market?

Y.S. Wong said he was feeling "funny" over the weekend before the Black Monday crash on Wall Street in 1987. In Asia, the fateful day was Monday, October 19, 1987, after which the Hong Kong Futures Exchange and the Hong Kong Stock Exchange closed for four days, although much-smaller markets around Asia stayed open and weathered the storm.

"I did my homework over the weekend," Wong recalled. "I came back from Asia's annual regional budget meeting, and looked at the Dow and how the U.S. market had behaved. For two weeks, the index had

been coming down, especially in the last three consecutive days, when it dropped sharply by 10 percent, despite the fact that people were bullish. And I looked up and said, 'If this is a bull market, how come it came down so sharply amidst an optimistic sentiment? I don't feel comfortable.'" Wong said his trading decisions were evenly split between fundamental and technical factors. "Neither showed a very good picture."

Wong's trading method to unload stock positions on that Monday morning raised a few eyebrows at Vickers da Costa, the securities arm of Citicorp at the time. "If the price was 10 dollars, I told them to sell everything at 9.50 or better. They hadn't seen anything like this before. But in foreign exchange, when we want to sell a big

position, we don't worry too much about the price—we just want to get rid of the position. For stock markets, especially in a good market, normally you bargain for cents—you place your order for people to buy."

The Hong Kong Futures Exchange was rescued through a controversial bailout. "After the collapse and then the bailout by the Hong Kong government, the stock market and the futures market reopened, and I was able to buy the Hang Seng index futures contract at the lowest price of the day," he said. "I was short, so I was able to do it." Looking back, Wong said he learned a valuable lesson. "Anything can happen. I didn't expect such a collapse ... but then it confirmed my belief... when you really don't feel comfortable, you should really get out."

Cash management in India

Citibank responded prudently. It had already learned its lesson in Latin America and the Philippines, where the international debt crisis had first erupted in 1982. Some restructuring was still going on at the end of the decade (see pp. 129–130). Moreover, a new system of managing risk was in place (see p. 153).

In the area of institutional and corporate banking, Asia was Citibank's main source of growth, reflecting benefits from developing infrastructure and distribution networks across the region. The bank highlighted transaction processing for big clients as a major business after commercial real estate and structured finance deals, followed by foreign exchange and risk-management products.

In the early 1980s, the growing use of personal computers allowed customers to "connect" their own operations to Citibank's to access information on their financial balances and accounts receivables, and eventually to initiate transactions electronically. By 1997, Citibank delivered the broadest range of cash management services electronically to customers across the region from a single platform. This service, called Citibanking, was in all

local languages, and migrated to the internet in 2001. Among the large customers targeted were American companies importing merchandise from Asia.

At the same time the extension of new financial technology across Asia enabled the bank to launch cash management products in India and expand distribution networks in Taiwan, Australia and Japan. Citibank's Australian branch meanwhile developed special expertise in commodities, in particular base metals such as zinc and copper, precious metals

Baptism of fire

Steven A. Bernstein, from the fixed-income sales division of Salomon Brothers in New York, was on his first trip to Tokyo when global equity markets collapsed in October 1987. At the time, the leading Wall Street securities firm was the biggest force in foreign fixed-income sales in Japan and Japanese institutional investors were among the largest participants in the U.S. Treasury Bond market. For Bernstein, who had just gotten off the plane, the visit turned out to be a rude introduction to Japanese work habits. "I knew it was going to be a big day," he recalled, adding that he arrived at the Salomon Brothers office at 7 a.m. on the Tuesday morning in Tokyo as "Black Monday" was coming to a close in New York. "Bond prices were moving by 200 or 300 points. We stayed in the office until 2 a.m the next morning."

Bernstein later worked in Japan for many years. He was a senior manager in the fixed-income division, and helped to oversee the establishment of Nikko Salomon Smith Barney (see p. 164).

From three months to three days

In the mid-1980s, getting a housing loan in Malaysia wasn't easy. "The waiting time was 3–6 months. No one was even sure of the best way to apply. Success seemed to depend on the whim of the bank staff that day," recalled Allen Tan, consumer banking head. "We saw a huge opportunity because of the country's rapid economic growth."

Citibank launched "Four Square" housing loans with radio and billboard advertising promising customers they would know the status of their application in three days, not 3–6 months. It was the first time anyone in Malaysia had developed a mortgage product and advertised it. "We had to change people's mindset from 'do I deserve a housing loan?' to 'I'm entitled to one,'" said Tan. Within two years, Citibank had captured nearly 80 percent of the housing loan market in the growing residential areas of Petaling Jaya, Subang Jaya and Bangsar.

Consumer banking at the Wheelock House branch, Hong Kong

such as gold, and energy commodities such as oil and gas. From 1992, the bank operated its global gold book out of Sydney.

Although income from Asia through the mid-1980s still flowed predominantly from corporate banking, especially foreign-exchange earnings in Japan (see p. 124), by the end of the decade, the foreign-exchange market was more stable. The consumer business was starting to contribute to regional earnings significantly, helping to offset lower revenues from currency and securities trading. The thinking which John Reed and others had brought to bear on the consumer business meanwhile bore early fruit, especially in Hong Kong and

Australia (see graph, p. 122). The bank had been granted a full Australian banking license in 1985.

The strategy for expanding the consumer business was to build an upscale brand from scratch, avoiding the mass market but using techniques like telephone sales and direct marketing to get new customers. "We hired sales people, taught them about banking and then told them to go out and sell," one former Citibanker said, comparing the new breed of bankers to Avon ladies.

Experience with consumer banking in the United States was instructive, and expertise in areas such as credit cards and mortgages was exported to Asia. But the key was service. "Some initiatives were quite basic, such as picking up the telephone within three rings," said Amy Tan, who ran the consumer business in Singapore when it was first designated a strategic priority. "But they all added up. Once we decided that if a cus-

Jump-starting credit cards

When Citibank decided to enter the card business in Singapore in 1988, the original thinking was for each country to have its own data-processing center. But with the simultaneous launch in four countries, the bank decided to set up a regional system on a temporary basis. Ajit Kanagasundram, who was in charge of the project, says he was told not to go "overboard" in developing the system as it would be dismantled after four years. The immediate goal was to "jump-start" the card business in Southeast Asia by avoiding the delays and expenses associated with setting up the processing infrastructure in each country. Using a borrowed mainframe computer, Kanagasundram and a few young and enthusiastic staff members set up the regional card center in Singapore in eight months.

In the event, the principle of centralized processing proved a winner. Within 12 years, the center had grown into a global unit, processing card transactions from two dozen countries in Asia, the Middle East, Europe and the Caribbean, with the number of cards covered reaching 7.5 million in 2000. "What started out as a temporary center for four countries in Southeast Asia ended up as our second-largest processing center for credit cards in the world," Kanagasundram said. An offshoot was the bank's Asia-Pacific computer center in Singapore, which began operation as the processing arm of the regional card center. The data center evolved to include consumer bank data processing in Asia as well as several other countries in the Middle East, Europe,

the Caribbean and Latin America. In 1999, the consumer data center was merged with the corporate data center and became one of the region's largest hubs for processing financial data.

For Kanagasundram, the key to the success of the regional card center was the ability to reduce costs through economies of scale. By 1990, the center had cut processing costs per card by 45 percent, at which point Singapore was given a mandate to extend the operation to other parts of Asia and the Middle East. By 1994, processing costs had been reduced to 32 percent of the 1989 level. "None of the country managers asked for decentralization of their credit card operations," he said. "Who wants costs per card to triple overnight?"

"Not Just Visa, Citibank Visa"

In the late 1980s, credit cards were not new to Asia but they were a missing piece in Citibank's consumer product arsenal. Pei-yuan Chia, appointed in late 1987 to head Citibank's international consumer operations, had managed the bank's United States card businesses and favored international expansion. The bank already had some experience in Hong Kong—it had acquired the Diners Club card business from Standard Chartered Bank in 1983 and Bank of America's Visa card portfolio in 1987. Pricing and the potential for losses in the initial years were major concerns. How could a premium-priced card product sell in what looked like a saturated marketplace? Furthermore, lists of names for direct mailing were almost non-existent, let alone credit bureaus which could help evaluate potential customers.

In 1989, Chia gave the green light to credit cards. Within 18 months, credit-card businesses were launched in Indonesia, Singapore, Taiwan, Thailand, Australia, India and Malaysia. Aggressive marketing campaigns supported each launch. Underlying the whole exercise was a firm strategic principle: that premium value and service would command premium pricing and that the aspiring consumer would welcome a card issued by a global, innovative and service-driven bank such as Citibank. As Rana Talwar, at the time head of regional consumer banking, later commented: "It became clear to us that, while countries are diverse in many respects, their mass markets share one thing in common: the consumer will pay for a product that provides value and benefits." Advertising campaigns carried taglines such as "Not Just Visa, Citibank Visa" and "Not Just MasterCard, Citibank MasterCard."

Hundreds of thousands of direct mailers were used, in some cases straining the capabilities of individual countries' post offices. One of the simplest but most successful vehicles was personal selling. Jeannine Farhi, who had moved to Asia from Citibank in the United States, said: "Our American counterparts were amused when we started direct selling. Nobody was doing that in the U.S. But in Asia, it is a wonderfully focused and effective way to gain customers." In markets such as India, direct selling soon accounted for up to 70 percent of applications from prospective customers.

By the end of 1991, Citibank's card launch had been a phenomenal success. In most of the new markets, the bank had overtaken American Express in terms of market share by customers. By 1992, Citibank had issued over a million cards: this represented 810,000 customers and accounted for 225 million dollars in revenue and 30 million dollars in earnings.

In Singapore, the "Citibank Yuppie" vied with the "Singapore Girl" as one of the cultural icons of the late 20th century. According to the *Straits Times* newspaper, Citibank commercials departed from the image that financial institutions had adopted for generations. "Citibank sold the idea of easy money: easy to manage through friendly bankers you could phone anytime, easy to get hold of with 'easy credit' and easy to spend with its photo cards."

Selling credit cards in a shopping mall in Makati City, the Philippines

More than just a card

What's the big deal about putting a photo on a credit card? Plenty, if your market consists of relatively affluent and sophisticated, globally aware consumers. Photocards were launched in the early 1990s. "Photos gave our card holders added security but also a sense of status," recalled Frits Seegers, who became consumer bank head for Asia-Pacific. "To bank with Citibank had anyway become something of a status symbol in Asia because we were seen as being inventive and offering better service," he said. "Credit cards are a perfect example—we knew our customers wouldn't be content with just low annual fees or lower interest rates." Firsts included linking card spending with free airline miles, instant credit extensions, and emergency card replacements within 24 hours. The perks kept pace with customers' lifestyles—besides discounts on restaurant meals or hotel visits or rounds of golf, cardholders also enjoyed more unusual offers, such as a 10 percent reduction off liposuction in Manila. In 2001 alone, Citibank added more than 1,000 special offers to credit-card holders across Asia.

Installment loans in India averaged only 600 dollars, but made a big difference in a country where motor scooters were still a luxury

South Korea was one of the first Asian markets targeted for Citibank's touchscreen ATM technology

tomer stood in a queue at our branch for more than 10 minutes, we would deposit a Singapore dollar into their account. There was a sense of urgency in everything we did. Our personal service had to match up to the premium products we were pitching."

In India, the bank introduced consumer installment loans at its four branches. With an average size of 600 dollars, these loans were small. But with strong demand for items such as motor scooters and home appliances in India, the number of borrowers grew to 150,000, ranging from railroad employees and miners to university professors. Repayment was through payroll deductions, with employers making lump-sum payments to the bank.

As consumer banking developed across the countries of Asia, cards became a major focus. The card business was expanded by a combination of energetic marketing, product innovation, and acquisition. In 1987, for example, Citibank acquired Bank of America's Visa card business in Hong Kong and expanded the business. The bank launched cards in Japan, the Philippines and Indonesia. By the end of the decade, credit-card solicitation and screening techniques from the United States were being applied to markets in Japan, Taiwan and Australia.

A new generation of touchscreen ATMs from New York was brought to Hong Kong and Singapore. The new ATM technology was extended to Taiwan. After the first international ATM transaction (between New York and Puerto Rico) took place in 1989, the bank designated Hong Kong, South Korea, Taiwan and Singapore as priority markets for the new technology.

Seeds of a software revolution

In 1985, Citibank became the first foreign bank in India to sign a computerization agreement with its trade-union members. This was a turning point for the Indian operation, which was then headed by Victor Menezes with Nanoo Pamnani serving as Senior Country Operations Officer. As it turned out, the timing was perfect—the bank was expanding its consumer operations worldwide and was just focusing on the potential for business in Asia.

At the same time, the agreement gave rise to the establishment of a software company. The idea came from Menezes, but it was left to Pamnani and Venky Krishna-kumar—who became chairman of the new company—to implement. One of the first big hurdles was to get government approval for the venture. Pamnani recalled explaining the benefits of online testing to one official, who appeared horrified. "But if you do that, you can export without us knowing," the official said. "That's true," Pamnani replied. "Welcome to the real world."

Some opposition to the development of Citibank Overseas Software Ltd (COSL) initially came also from within the bank. In 1986, vice chairman Larry Small was in Singapore reviewing regional operations. "What's this COSL?" he asked the staff, who explained the background. "Why are we in this? We're a commercial bank. Close it down," he

COSL in India

ordered. So some 50 employees were taken off the books to become consultants to the bank. After two years, they were redesignated as full-time contract employees. In time COSL justified the bank's faith in it—it became a flourishing business. By the turn of the century, Citibank was India's third-largest software exporter with annual exports above 165 million dollars.

COSL itself focused on Citibank businesses worldwide while its 48.4-percent-owned subsidiary i-Flex Solutions Ltd concentrated on software for the global financial services industry in general.

The Salomon Brothers trading room in the Urbannet Otemachi building in Tokyo, late 1980s

While consumer banking was beginning to pay off and traditional corporate banking remained an important source of income, it became clear that the missing link in Asia was capital markets, including mergers and acquisitions.

Although Citicorp's Vickers da Costa affiliate was among the first six foreign stockbrokers to get seats on the Tokyo Stock Exchange, it was a minnow compared to most of the new American and European firms stampeding into Japan. Among them was the Wall Street firm and future merger partner Salomon Brothers, which had been in Tokyo for several years. It missed out in the first round of bidding in 1985 and would have to wait another three years for a highly coveted membership on the exchange. But all of these companies were relative newcomers to the Japanese market. Smith Barney had been dealing with the Japanese government and local companies since the 1920s (see p. 131).

When Deryck Maughan arrived in Japan in 1986, Salomon Brothers Asia had 60 people in Tokyo. "It was largely international fixed-income sales and trading with a small yen bond desk. We had a very small capital markets desk for underwriting bonds," he said, describing the operation as "profitable and well-regarded" but still very much a "niche" player until 1988, when it acquired an exchange membership.

Cargo in distress

The 1980s saw one brief excursion beyond the bank's core activities reminiscent of the "congenerics" of earlier years (see p. 114). New York decided that Citicorp Securities should get into the business of commodity trading, and established Citicorp International Trading Company (CITC). Modeled on the great Japanese trading houses, the new initiative would be an international trading company and in Asia the operations were in three centers: Hong Kong, Singapore and Manila. In due course, Citibankers in the Philippines were trading molasses, castor beans and bunker oil.

Norberto Nazareno recalled that molasses was a big hit, and very profitable: "We were buying from sugar planters and exporting to Korea and Japan."

But the oil trading raised more than a few eyebrows. "The Caltex guys were asking, 'What are our bankers doing in our business?'" said Nazareno, who later became president of the government-owned Philippine Deposit Insurance Corporation (PDIC).

The bank (CITC) decided to financially engineer and to lease an oil-storage tank owned by a nickel mining company on an

Norberto Nazareno

island in the southern Philippines, and operate it like a gasoline station where the mining company would pay cash, but only for what they had used. It looked like one of those classic "win-win" scenarios.

"There was no credit risk," he said. "We started bidding for bunker oil and booking the deals out of Hawaii." The first shipment, worth eight million dollars, was a huge success, yielding a tidy profit. A second shipment was booked. The oil tanker was sailing for the Philippines when the workers at the nickel mine went on strike. The oil couldn't be offloaded, and the bank suddenly had a "distress cargo" on its hands. The shipment would obviously have to be sold off to someone else. "The problem was, it was for a high-sulfur low-quality oil that wasn't used by any other country but the Philppines. ... It was out in the middle of the Pacific with no place to go."

While, providentially, the distress cargo was purchased at cost by the National Power Corporation, like many of the congeneric investments of the 1970s the commodity operation was short-lived. As Nazareno said, "After four years, we had to close it up."

"Over the course of 1986 to 1991, we first of all built up the Japanese operation quite considerably to about 700 people," Maughan recalled. "We were active in negotiating the opening of the markets in terms of bond auctions instead of syndicates, and on the Tokyo International Financial Futures Exchange, of which I was a board member. I led the international securities firms in their regular meetings with the Ministry of Finance. Salomon took a more forward-looking position and began to build out equities, investment banking as well as fixed income."

At the same time, Salomon made a clear decision to build domestic distribution in Japan. Assisting Maughan were Shigeru Myojin, a highly successful trader who would later become Salomon's head of global trading in London,

Toshiharu Kojima (left) and Deryck Maughan at a seminar in 1989

and Toshiharu Kojima, who would emerge as chief executive of Nikko Salomon Smith Barney, a joint venture with one of Japan's leading securities companies.

"We expanded our product line, and we went local," Maughan said. "Because of the lack of maturity or sophistication in the local market—which was all to do with futures, shorts, repos and swaps—it was a very profitable operation for us. We established ourselves as one of the leading fixed-income houses in the region and also had a decent equity operation.

"At the same time, I remember going to New York and saying, 'We're not really addressing the Asia-Pacific region,'" Maughan recalled. Between 1988 and 1991, Salomon opened offices in South Korea, Taiwan and Singapore. It also reopened in Hong Kong and strengthened the office in Australia.

In a bid to reassure the public, Citibank invited the press into one of its vaults to show that it still had lots of cash. This picture of bundles of HK1,000 dollar notes was subsequently splashed across page two of *Ming Pao*, one of the leading Chinese-language papers in Hong Kong

Crisis management

Antony Leung, who became Hong Kong's Financial Secretary, got used to pressure. In 1973, the year he joined Citibank in Hong Kong, the local stock market collapsed. "I experienced a meltdown while I was a trainee," the veteran investment banker recalled. And when he was the bank's regional treasurer in 1983, he witnessed the panic selling of the Hong Kong dollar. The government stepped in to halt the collapse by pegging the currency to the U.S. dollar.

Although Leung witnessed the collapse and closure of the Hong Kong stock market in 1987 firsthand as a director of the local futures exchange, he reckons the most challenging crisis he faced was the run on

Citibank in 1991 when he was the corporate officer for the territory.

When a United States senator referred to Cititbank as "insolvent," a number of clients withdrew their deposits, the BCCI collapse still fresh in their minds. As Leung recalls, "A lot of the staff also had doubts. ... Even more doubts emerged later, when the bank announced a loss of almost half a billion dollars ... but it was a great occasion for building comradeship."

For Leung, however, one of the most instructive lessons was how to deal with the public in times of crisis. "I had my media training then," he said. "It was very educational. A lot of these things you don't learn in the textbooks."

At the inauguration of the model branch in the Philippines, 1995, from left: Stephen Long, Pei-yuan Chia, the then Philippine President Fidel Ramos, Rana Talwar, Shaukat Aziz, and the branch manager Victor Lim

The beginning of the 1990s was a difficult time for Citicorp in the United States, in part due to exposure to the troubled real-estate marketplace in North America. In 1991, described by chairman John Reed in the annual report as a "transitional, turnaround year," the company recorded a loss of almost half a billion dollars and suspended its dividend for the first time ever. The stock price dropped as low as eight dollars, and many employees took advantage of the staff equity plan at the time. By the end of 1997, the shares were worth more than 126 dollars. Dennis Martin was one of 12 senior Citibankers working closely with Reed to manage a difficult situation. "It is difficult to explain [to local staff], when you have growth in a region, that at that point you don't want to invest in the business; and it is important that, as a global entity, we survive as a global entity. ... We decided—John Reed decided—to earn our way out of the crisis, and not sell any of our franchises. Because, for example, if we sold Latin America or Asia, then we would be missing one of the legs of our global quest. ... Then we'd wake up the next day without one of the best franchises there is, and that's Asia. It was a balancing act—maintaining our franchise, trying to do our best for our local people, and surviving as a whole, which we did." Martin went round Asia explaining the situation personally. "We managed to survive and keep most of our greatest asset, which was our local people." But the bank's Asian businesses continued to do well, and made a crucial contribution worldwide in helping the bank to weather the storm. A recovery plan was devised.

The bank's difficulties in 1991 led to a brief run in Hong Kong, although a contributing factor was the recent failure

Hong Kong depositors queuing up to withdraw their savings in 1991. Many people in Hong Kong were already jittery following the collapse of BCCI

Mongkok cash drop

Hong Kong is one of the most crowded places on earth, and Mongkok, with its large concentration of high-rise apartments, restaurants, nightclubs, retailers and other small businesses, is easily the most densely populated part of the city. The narrow streets and alleys are a seething mass of humanity with hawkers, shoppers and businessmen competing for space with a variety of distinctly less savory characters.

When Citibank suffered a run on deposits in 1991, the Mongkok branch was especially hard hit. Laymond Chan was managing the branch at the time.

"The premises were so small. People wanted their money and were very aggressive," he recalled. When cash deliveries to the branch were delayed, the queues of depositors lengthened so Chan contacted the manager of a neighboring branch of another bank and asked him if he'd cash a bank check. The manager agreed but said he wouldn't be responsible for anything that happened once Chan left with the cash. Accompanied by just two of his staff, Chan went out into the street and into the adjoining bank carrying nothing more than a Chinese shopping bag.

In two daring trips, they managed to bolster the branch's cash reserves by about 20 million Hong Kong dollars. "My staff were very nervous," Chan said. "But I had no choice."

The distinctive "blue wave" color scheme on the exterior of a model branch in Taiwan

Pei-yuan Chia

of the international bank BCCI, which had a prominent consumer business in the territory. The situation was quickly defused. Antony Leung, the bank's Hong Kong head, went on television; all the Hong Kong branches stayed open and paid customers in cash in full. The deposits that had been withdrawn came back within a few months.

Back in New York, management was streamlined with Pei-yuan Chia named as senior executive vice president with responsibility for the global consumer business. Chia had joined the bank in 1974 as a senior marketing officer in the new consumer services group. The very high profile gained by Citibank's consumer business in Asia in the 1990s owes much to Chia, who vigorously promoted the "blue wave" color scheme of the retail branch exteriors, as well as the notion of the "model branch." This was intended to bring uniformity to the fittings and furnishings of all the bank's branches. Over time, the strict imposition of the model-branch standards was relaxed; but the general idea survived, and helped to establish throughout the region a highly visible and recognizable presence on the ground, despite limitations on the size of Citibank's branch network.

At the same time, the bank named former Dutch finance minister Onno Ruding as vice chairman in charge of the corporate banking business worldwide. Ruding had been on

A new mantra

In the mid-1990s, Citibank's management turned its focus to long-term strategy. The late 1980s and early 1990s had been turbulent and in 1994, Reed asked David Gibson, then running operations in eastern Europe and Africa, to articulate a new direction for growth in the international business.

With three other region heads, Shaukat Aziz, Alvaro de Souza and Dennis Martin, Gibson appointed a team. One of its members, Piyush Gupta, recalled: "In many cases we had been one of the first international banks to set up a presence in a country and our competitive strength was building a strong local business. Gibson saw the challenge simply as how to keep that advantage when markets matured and competition got tougher. He thought we weren't investing enough in

David Gibson

market development and that acquisitions were the key to achieving the level of growth we wanted." Investment and acquisitions were to be at the heart of the new plan.

"We did the plan in three months, working intensely," said Gupta. "To get the four region heads in the same room together, we had to fly them into Heathrow for the weekend and book a conference room at the airport. They had to be back at their desks on Monday to run their businesses." The result was that on April 18, 1995, the "embedded bank strategy" was presented to the board of directors.

The new strategy set out that Citibank should create roots in every country as deep as any local bank. Developing market share was a priority, as was broadening customer and product

Dennis Martin

bases. Also stressed were commitment to broader local networks, promotion of local managers to the most senior positions, and being deeply involved in local communities.

The bank would develop localized solutions for local needs and not just rely on its branch network—in any case limited in most countries by regulations.

Gibson traveled widely to explain the concept. "Obviously my own focus was its benefits to the corporate bank; but it embraced Citibank's total presence because if we were an embedded bank, both businesses would benefit." One prize for local innovation went to Indonesia, where the initial public offering of shares in Telekom Indonesia was facilitated by a temporary 20-teller branch set up on an abandoned air force base, which handled crowds exceeding 60,000 over seven days.

Promotional key chain:
"Perfect Service Everyday: Citibank"

the board since 1990 and had served with several multilateral financial institutions, including the Asian Development Bank and the IMF. As part of the recovery plan, the company intended to build on foundations such as Hong Kong's trade processing center and customer relations in Japan, where it was the leading and most profitable foreign bank.

As part of the concentration of resources and control during the recovery from the difficulties of 1991, the responsibilities of the senior corporate officers were assumed by the regional heads of the corporate and consumer operations, Shaukat Aziz and Rana Talwar respectively.

Despite the problems in the United States, 1991 saw a continuing expansion of the bank's presence in Asia. The most symbolic development of the year came in June with the upgrading of the representative office in Shanghai to full branch status. After an absence of 38 years, Citibank was finally back in

town. It was the first American bank to be operating fully in Shanghai since the Korean War: older people still recalled the "Flower Flag Bank" and its distinctive banknotes. "Citi is a very famous name in China. But the Chinese name is better than the English name," a senior Chinese official told Citigroup's visiting chairman Sanford I. Weill nine years later. During the same visit,

The bank's commitment to Hong Kong was symbolized by the opening, in October 1992, of Citibank Plaza, the largest real-estate development ever undertaken by an American corporation in the territory

another senior Chinese official said it was the strongest foreign brand name in China after Coca-Cola (which literally translates as "Good Taste, Good Life.")

Although the new Shanghai branch suffered from the same limitations on business as other foreign banks, Citibank was reinforcing its presence in China still further. As well as the full branch now in Shanghai, there was another in Shenzhen, the special economic zone bordering Hong Kong (the representative office had been upgraded in 1988). Other representative offices were in Beijing and in the southern coastal city of Xiamen, facing Taiwan, where an office was set up a few months before the upgrading of Shanghai. A representative office was also opened in Guangzhou, where IBC had opened its second Chinese branch some 90 years before. Both Beijing and Guangzhou were later upgraded to branch status. A major development in China took place in 1996, when Citibank was among the handful of foreign banks licensed to make loans in renminbi. Foreign banks could previously only accept deposits, and the license meant new opportunities even if they were limited—only certain borrowers could access local currency funds.

With the Petronas twin towers in the background, Menara Citibank, the headquarters in Kuala Lumpur

By 1992, the bank had 1.6 million retail customers as well as 99 branches and offices in the Asia-Pacific region. The card business in Asia now had more than 1.5 million accounts and was posting a significant profit with sound credit quality despite rapid growth. More branches opened in South Korea and Australia, as well as Taiwan, a big new market for consumer loans. Citicard Banking Centers in Singapore, Hong Kong and Japan were linked to those in the United States, Europe, and Latin America.

In Japan, ATM services were extended to nine o'clock in the evening, two hours longer than at most Japanese banks. The huge investments in Japan started to bring notable results in 1993, with local customers performing 223,000 overseas transactions. There was now a 21-branch network serving 300,000 customers. That year Citibank became the only bank in Tokyo to offer ATM and telephone banking services 24 hours a day.

Far right: Marine Tower, in the newly built Pudong area of Shanghai, home to Citibank's corporate headquarters in China since 1997. Below: In 1993, Citibank became the first international bank in the modern era to locate its China headquarters in mainland China rather than in Hong Kong

Private banking

The Citibank Private Bank's predecessor, the International Services Division, entered Asia in 1972, with an office in Hong Kong. It expanded operations to Singapore in 1976, and was renamed International Private Banking in 1978 before further expansion to the Philippines in 1980 and Thailand in the mid-1980s.

The Citibank (later Citigroup) Private Bank was set up in 1985, with David Gibson in charge in New York. Up until then, private banking for wealthy customers had been conducted more or less autonomously within each geographical entity, either within the corporate bank or as part of asset management.

The plan now was to offer wealthy clients investment, treasury or loan products sourced from any part of the world. Thus, a Hong Kong client could have a portfolio of fixed-income bonds managed in London or Zurich; an interest rate swap transaction could be handled in London or New York; or real-estate investment opportunities could be snapped up wherever they might occur.

From 1989, Nanoo Pamnani was division head for the private bank for all of Asia except for Japan, which was managed by Tatsuo Kubota. Pamnani recalled, "The bank decided to develop Singapore as a management hub at this time, in terms of processing as well as relationship and product management, and in so doing unleashed enormous private banking growth, particularly in Singapore and Indonesia. Southeast Asia suddenly took off. Hong Kong and Taiwan remained very significant."

Within a few years, Citibank was operating the largest non-Swiss private bank in Asia. In 1992, Asia accounted for 11 percent of the 75 billion dollars in total assets under management worldwide. By 1995, the private bank was operating in Japan, Taiwan, Hong Kong, Singapore, Thailand, the Philippines, Indonesia and India, and at the end of the decade was well established in all the major regional markets, including Australia.

Deepak Sharma, head of Citigroup Private Bank, Asia Pacific, from late 1996

Left: At night, the new Citibank Tower, the Thailand headquarters in Bangkok. Top: Buddhist monks visit Citibank Tower in Bangkok, in 1996. Above: A Shinto priest conducts a ceremony marking the opening of the new Citibank building at Sea Fort Square, the Japan headquarters in Tokyo. Below: Aerial view of Sea Fort Square

Total assets in Asia-Pacific (1980–97)

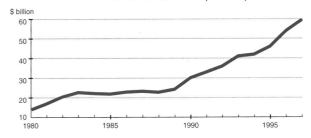

$ billion

Assets in Asia-Pacific began to grow sharply in 1990 as the consumer business expanded, especially in Japan which accounted for some 40 percent of regional assets of 60 billion dollars in 1997. By contrast, assets in South Korea, Malaysia, Thailand, the Philippines and Indonesia combined came to 25 percent

Source: annual reports

Expanded ATM operating hours was one of the distinguishing features of the bank in the 1990s

As the consumer banking operation developed in Asia, it started to give rise to new products which were then exported to other markets. Priority services developed in Hong Kong and Singapore for upmarket consumers, for example, were extended to other Asian markets, then to several Latin American markets including Argentina, Brazil and Chile. The concept was later extended to Europe. By the end of 1993, 24-hour phone service seven days a week was available in all Asian markets.

By this time, the card business had 2.5 million cards in 11 countries in Asia, with a market share of more than 30 percent in several. In addition to card relaunches in the Philippines and Australia and the launch of photocards in Hong Kong, Indonesia and Japan, the bank joined forces with Japan Travel Bureau (JTB) to inaugurate an international prepaid card for travelers from Japan. At the same time, multicurrency accounts developed in Hong Kong were extended to Japan, Singapore and the United States, with time deposits in nine different currencies.

Branch revenue in Asia was soon running at twice the global average and cards was the fastest-growing

business. By 1996, the bank had seven million cards in Asia including India—more than twice the number in Europe—with the processing of card transactions in 12 markets centralized in Singapore. In Shanghai, the bank opened two Citicard Banking Centers and so became the first foreign bank to offer cash withdrawals in renminbi—the people's currency adopted after 1949 in the wake of the inflationary chaos of the post-war period.

An emphasis on service lay at the heart of Citibank's reputation, both in consumer banking and other areas of the business. In a 1992 survey of six banks in Hong Kong, it was rated top bank for customer service, and was also rated by Japanese companies as top foreign bank for corporate finance.

In its annual report for 1992, Citibank noted that the substantial withdrawal of most Japanese banks from international

A Foreign Service

Bill Rhodes once described working for Citibank as being part of the "foreign service." In a *Euromoney* magazine interview, he said: "In many of the countries where we operate, working for Citi is a very special opportunity because of the training you receive and because we are a meritocracy."

Shaukat Aziz, who joined the Karachi office in 1969 and later became Asia-Pacific corporate banking head, recalled in a *Euromoney* interview: "Citibank was a talent machine, it attracted the best talent from everywhere in the world. There were no bars on origin or nationality, performance

Shaukat Aziz (left) with Singapore's Senior Minister Lee Kuan Yew (center) and John Reed

was the only criterion. You could deal at a global level with the best in the business. " He added: "It was a tremendous learning experience to be running businesses in groups of countries. You were required to look at the macroeconomic situation, to see the opportunities and crises in many countries. ... You got tremendous authority."

Continuing the practice of giving achievers early responsibility, in 1998, for example, the bank introduced a "Fast Track" program to give talented young employees in Asia the chance to work in New York or London for two years before returning to a middle-management position.

Offshore platform in the Camago Malampaya natural gas field, operated by Shell and Occidental Petroleum in the Philippines

markets had provided opportunities for Citibank to expand relationships with Japanese companies.

Citibank also strengthened its relationships in emerging economies such as the Philippines, where it played a major role in developing infrastructure. As well as power and transportation projects, the bank also helped to finance the development of the Camago Malampaya natural gas field by Shell and Occidental Petroleum in the late 1990s. This was the biggest

foreign investment in the Philippines for a single project.

Elsewhere in Southeast Asia, Citibank had returned to Vietnam after an absence of 18 years. In 1993, a representative office was opened by Shaukat Aziz, then head of the corporate bank for Asia-Pacific, in November. A second representative office followed in Ho Chi Minh City. In early 1995, Hanoi became a full branch with a staff of 18. Ho Chi Minh City was upgraded two years later. Located on the 15th floor of the Sun Wah Tower, the second Vietnamese branch overlooked the building evacuated 20 years earlier (see p. 106), now occupied by the Vietnam Bank for Agriculture.

Singapore was meanwhile emerging as a key regional center for the bank. In 1996, the city state appeared for the first time on the list of countries with outstandings exceeding one percent of total assets. Total outstandings were at a high of 3.4 billion

Regional hub

During the second half of the 1990s, Singapore emerged as a regional processing hub, the location of three of the five regional management offices and eight of the 11 regional processing activities, including cash products, securities and data processing. All the bank's credit card transactions in Asia were handled there.

"In the late 1980s and early 1990s the bank started to define cash, trade and securities as a transaction banking business," said Venky Krishnakumar, who oversaw the regional processing empire. "Before that, the operation component was subsumed by the product. The focus had switched to the product and we began to lose some inherent strengths in processing. So we re-established processing as distinct from the product."

Regional trade transactions were processed on the Malaysian island of Penang, part of a network that included Lewisham in Britain and Tampa, Florida. Foreign exchange and other treasury products for 13 economies in the region were processed in Sydney, part of a network linking Australia with London and New York.

The Singapore cash-processing center came under a different global network along with Dublin and Buffalo, New York. The area handled by Singapore itself stretched from Japan, South Korea, China, Taiwan and Hong Kong to the six main ASEAN countries plus Australia and New Zealand. In 2000, the center gained the Singapore Quality Award, for its zero-defect processing record.

A senior Singapore politician once told chairman John Reed that Singapore was

effectively a "six-star hotel" where guests had to pay the prices and act like they belonged. "This is the Switzerland of Asia," he said. And with the government easing foreign bank restrictions on Citibank and three other banks, Citibank was viewed as a "privileged occupant of this high-class hotel."

Venky Krishnakumar (center) and Vincern Fernando (right) at the presentation of the Singapore Quality Award

New...
Funds Transfer Service To VIETNAM

TIN MỚI...
Dịch Vụ Chuyển Ngân về VIỆT NAM

CITIBANK

Building on the success of its services for Indians living abroad, Citibank branches in New York began offering transfer services to Vietnam for Vietnamese living in the United States

CitiGold Priority Banking section in Kuala Lumpur, 1996. The consumer bank moved to the new Malaysia head-quarters in Menara Citibank in 2001

dollars, including 1.7 billion dollars invested in the Singapore franchise and related funding, which was 30 percent more than the bank's investment in Japan the same year. Over the next few years, the bank would open an expanded trading floor and gain "qualifying full bank" status in Singapore. The significance of this was that the bank was now able to increase its branch and ATM networks while competing on more equal terms with local banks. In neighboring Malaysia, where Citibank's operation had been incorporated into a local subsidiary in 1994, Islamic banking products were developed. These included Al-Wadiah savings accounts and leasing products targeted at small and medium-sized companies.

Managing risk

Citibank largely avoided the pitfalls of reckless lending to unproductive sectors of Asian economies such as the high-flying market for real estate. When the bubble burst in 1997, the bank was less exposed to the Asian crisis than many competitors from Europe and Japan. One reason, many Citibankers said, was that the bank had learned a lesson during the global debt crisis which engulfed most of Latin America after the go-go years of the 1970s. The collapse of Japan's bubble economy in 1990 provided another lesson, as did Citicorp's own exposure to real estate and leveraged buyouts in the United States around the same time. But another factor was an initiative by the bank's credit policy committee.

Developed in the aftermath of Citicorp's loss of almost half a billion dollars in 1991, the "windows on risk" initiative was designed as a global report that consolidated and enhanced portfolio information for in-depth review by management several times a year. From 1994, the reports were used to control concentrations in particular countries, industries, products and clients. They were also used to determine portfolio actions and to achieve a balance between the risk profile of Citicorp in relation to its budgets, operating earnings and capital.

A key outcome was a management consensus on the outlook for the external environment over the coming 18 months based on such factors as the latest position of each country or region in the business cycle and different scenarios for major economies. In its outlook for 12 global industries over the coming 12–18 months, the management review would seek opinions of outside experts as well as internal analysts and the bank's senior lending officers from around the world. It would also discuss possible "tripwires"—critical events likely to happen in the coming 3 to 18 months—and would analyze general economic and geopolitical events in the more-important countries. The final part was a two-year outlook on "what if" scenarios—possible highly unfavorable economic or geopolitical developments.

For Citicorp, the whole process represented a commitment to "controlling risks and to avoiding future surprises. ... Citicorp has a much clearer view of the environment in which it operates and the risks inherent in its businesses."

"Windows on risk" was first applied to Asia in 1996, and proved invaluable in controlling the bank's exposure to the financial crisis that erupted the following year.

Not the worst-case scenario

Stephen Long recalled nervousness in New York in the early 1990s, as the date for the handover of Hong Kong to China was coming nearer. John Reed had instructed that an asset limit be put on the Hong Kong franchise, and every month there was a meeting of the Assets and Liabilities Committee to review the "worst-case scenario." By 1995, when Long became North Asia division head, it was clear to him that these concerns were limiting the growth of the business. "I wanted to know, 'Did John Reed really mean this?'" So, having pondered the most diplomatic way to approach the problem Long got Pei-yuan Chia to give Reed a call. "So that way I got a 'reinterpretation' which allowed the business to grow."

Long was proved right. When 1997 came along, it was Southeast Asia and Korea, and not Hong Kong or China, that showed signs of instability.

Stephen Long

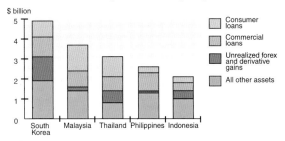

Selected local country assets in Asia (1997)

$ billion

Legend:
- Consumer loans
- Commercial loans
- Unrealized forex and derivative gains
- All other assets

In 1997, traditional loans, especially consumer loans, dominated the local assets portfolios in Malaysia and Thailand. In South Korea, the Philippines and Indonesia, the majority of local assets were unrealized gains on foreign-exchange contracts and derivatives, along with "other assets" such as deposits with other banks, securities and customer acceptance liabilities

Source: annual report, 1997

The Asian economic crisis was a traumatic experience for governments and businesses alike, and when it erupted in 1997, many foreign banks fled the region. It had the effect of temporarily derailing the acquisitions component of the embedded bank strategy. However, as Stephen Long, then corporate bank head for North Asia, remembered: "The big difference during the crisis was that our international competitors did not have the embedded strategy, which allowed us to develop local currency liquidity and reduce cross-border exposures, among other things. We were able to continue to support our customer base and grow market share during the downturn." It was an opportunity for Citibank to demonstrate its commitment to its Asian markets—and its ability to respond quickly to a situation. The bank, which had 6.2 million accounts at 93 branches in 13 Asian markets, excluding India and Pakistan, was there for the long haul. It may have faced constraints in expanding its branch network in the region, but its understanding of consumer needs enabled such hurdles to be surmounted—indeed they were a stimulus to greater ingenuity.

Among the bank's main exposures in the markets worst hit by the crisis were consumer loans in Thailand and Malaysia, as well as commercial loans in the Philippines and other items in South Korea, including unrealized gains on foreign-exchange contracts and derivatives, and deposits with other banks.

As part of its strategy of developing the market despite the difficult economic climate, the bank attached great importance to new technology, in the form of ATM outlets and phone banking. The bank forged alliances with local financial institutions,

Hearing the alarm bells

When head office became concerned about the potential for financial problems in Asia, Citibank invited American economist Paul Krugman to address the Windows on Risk committee. William Rhodes, who chaired the committee, had been alerted to the dangers during a visit to South Korea and Thailand earlier that year.

"There was too much real-estate lending going on, together with other problems" Rhodes said. "The banking sector was over-extended." Krugman's warning was clear: "This could blow."

The bank decided to draw up three scenarios for Asia—business as usual, a mild recession or a deep recession—and evaluated their impact on country exposures. As the early-warning signals started to flash more often, it became clear that Thailand and South Korea were in deep trouble. Any last-ditch attempt to convince authorities of the impending disaster failed at the annual meeting of the Asian Development Bank (ADB) in the Japanese city of Fukuoka in April 1997.

Rhodes said the specter of a Mexican-style collapse was raised once, but quickly dismissed by an Asian finance minister. "The problem with you, Bill, is that you spent too much time in Latin America," the minister said. "We're different. We have a strong work ethic and a higher rate of savings."

It was a familiar refrain throughout Asia at the time. The Japanese had insisted they were different until their stock market crashed in the early 1990s, triggering a collapse in real-estate prices and the worst recession since World War II.

And as questions were raised by some observers about whether the "tequila effect" might spread to Asia, they had been largely treated with derision.

Real estate

From 1996, Dennis Martin was overseeing the "emerging markets" for the corporate side of the bank, including Thailand. "Good business people talk to their customers and walk the street. In Thailand, we had exposure in real-estate; we had developed loans for middle classes and low-income customers, and for some office buildings. I saw a picture of an office in the window of a Bangkok antiques store I went to sometimes. I asked, 'What is this building?' The nice woman said: 'We are going to tear down this building and build an office building.' So I went back to the bank and said, 'Guys, we're out of the real-estate business—if ladies like this start getting into the real-estate business, this place is going to be overbuilt to hell.' And sure enough that happened."

Sleepless nights

The first major test of the international financial system's ability to cope with the 1997 crisis came at the end of the year when South Korea came perilously close to default. The country had the world's 11th largest economy—bigger than all Southeast Asia economies combined—and such a development would have had unthinkable repercussions.

Michel Camdessus, managing director of the International Monetary Fund (IMF), oversaw tense negotiations with the Koreans from his hotel suite in Kuala Lumpur, where he was staying for an emergency meeting of Asia-Pacific finance ministers in December. A deal for emergency assistance on certain conditions was finally put together, and Camdessus traveled to Seoul to make sure everyone from both the outgoing and the incoming governments was committed. The first hurdle crossed, attention now focused on the "second line of defense"—the creditor banks who were pulling loans out of South Korea at the rate of hundreds of millions of dollars every day.

Citicorp's William Rhodes, a 15-year veteran of debt restructurings in Latin America and the Philippines, recalled the episode

Citibank headquarters in Seoul

For his efforts during the 1998 IMF crisis, Rhodes received Korea's Order of Diplomatic Service Merit's *Heung-in* medal from Kyu Sung Lee, the then Minister of Finance and Economy

well. "There was one weekend I didn't sleep at all," he said. His first inkling that something was seriously amiss came with a couple of phone calls from United States deputy treasury secretary Larry Summers and Japan's vice minister of finance for international affairs Eisuke Sakakibara.

Summers and Sakakibara had a request. Could Rhodes call the Japanese commercial banks and ask them to stop pulling their short-term loans out of South Korea as they fell due? The Japanese banks had the biggest exposure to the country. They had their own problems with bad debts, and Japan had recently seen the twin failures of a leading bank and a top securities firm. In the circumstances, the Japanese banks were in no mood to be generous, and they were being uncharacteristically concerned. In an unprecedented move, they were refusing to follow the "advice" of the Ministry of Finance (MOF).

Summers and Sakakibara knew the banks' refusal to roll over Korean loans threatened to "blow the whole thing up," Rhodes said. "South Korea was losing almost a billion dollars a day. It was that bad." But there was an outside chance—the Japanese bankers might not listen to their Ministry of Finance, but apparently Summers and Sakakibara thought they would listen to Rhodes.

Through his efforts in the Latin American debt crisis of the 1980s, Rhodes had come into personal contact with numerous Japanese bankers involved in restructuring their debts with countries like Brazil, Mexico, Argentina, Peru, Uruguay and Venezuela. Some Japanese banks had been almost as exposed as Citibank in South

America. He had maintained contact with them over the years, and most had become top executives. "I got them to agree to basically hold while I got talking to the Americans and Europeans," Rhodes said, referring to the other banks. "The first time around, the MOF couldn't bring it off." Rhodes' personal acquaintance with many of the Japanese bankers proved very useful. "When I gave them my word, they believed me. Then they asked me to line up the Americans and the Europeans."

In early January, Rhodes was formally asked by deputy prime minister and finance minister Lim to chair the negotiations. After round-the-clock meetings, by the end of January Rhodes and South Korea's deputy finance minister Chung Duck Koo could announce that a group of creditor banks had reached an agreement in principle whereby local banks would offer to exchange short-term credits for new loans with maturities of up to three years. The deal was worth 24 billion dollars and eventually involved further negotiations providing for South Korea's return to the international bond market.

In a quirk of history, future merger partner Salomon Smith Barney played a lead role in the subsequent four-billion-dollar global bond issue. Rhodes and Salomon chief executive Deryck Maughan would become Citigroup vice chairmen with offices on the same floor at the Park Avenue head office. "Bill was doing the loans, and at Salomon we were doing the bonds," recalled Maughan. "Six months later, Bill's next door and we're partners. We laugh about it, because we weren't going to do the bonds if he didn't do the loans, and he wasn't going to do the loans unless we did the bonds."

The Citicard Banking Center at the Seoul headquarters

including post offices in many countries. This effectively supplemented the branch network.

One of the most dramatic examples was in Japan, where Citibank had been pressing to link its ATMs to local bank networks since the early 1990s. It later embarked on a new strategy of linking up with ATMs operated by the huge Japanese postal savings system, breaking a long-held taboo which prevented such links from being developed with Japanese banks. In due course, Citibank found itself with direct access to a wide customer base—one that domestic banks couldn't reach because they had shut the post office out of their ATM networks. "We went from 20 branches to 22,600 overnight," recalled Frits Seegers, who ran the Japan operation before taking the helm of Asia-Pacific's consumer banking operation.

Indonesia, which had seemed initially to be coping well with the crisis, was, in the end, one of the countries hardest hit. Economic and political pressures coincided, and by May 1998 Jakarta was in turmoil. Most foreign banks shut up shop. Citibank took a determinedly positive stand, opening 61 new

Citibank customers using ATMs at a local post office in Japan

"branches," mostly in Jakarta, Surabaya and Bandung—not the banking palaces of earlier days, but mostly kiosks sufficient for an ATM, a telephone for remote banking, and a clerk. By 2000, Citibank customer accounts had multiplied by 300 percent, and the bank recouped its money on its investment in new branches after a year of operation. By the end of the century, it was the eighth-largest bank in Indonesia, with the largest foreign-owned franchise in the country. It employed 1,200 people,

The launch, in 1998, of Citibank's co-branded credit card with the Indian army and Indian air force

Citibank billboard advertising the Eazypay program, located in the most prestigious area in Jakarta, Jalan Thamrin—Hotel Indonesia's traffic circle

99 percent of them Indonesians. "Despite the regulatory and political issues facing the country, it was the staff who strengthened our confidence in the bank's long-term prospects in Indonesia," Seegers said.

In 1998, *IFR Asia* voted Citibank "Bank of the Year." It wrote: "Being there for its customers in a distressing time is a significant measure of a bank's commitment. This is where Citibank stood head and shoulders above its peers, especially in the region's loan markets, which have historically been the dominant financing market. As the region's loan market

The Asian framework

After the Asian financial crisis erupted in 1997, the bank decided to adopt a detailed framework to deal with specific regional developments. In February 1998, a group of senior managers gathered at the Oriental Hotel in Bangkok. The Thai baht had collapsed seven months earlier, South Korea had just been pulled back from the abyss and the situation in Indonesia was deteriorating. In November 1997, deputy finance ministers and central bank governors from the region had come up with their own "Manila framework" for dealing with the crisis during a meeting in the Philippine capital. The Citibank managers came up with their own detailed plan, and the "Asian framework" was born.

"We asked ourselves a question," recalled Stephen Long. "We had a crisis and that crisis was probably going to continue. Our portfolio was in pretty good shape. What should our strategy be?"

The bank wasn't going to cut and run. Under the embedded bank strategy (see p. 146), it was aiming for a market share of

4–6 percent in many Asian markets. But it was still short of that target in most of the key markets, notably Thailand and Indonesia (barely three percent) as well as Malaysia (two percent) and South Korea (less than one percent). The crisis was an opportunity to increase market share at substantially reduced cost. Citibank was already well placed to benefit from the "flight to quality" triggered by the crisis. Among other driving forces behind the new opportunities were regulatory changes, an absence of liquidity in domestic markets and the recapitalization needs of local companies. At the same time, weaker competition meant lower acquisition costs and increased ability to hire good local staff.

In the short term, immediate opportunities were identified in such areas as treasury and capital markets. Direct investment was also highlighted, with the bank getting the green light for up to 100 million dollars in new equity investments.

In the longer term, the Bangkok meeting identified opportunities to support the embedded bank strategy and position

Citibank for the future as a large local-currency bank in key Asian markets. The biggest long-term opportunities were seen in the areas of trade finance, cash management, emerging local corporates and loan products. In the area of trade finance alone, the bank arranged a billion dollars worth of lines in an attempt to build long-term customer loyalty while supporting government efforts to generate foreign exchange through increased exports.

"To make sure we continued to support our customers, we also increased our balance sheet by another 20 percent or so, which translated into billions of dollars," said Long. "We've learned over the years that if you're disciplined with your target market, you can get through these crises and actually come out stronger than you were when you went into them.

"That's exactly what happened. We supported our customers, we increased our exposure to them, we never pulled back and we continued to market. We worked through the crisis, and our customers worked through the crisis."

Citibank was one of the first foreign banks to relocate its Shanghai branch to the gleaming new city of Pudong. It also acquired prime space in old Shanghai, on the ground floor of the Peace Hotel, facing the Bund

(excluding Australia) shrunk by 73 percent in the first nine months of 1998—a contraction of 62 billion dollars—Citibank was the only institution which increased business."

Dennis Martin was head of corporate banking in the emerging markets at the time. "You have to stay with the customers that have the managerial aptitude to be flexible and run with the crisis, and who have a good product." Despite weaker currencies and shrinking economic activity in most of Asia, the bank's net income from the region amounted to 347 million dollars in 1998. The financial crisis triggered a massive "flight to quality" during the same year, average customer deposits jumping to 36.1 billion dollars, up from 30.5 billion dollars in 1997.

Both India and China were less affected by the crisis than the other markets in Asia. By 1998, Citibank was the most profitable consumer bank in India; it had the largest business with Indians overseas; it was also the largest consumer lender, with household loans amounting to 3.9 billion dollars. Indeed, with a million customers, Citibank had a

Hardened by global experience
In the senior team that coped with the Asian economic problems in the late 1990s, Bill Rhodes was not the only veteran of the South American debt crisis.

During the 1980s, Victor Menezes had worked in New York as senior corporate officer for South America, and helped to put in place financial solutions that brought the bank through the South American problems in one piece. Dennis Martin, an Argentinian in charge of international corporate and investment banking in 1997, had run corporate banking operations in Latin America. "In Latin America we lived in crisis," said Martin. "The fact is you were jumping from one fire to another. So in Asia we could tell the story of what reasonably to expect, and take action so our losses were as small as possible." Martin positioned Stephen Long, formerly in Central America and the Caribbean, as head of the North Asia division of the corporate bank; and Michael Contreras, also with experience in Central America, in charge of Southeast Asia-Pacific.

Senior people in Indonesia, the Philippines, South Korea and Thailand had all had Latin American experience.

larger consumer base in India than any other foreign bank.

China remained a focus for strategic development. The upgrading of the representative office in Guangzhou in 1998 gave the bank access to the local interbank market. Approval for carrying out local currency lending was extended to Shenzhen and a representative office was later set up in Chengdu, the capital of the southwestern province of Sichuan where the late Chinese leader Deng Xiaoping grew up.

Salomon Brothers, acquired by Travelers and merged with Smith Barney in 1997, had also been expanding its Asian footprint to China. Offices were also opened in Thailand, Indonesia and Malaysia, and a second Australian office was opened in Melbourne (see p. 144).

As the world was coming to terms with the Asian crisis, a merger between Travelers and Citicorp was announced in 1998, forming a new financial-services giant called Citigroup Inc. Among the challenges to staff was the merger's timing in relation to external events: the Asian crisis was at its most severe and the Korean debt position was demanding of management's time, as was the introduction of the euro in Europe. Under the new worldwide structure,

Above: Shanghai Stock Exchange. Citibank played a leading role in developing the exchange's clearing system. Left: An investor studies the latest price on the stock market

Interior of the Jurong East branch in Singapore, advertising Citibank's 24-hour hotline

Mortgages online

In the 1980s, with only a few branches in most countries, Citibank pioneered the use of remote channels to reach customers. It introduced the first "touchscreen" and dip-card ATMs and operated the first customer hotline operating 24 hours, seven days a week. By the late 1990s the holy grail was internet banking. Citibank was the first to launch it in Hong Kong, and by 2001 it was in every Asian market and winning awards. Frits Seegers, head of the Asian consumer business, said: "We had to be smarter in how we talked to our customers because we were limited by the reach of our branch network. We had to show customers we were always available and could meet all their banking needs— even if they couldn't walk into a branch. In some ways this was an advantage. It made us flexible and quick to recognize the potential of new technologies."

Frits Seegers, head of the Asian consumer business

As with ATMs and phone banking, Citibank aimed to make internet banking simple and customer-friendly. Seegers added: "We made it available to our whole banking and cards base. A PIN, a few clicks of the mouse, and you could view accounts, make transactions, pay bills and now, buy mutual funds online. In Japan we booked 25 percent of mortgages online. Customers could pay bills or switch currencies through i-mode phones. If you applied for a credit card online you received an instant response. The idea was we would offer services any way, any time, through any gateway and on any device."

In Japan, Citibank took the lead in banking over the internet, widely available on mobile phones

New lease of life

In 1988, Citibank's 24-hour phone-banking center in Taiwan was born with eight operators. By 2001, it had 400 operators taking more than 50,000 calls a day.

The center had found a new role for itself in 1999 when it ran hotline services for victims of an earthquake which took place on September 21. With its epicenter in Nantou in central Taiwan, the quake killed over 2,000 people and left thousands of others homeless. As relief agencies struggled to get aid to the area, Citibank opened its phone center to accept public donations of food, tents and other supplies. Working with a local cable television network, some 180 Citibank volunteers received 4,500 calls

Investing in technology

Investing in technology has been a consistent priority. "When Asia's financial markets were in crisis in 1997, we didn't cut our technology spending," said Simon Williams, regional consumer bank head from 1997 to 2001. "We were in the midst of consolidating 15 different software systems to one, and we invested to create a standard platform: this meant we could offer faster, better customer service across the region."

In Singapore, the bank launched CitiAlerts, a service which sent direct to customers' mobile phones not only account information, but also the latest financial news, live foreign exchange rates and updates on their personal stock portfolio movements. It was a global first.

By the end of Citibank's first century in Asia, remote channels, such as telephones, ATMs and the internet, accounted for some 95 percent of the 10 million transactions performed each month. The ratio is among the highest of any retail bank in the world.

during a two-week period while making another 2,100 calls to match the supply of public donations with demand. The bank's branch in the nearby city of Taichung survived the earthquake, although electricity and water supplies were disrupted.

After the disastrous earthquake on September 21, a grant of 200,000 U.S. dollars was approved by Citigroup Foundation to help rebuild Puli Community College, located in Central Taiwan

The new Bandra Kurla Complex in Mumbai (formerly Bombay), Citibank's main corporate premises in India

Advertising the merger in 1998 of Salomon Brothers Asia Ltd. and Smith Barney International Inc.

Citigroup was valued at 50.6 billion dollars. Citicorp alone accounted for 45 percent of the parent holding company while Salomon Smith Barney accounted for 17 percent. Travelers Insurance Company and Travelers Property Casualty Corporation made up most of the rest. Among the goals of the merged organization was to double earnings every five years while achieving a 20 percent return on equity.

For new Citigroup chairman Sanford I. Weill, the merger created not a larger version of Citicorp or Travelers, "but a new company altogether, with more exciting growth possibilities than either predecessor had alone," with 230,000 people working in more than 100 countries. "The new model of financial services we are building rests on three pillars that, put together, give us significant advantage," he said. Weill cited the group's broad distribution channels, its unparalleled global imprint, and its unrivaled breadth of products and services. This "gives us enormous strategic flexibility for growth."

The merger created a formidable combination of Salomon Smith Barney's capital market expertise and Citibank's "embedded" commercial banking footprint in Asia. It didn't take long to reap results. By 1999, the bank could count 15 major deals which combined resources in these two areas. A notable example was a five-billion U.S. dollar syndicated loan for Japan Tobacco—a loan Citibank wouldn't have expected without an introduction from Salomon Smith Barney and its new partner Nikko Securities (see p. 164). Apart from the sheer size of the facility, Citibank and Salomon Smith Barney underwrote the entire amount before inviting a group of sub-underwriters into the deal. In the same year, Neptune Orient Lines (NOL), a long-time shipping client of Citibank in Singapore, was introduced to Salomon Smith Barney to discuss a recapitalization plan. The result was a 500-million U.S. dollar follow-on offering of primary shares which Salomon Smith Barney lead-managed and for which Citibank pro-vided the securities

The new Surabaya branch, opened in 2001

services. Another important transaction in 1999 in which Salomon Smith Barney acted as global bookrunner was the 1.75-billion U.S. dollar global offering for Siam Commercial Bank of Thailand, which utilized the government's Tier One Capital Support Program to recapitalize the troubled bank.

Container handling at Neptune Orient Lines, introduced to Salomon Smith Barney by Citibank

This innovative transaction won 11 institutional awards from publications around the globe.

The importance of the Citibank/Salomon Smith Barney nexus was demonstrated again memorably when Singapore Airlines (SIA), Swissair and Delta Airlines made the decision in 1999 to unwind the cross-shareholding they had entered into in 1989 as part of their global strategic alliance. As sole placement agent and arranger, Salomon Smith Barney helped Swissair dispose of its shareholding in SIA and Delta of its shareholding in SIA via overnight block trades. Singapore Airlines disposed of its shareholding in Delta via a private placement back to Delta. Each of these trades posed its own settlement issues, but a particular challenge was how to take in the 35,186,330 shares which were in physical form from Delta's agent bank Standard Chartered, and make them available in Singapore in time to settle the requirements of the Singapore Stock Exchange. Citibank's Worldwide Securities Service

(WWSS) came to the rescue. The physical shares were transferred to Citibank and converted to scripless stock in time to make settlement and avoid the necessity of buying replacement stock (potentially much more expensive than the original 317-million U.S. dollar stock) in the open market.

The merger also created one of the largest global money managers. In 2000, the Citibank Private Bank and Salomon Smith Barney/Citi Asset Management announced a rebranding to become the Citigroup Private Bank and Citigroup Asset Management. The new Citigroup Asset Management Group combined three companies with complementary expertise—Citibank Asset Management, Salomon Brothers Asset

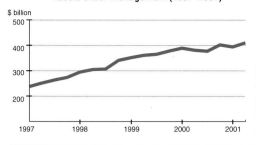

Assets under management (1997–2001)

$ billion

As of mid-2001, Citigroup Asset Management was ranked 10th-largest global money management group, with over 400 billion U.S. dollars under management

Source: annual reports

Management and Smith Barney Asset Management. Covering both retail and institutional businesses, it had more than 409 billion dollars under management by mid-2001.

The last years of Citigroup's first century in Asia were marked by expansion, particularly on the consumer side of the group, through credit cards, priority banking and wealth management services. One of the most exciting opportunities came with the development of internet applications, allowing the group to extend its reach across an even wider customer spectrum in Asia. Remote banking was no longer an impractical dream, and was set to revolutionize the delivery of financial services to companies and individuals alike.

Private banking was especially strong. "We saw 65 percent compounded growth in net income between 1998 and 2000, and 30 percent increase in customer acquisition," said Deepak Sharma, the regional head of private banking.

The merger re-energized a central component of the "embedded bank strategy"—it gave Citibank a new expertise and appetite for acquisitions. In 1999, the company

repurchased the Diners Club franchise in Japan that it had sold off profitably a decade earlier. Agreement was reached the following year to acquire the global investment banking business and related assets of the British merchant bank Schroders. In Asia, this included a well-established business developed in the 1970s in partnership with Hong Kong's China Light and Power, and Standard Chartered Bank. The company also formed an important strategic partnership with the Fubon group, one of Taiwan's leading financial-services companies.

The acquisition of Associates International Holdings brought into the group more than 1,000 consumer-finance outlets across Japan and an additional presence in Hong Kong, India, Taiwan and the Philippines.

In corporate and investment banking, the new partnership with Nikko enjoyed a 30 percent share of equities issued in Japan in 2000. Elsewhere in Asia, the company opened investment banking offices in Manila and Mumbai, and expanded its Taiwan operations.

In Korea, Salomon Brothers had opened an investment banking

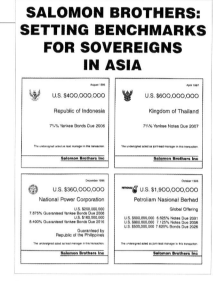

SALOMON BROTHERS: SETTING BENCHMARKS FOR SOVEREIGNS IN ASIA

Salomon Brothers was a dominant player in sovereign issues during the 1990s, bringing Malaysia and Thailand to the international capital markets

Dragon bond master

After Salomon Brothers returned to Hong Kong, it hired Albert Cobetto to work in the fixed-income business.

Cobetto had been involved in the first issue of a "dragon bond" (an Asian currency bond issued by a foreign issuer) for the Asian Development Bank back in 1992, and was now considered a veteran of the market, having led 15 deals in a single year.

"There was strong liquidity in Asia for Asian credits and we had a really simple but effective fund-raising alternative for the

Asian borrower," Cobetto recalled. He noted Salomon's role in bringing both Thailand and Malaysia to the international capital markets. "Salomon had a strong fixed-income group in the United States and Europe, but wanted to improve its standing in the Asian market. It was the perfect platform." During Cobetto's first year at Salomon, this platform was widened when the firm underwrote the first global issue of the ADB.

In 2000, Cobetto moved on to head BondsInAsia, an online bond-trading platform with Citigroup as a major shareholder.

Net income from Asia-Pacific consumer banking (1996–2000)

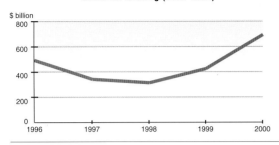

At this time, the Asia-Pacific region (excluding South Asia) was the biggest contributor to international consumer earnings. By 2000, net income from the regional consumer business was approaching 700 million dollars, including almost 140 million dollars from Japan alone

Source: annual reports

Dr. C.S. Park, chief executive of Hynix Semiconductor, and Bill Mills presenting Hynix's GDR issue, part of a landmark restructuring of the former Korean chaebol subsidiary undertaken by Citigroup's investment bank and Citibank; it won a deal award from *CFO Asia* in 2001

representative office in Seoul in 1989, and later participated in a joint-venture securities company which started business in 1996. Meanwhile, in another part of Seoul, Smith Barney entered into a securities joint venture with Korea Exchange Bank called KEB Smith Barney in 1996, which opened for business in 1997. Following the acquisition of Salomon Inc. by Travelers in 1998, the merged firm of Salomon Smith Barney became a partner in the KEB joint venture. On December 12, 2000 it bought the remaining KEB interest in the joint venture and renamed the company Salomon Smith Barney Korea Ltd. The firm is a fully licensed securities company, and a member of the Korean Stock Exchange. "Korea is a priority for us," said William J. Mills II, Chief Executive Officer of the investment banking arm of Citigroup in Asia Pacific, what was, until 2001, Salomon Smith Barney. "We think its long-term growth prospects are good—the post 1997 economic crisis

Americans and Japanese

Some five months after the announcement of the merger between Citicorp and Travelers Group in April 1998, Travelers concluded an agreement to spend 217 billion yen (1.8 billion dollars) on a strategic investment in Nikko Securities Co. Ltd., one of the big three securities houses in Japan. In a country where direct foreign investment was only just starting to take off, the deal was huge. The group paid 67.2 billion yen for 9.5 percent of the company, although this later rose to more than 20 percent through the conversion of some of the 150.1 billion yen worth of convertible shares that were the main part of the deal. In October 2001, the company changed its name to Nikko Cordial Corporation.

Toshiharu Kojima

The two companies also set up a joint venture that effectively merged their existing institutional businesses. The new company, Nikko Salomon Smith Barney, was 51 percent owned by Nikko but run by veteran Salomon Brothers Asia executive Toshiharu Kojima, who used to work for Nomura Securities in Brazil. The Portuguese-speaking chief executive is also credited as one of the two main factors behind the early successes of Salomon Brothers Asia, where he worked

Nikko Salomon Smith Barney, Japan

as head of sales. While the joint venture ran the institutional side of the business, Nikko managed all of the retail and asset management business through its own network.

Depending on whom you talked to, Nikko and Salomon Smith Barney were, together, either the No. 1 or the No. 2 securities company in Japan. "Nomura would say they're No. 1. We say they're a very good No. 2, and we did beat them two years running as the lead equity underwriter in Japan," said Citigroup vice chairman Deryck Maughan. "Nomura has a fabulous Japanese franchise but doesn't have what we have in the United States or Europe. Similarly, Goldman has a fabulous business but doesn't have what we have in Japan. No foreign competitor has the embedded relationship of Nikko in Japan. Citibank is a local bank throughout Asia and Nikko is a local securities company. If you combine those local relationships with global product capability, you have a great business proposition."

The new Citigroup headquarters in Sydney, Australia

Colin Powell with the Society for the Promotion of Area Resource Centres (SPARC) in Mumbai (see p. 184)

restructuring is progressing well." In 2001 Korea's sovereign credit rating was upgraded to BBB+.

In Australia, Salomon Smith Barney acquired the equity and fixed-income operations of British securities firm County Natwest. The deal, arranged by then regional head Robert R. Morse, boosted Salomon's limited investment-banking staff presence in Australia from 12 to 400. The company also acquired HSBC's retail brokerage, following the earlier purchase of the asset management business of J.P. Morgan and Co. with 4.8 billion dollars under management.

By the turn of the century, around 10 million people living in the region were saving with Citigroup, and it was securely in place as the largest pan-Asia issuer of credit cards. Asia's net income from consumer operations alone was approaching 700 million dollars a year with more than 47 billion dollars deposited in almost 10 million accounts. In July 2001, CitiGold was relaunched in Hong Kong, with an expanded offering including wealth planning and portfolio tracking.

Citigroup's profile was high, and its operations in Asia received many awards and accolades. Deryck Maughan saw huge potential in the new business combinations brought about by the Citigroup structure. Citigroup was now "the largest foreign financial-services company in Japan by some measure, and we're very pleased with the way it's worked out.

"In Asia outside of Japan, Salomon Brothers has essentially become the investment banking arm of Citibank," Maughan added. "Citibank has a fabulous reputation throughout Asia. It

EQUITY IN ASIA.

Salomon Brothers

Unimat, one of three Japanese consumer finance companies acquired by Citigroup in 2000, dominates the skyline over Shimbashi station in Tokyo. Shimbashi was the terminus for Japan's first railroad, which was financed by a bond issue underwritten by British merchant bank Schroders in 1870. The global investment banking business of Schroders became part of Citigroup

AIC, DIC and Unimat

When Citigroup acquired Texas-based Associates First Capital Corporation in late 2000, it suddenly had more than 1,000 consumer finance outlets across Japan. Moreover, the Associates' Japanese business accounted for a significant part of its total earnings.

Associates had assets of more than 100 billion dollars in 14 countries, and a unique Japanese franchise. In 1979, it had started up a consumer finance business called AIC Corporation, which had 631 outlets by 2001. Three years earlier, it acquired another consumer finance company from struggling retail giant Daiei Inc. as part of its corporate restructuring. Known as DIC Finance Corporation, the Osaka-based company had

another 350 outlets. And shortly before the Citigroup takeover, it acquired Unimat Life Corporation, a finance company for women with another 134 outlets in Japan.

Citigroup vice chairman Deryck Maughan

Japanese consumer finance companies AIC, DIC and Unimat now all come under the Citigroup umbrella

described AIC as a "unique asset" within Associates. "They've grown it from scratch, and it's run on international lines in terms of product quality, client services and accounting standards. But of the 6,000 people who work there, 10 are foreign. The rest, of course, are Japanese. It's a very Japanese company. It's been remarkably successful, and they've gone at a very strong organic growth rate," he said.

"It's a curious thing. We bought it [Associates] because of its strong U.S. business. But I think we all clearly had in mind that this was a great way to buy a big consumer finance operation in Japan. Rather than try to build one or build a Japanese one, we got one built to American standards through this acquisition."

Total assets (1986–2000)

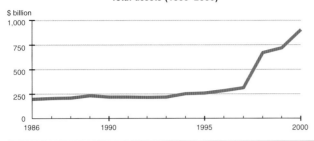

$ billion

Growth in worldwide total assets was fairly subdued until 1997. With the merger, the balance sheet more than doubled between 1997 and 1998

Source: annual reports

has very broad client relationships, it has good relationships with local governments and Salomon was their missing product. Citibank had foreign exchange, retail banking and corporate banking, but it didn't have capital markets or mergers and acquisitions. ... The combination of a bank and a securities company in Asia has been extremely productive—Citibank and Salomon Smith Barney together have been very dramatically growing their franchise since the merger of 1998. They were sort of made for each other." In 2001, Salomon Smith Barney adopted the Citigroup brand.

As Citigroup neared the completion of its first century in Asia, the economic climate seemed full of uncertainties. National economies faced the possibility of a major global downturn in late 2001, exacerbated by a slowdown in the United States, a big export market.

Living with such uncertainties was nothing new for Citigroup. Approaching change with a positive attitude had become part of the organization's culture over a century in which wars, political upheavals and successive economic highs and lows had posed challenge after challenge.

Spectacular growth, particularly in the later decades of the century, had transformed the region into one of the most dynamic parts of the world. Citigroup was poised to contribute to its continuing development: in south and southeast Asia— including India, Singapore and the Philippines, where it had operated for a hundred years; in north Asia—including Japan and Hong Kong, franchises with equally long histories, and markets such as Taiwan and Korea, which were showing huge potential by the end of the century. And in what could

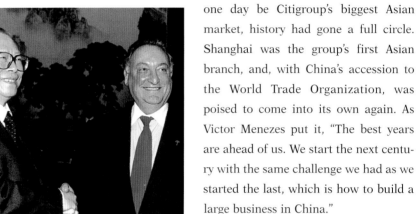

Chinese President Jiang Zemin with Citigroup chairman Sanford Weill in Beijing during Weill's visit to China in 2001

one day be Citigroup's biggest Asian market, history had gone a full circle. Shanghai was the group's first Asian branch, and, with China's accession to the World Trade Organization, was poised to come into its own again. As Victor Menezes put it, "The best years are ahead of us. We start the next century with the same challenge we had as we started the last, which is how to build a large business in China."

For a century Citigroup and its ancestor companies have been participants in the economic transformation of Asia. In the process Citigroup has transformed itself, and it will continue to do so. The lessons of experience have been learned and applied, so that Citigroup has become arguably the leading international provider of financial services in the region. Its roots in Asia run very deep.

Robert Rubin addressing the audience during a visit to the Citigroup operation in Mumbai, India

The Next 100 Years

Citigroup has an extraordinary and vital franchise in Asia. We are clearly where we are today because of the cumulative efforts of a great many people over the last century, who set out to build a unique banking network across Asia. When you stand on the shoulders of giants, you can see further; and we have that good fortune.

Our strategy, in Asia as elsewhere, is to become an "embedded bank" wherever we do business. This means establishing roots as deep as any local, indigenous bank. That means riding out economic cycles, and growing our customer base and product diversity in volatile periods as well as through growth cycles. It means hiring and promoting local staff and playing a role in the local community. When we open for business in a country, we mean to stay there. After 100 years in Asia I hope people think of us as a local bank.

We are also customer-centric. We genuinely listen to our customers and respond to their needs in a modern and efficient manner. It is our customer base that constantly moves the bank forward—as their demands grow and change, so must we.

Even as we establish ourselves as an embedded bank, our global character is also important to our customers in Asia. They want a bank that can match their ambitions, a bank that is at home in 100 countries and can service their needs in 100 countries. Citigroup can provide that. The balance of global, local, and regional considerations is an essential characteristic of Citigroup.

Goals for the second hundred years

In a way, Citibank begins its second century in Asia with the same challenge we had in the last century: which is, how do we build a serious and large business in China? This is probably our number one objective as we begin our second century in Asia.

Of course, while we are building our business in China we do not intend to stand still elsewhere in Asia. We have ambitious goals across the region. We aim to expand our customer base, and provide services to more people and businesses across the region. We want to be known as the best place to work in Asia. All these efforts will further enhance our name. Citibank is already among the top five of all brands in the region, including consumer brands, and we are the leading brand among financial services. The Citigroup brand is also rapidly gaining higher recognition.

I also believe Asia will be driving technological innovation for Citigroup around the world. We don't sit in New York and "innovate." Innovation happens where it should happen—closest to the customer—and then moves around the world. I look forward to having Asia lead that charge, to its role at the forefront of technological development.

Succeeding in Asia will mean a great deal to Citigroup. Asia will be a larger and larger percentage of Citigroup's total business. Back in the 1930s, when much of the world was in the depths of the Depression, there was one year when our branch in Shanghai was able to pay the dividend of the whole company. While I sincerely hope we are never again in that position, I can envision Asia being that important a player in Citigroup's global business.

But 100 years in Asia has done more than provide us with revenues and growth. It has made us who we are. It has made us a global bank. If you look at who became senior managers of the bank during the last 100 years, many of them had experience in Asia. As a source of talent and experience, Asia has been enormously valuable.

And most fundamentally, our long presence in Asia has had a profound effect on our culture. We'd have been a very different company if we had just been in North America; even if we'd been in North America and Europe. One hundred years in Asia gave us a vision of genuine global reach. It shaped our identity.

Dynamics of success

Our future growth will be driven by our skills in marketing and distribution—how to attract customers, how to serve them. From a management point of view, simplicity and transparency are important. We like to make sure that people are focused on performance. We encourage that by using a number of performance measures—financial; customer franchise growth; strategic cost management—and everyone understands that this is what we measure.

We also understand that we are very much dependent upon the judgment and quality of the people on the ground to do the right thing for the company and the right thing for the customer.

It always seems to come down to people. Citibank has a distinct culture that attracts a certain type of person. It is a genuine meritocracy; there are no limits to where you can go, what you can achieve. It's a culture that is focused on customers, shareholder value, and employees. This culture will be just as important in our next 100 years in Asia as it has been throughout the history of our company.

I often think about the people who went out to Asia in 1902. A lot of people took tremendous risk to build our business; and we need the same kind of boldness to build the business going forward. We are the beneficiaries of their work, but we must not rest on their laurels. We have to step up to the challenges of the new century; and we can.

VICTOR J. MENEZES
Chairman and Chief Executive Officer
Citibank, N.A.

CITIGROUP IN ASIA TODAY

Celebrating Asian Enterprise shows just a few examples of the group's huge range of corporate clients, which includes multinationals and many other medium-sized and smaller enterprises. **Community Values** demonstrates Citigroup's general sense of responsibility to the societies where it operates, which it expresses through support for education, the fostering of economic self-sufficiency through microfinance initiatives, and the encouragement of volunteer work by its staff. **Making Things Happen** illustrates the unrivaled technical expertise at the heart of the operation, all of which goes to support **Customer Service With Innovation**.

Celebrating Asian Enterprise

One of the great global brands comes to China. The manufacture of Buick cars in Shanghai symbolizes the growing links between China and the world economy. **Shanghai General Motors Co. Ltd.** was set up by China's Shanghai Automotive Industry (Group) and General Motors Corporation of the United States in 1997, with each partner holding 50 percent. In 1998, Citicorp arranged for 821 million U.S. dollars of limited recourse financing for the project, including the first major renminbi syndication. And more recently in 2001, Citigroup led a syndicated refinancing facility for 600 million U.S. dollars.

Citibank has long-standing relationships with international companies in Singapore, which has always welcomed inward investment. One such company is **Eastman Chemical Ltd. Singapore**, which produces chemicals used in making solvents, plastics and other chemical materials found in a variety of products ranging from drugs to paints. The 200-million-dollar complex on Jurong Island, Singapore has an annual capacity of 150,000 tonnes, almost a fifth of the company's parent plant in Texas. Citibank has been the main banker for Eastman Chemical Ltd. since 1982, providing cash management as well as trade finance and services.

1–4: Located in the Jinqiao Business District in Pudong, Shanghai General Motors' state-of-the-art facility comprises vehicle, engine and transmission assembly operations

5: The first Buick came off this facility in December 1998. Today, approximately 100,000 cars are manufactured each year

6: Shanghai General Motors staff enjoy their lunch at the facility

7: Daily measurements are taken at each of the five Eastman Chemical plants on Jurong Island, Singapore

8: Manufactured products are stored in the tank farm

9: The workshop-cum-maintenance area within the plant handles repairs and fabrication of parts

10: Plant processes are closely monitored from the control room

11–12: Product samples are sent for testing at the Quality and Analysis Services laboratory, which is also in the Jurong Island plant

13: Spare parts are kept at the store, which is located next to the workshop-cum-maintenance area

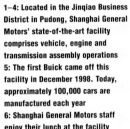

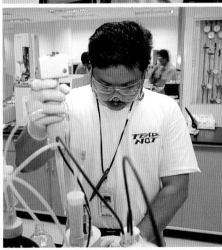

7-Eleven a Japanese brand? Founded in 1973, 7-Eleven Japan came to international prominence in 1991 when it acquired Southland Corporation, the operator of the 7-Eleven franchise in the United States. Majority-owned by leading Japanese supermarket operator Ito-Yokado, the company is the largest operator of convenience stores in Japan with revenues of 358 billion yen in fiscal 2001. Citibank's long-standing relationship with the Ito-Yokado Group covers a variety of the Group's strategic financial needs across the globe.

Established in Guangzhou in 1906, **Li & Fung Ltd.** is one of the biggest consumer products trading companies in Asia with annual sales of more than three billion U.S. dollars. A separate retail business, started in 1985, includes Circle K convenience stores and Toys "R" Us outlets. After the acquisition of the regional marketing operations of Britain's Inchcape PLC, a distribution company was set up in 1999. The bank's relationship with Li & Fung Ltd. goes back to their earliest days.

1–3: One of over 7,000 7-Eleven stores in Japan: shown here is a typical 7-Eleven store in Shin-Urayasu, Tokyo, Japan

4–6: Inside the store a wide range of items is sold, from magazines to varieties of cold noodles such as "hiyashi chuka" and "zaru soba"

7: A 7-Eleven staff member uses a scanner to check-in freshly delivered food before putting it on the shelves

8: Staff also prepare "oden" in a simmering-tray

9–14: Li & Fung Ltd. sources consumer products on behalf of customers who are mainly retailers from the United States and Europe. Shown here are samples brought in by product specialists at the Li & Fung office in Cheung Sha Wan, Kowloon, Hong Kong. Garments, giftware, household goods, and toys and games are some of the products found in Li & Fung's office complex

1			9			
2	4	7	10	11	12	
	5					
3	6	8	13	14		

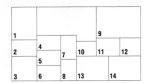

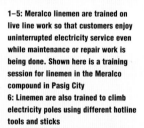

[Celebrating Asian Enterprise]

Citibank has long promoted the development of national infrastructure in Asia. Founded in 1903, **Manila Electric Company (Meralco)** is the second-biggest company in the Philippines with revenues exceeding 10 billion pesos. In 1961 Citibank financed the purchase of the company from its American owners by local investors led by Eugenio Lopez. The bank's relationship with Meralco now spans cash management services, trade, treasury, loans, securities and corporate finance.

Top-tier local corporates and global relationships are still the mainstay of business in India; but Citibank has led the way in bringing world-class service to smaller and medium-sized enterprises. **Royal Container Carriers**, established in Mumbai in 1994, specializes in transporting containers. With a latest annual revenue of 75.6 million rupees, its clients include companies such as Maersk Lines and Tetrapak Ltd. The bank's relationship with the company began in 1998 with a commercial vehicle loan. This led to a refinancing of 5 million rupees on the existing fleet and later to a working capital facility.

1–5: Meralco linemen are trained on live line work so that customers enjoy uninterrupted electricity service even while maintenance or repair work is being done. Shown here is a training session for linemen in the Meralco compound in Pasig City

6: Linemen are also trained to climb electricity poles using different hotline tools and sticks

7–8: At the Meralco headquarters in Pasig City, employees monitor, coordinate, operate and control the entire distribution network in real-time mode with the aid of SCADA-DAS (Supervisory Control and Data Acquisition-Distribution Automation System). Meralco is the only electricity utility company in the Philippines to be equipped with such a system

9: Drivers from the Royal Container Carrier company head off for their destinations in rural India after containers are loaded on the trucks

10: A Royal Container Carrier company office in Mumbai, India

11: Fork lifts are used to load the containers onto the trucks

12: Mr. Bhuphinder Singh, one of the many truck drivers with the company, waits in front of his truck

13: Chilies and lemons are believed to ward off the evil eye

14: A driver cycles to his truck at the beginning of the work day

15–17: The truck drivers personalize their trucks with decorative paintings and patriotic messages

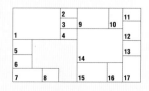

Community Values

Citigroup is a major player in many national economies, and believes this status carries with it responsibilities to local communities. The Citigroup Foundation makes grants mainly in support of sustainable community development and education. In Hong Kong, Citigroup has been a supporter of the HOPE *worldwide* Center for Kids, and also the Summerbridge program, which provides free English tuition to high-school students.

In the Philippines, Citigroup is involved with the Tuloy sa Don Bosco Foundation, which, among other activities, provides classes in practical skills and music lessons for street children in Makati.

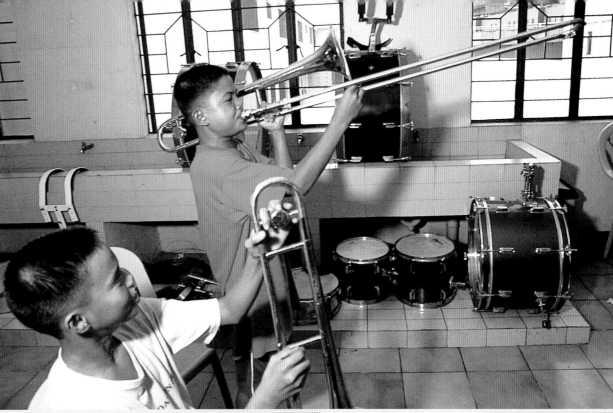

1: The reception area of the HOPE *worldwide* Center for Kids

2: The children at the center receive coaching for their school work in the study room

3: They also enjoy computer games in the cyber room

4–5: Boys from the Tuloy sa Don Bosco Foundation school in Makati City, Philippines have music lessons while the girls receive vocational training

6: The Summerbridge program for high-school students started in Hong Kong in 1992 and Citibank has supported it since 1995. Lasting five weeks every summer, it consists of daily English lessons conducted by student volunteers

7–8: Summerbridge participants are encouraged to converse only in English for the program's duration

1			4	
			5	6
				7
	2	3		8

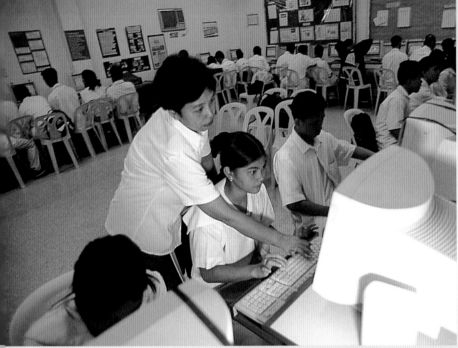

[Community Values]

Citigroup believes in fostering innovative educational programs. In the Philippines, Citigroup has donated computers and has provided computer-training courses at local high schools. In China, it offers a banking course at Shanghai's renowned Fudan University. In Singapore, Japan, Taiwan and Korea, also, university students are introduced to the world of banking.

One of the keynotes of Citibank's long presence in Asia has been its emphasis on developing human capital. This is achieved by the training and promotion of local staff within Citigroup itself, by helping with the development of financial and regulatory infrastructure in many of the countries where it operates, and—as shown here—by actively supporting education in the community, from junior to university level.

1–2: The Citibank Center for Education in Krus Na Ligas Public High School, Philippines. Over 30,000 students have benefited from use of the computers
3: Teacher training is conducted by Citibank volunteers
4: Staff volunteers in Singapore conduct classroom talks on consumer banking products
5: Students from the Anglo-Chinese School (Independent), Singapore, tour the bank's facilities at Capital Square
6–7: A Citibank-Fudan banking course is offered at Fudan University, China
8: Sanford I. Weill with the winners of Citi-scholarships at Fudan University
9–10: MBA graduates from Fudan University at their convocation
11: Business specialists from Citigroup lecture at a financial services course at Keio University in Tokyo

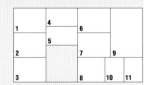

复旦 -- 麻省理工2001届工商管理硕士毕业典礼
Fudan-MIT International MBA Class 2001 Commencement

[Community Values]

Citigroup strongly supports the involvement of its employees in voluntary social work. In Singapore, 30 Citibank employees volunteered at the "Special Olympics," for people with special needs. During the four-day event, the volunteers acted as liaison officers to 12 local schools, and helped teachers supervise the children. In preparation for the games, the volunteers also coached the children in soccer. In Hong Kong, the voluntary activities of Citigroup gave rise to a corporate citizenship awareness program launched by the territory's Social Welfare Department. Citigroup also operates volunteer programs in every other Asian country in which it operates.

1–2: The 5th National Special Olympics Games was held at the Toa Payoh Sports Stadium in Singapore on June 1–4, 2001

3: Citibank volunteers were also cheerleaders during the Games

4–8: About 650 local and foreign special athletes competed in the Games. Foreign participants included athletes from Japan, China, South Korea, Taiwan, Hong Kong, Macau and Malaysia

9: In all, nine sporting events were offered for competition, including badminton and soccer. Athletics in the Special Olympics included wheelchair races

1	2		4	5	6
				7	
3			9	8	

[Community Values]

In promoting microfinance and microenterprise development, Citigroup draws on resources and skills used in running its businesses, while local communities remain in the driver's seat. The Society for the Promotion of Area Resource Centres (SPARC) is based in Mumbai, and is just one of the many programs supported by the group in India. Others include Friends of Women's World Banking (FWWB) in Ahmedabad, Working Women's Forum (WWF) in Chennai, Sharan in New Delhi, and Sasha in Kolkata. Subsequently, with the Grameen Trust (an offshoot of the Grameen or "Village" bank, a microcredit bank first established in Bangladesh), Citigroup has promoted micro-credit programs in other Asian countries such as China, Indonesia, Malaysia, the Philippines, Korea, and Vietnam.

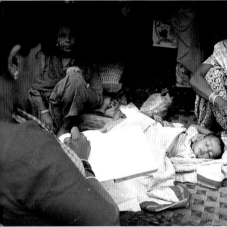

1–2: In the district of Sipitang, Sabah, in Malaysia, microcredit has helped several people, including those shown here, set up businesses

3: A woman weaves rattan for hats in a village in Central Java, Indonesia. She has benefited from Citibank Peka, a community program

4–5: A group of woman workers in Quezon City, the Philippines, make footrugs out of scrap materials for sale to grocery stores

6: A woman in Chennai has set up a flower shop with funding from the Working Women's Forum (WWF), a partner of Citibank India since 1998

7–9: In Mumbai, one of the initiators of the SPARC program visits her clients before they leave for work. She notes down the sums advanced

10: People whose homes have been demolished come to SPARC's office to have their grievances addressed

11: A delegation on an exchange program from Cape Town, South Africa, visits the SPARC office in Mumbai

12: In the SPARC office, credits noted earlier are transferred into passbooks

1	4	7		
2		8	9	
	5	6	10	12
3		11		

Making Things Happen

Trading and treasury operations are nerve centers for all banks. Advanced information and communications technology are crucial —a difference of a mere few seconds can be worth millions of dollars. As well as changes in supply and demand, traders of everything from cash to bonds must be able to react immediately to the latest news from around the globe. According to a BIS survey, daily foreign exchange turnover averaged around 50 billion dollars each in Singapore and Hong Kong in 1989—less than half the level of Tokyo. By 1998, the average turnover in Singapore was 139 billion dollars, only 10 billion dollars short of Tokyo, while Hong Kong was averaging almost 80 billion dollars a day.

1–5: Salomon Smith Barney's Equity trading floor in Exchange Square, Hong Kong

6–10: Treasury trading floor in Citibank Plaza, Hong Kong

11–18: Treasury trading floor in Centennial Tower, Singapore, the largest of all the Citibank treasury trading floors in Asia-Pacific

19–21: Treasury trading floor in the Bandra Kurla Complex, Mumbai

1		7		10		
	6		9	11	12	
2		8				19
			15	14	13	
3			16			20
4	5		17	18		21

[Making Things Happen]

Back-office operations are generally not seen as a business in their own right although they are an important aspect of banking. In recent years however, technical innovations and economies of scale have made regional processing a new growth area for Citibank. In the Asia-Pacific region, most treasury processing is centralized in Sydney while trade finance processing is done in Penang. But the main regional processing centers are in Singapore and Mumbai. In Singapore, the company processes card transactions from two dozen countries in Asia, the Middle East, Europe and the Caribbean. The number of card accounts serviced reached 7.5 million in 2000. In addition to credit card transactions, Singapore is also the bank's Asia-Pacific regional hub for cash products, securities and data processing. At the same time, Mumbai serves as a data-processing center for South Asia, the Middle East and parts of Africa and Eastern Europe.

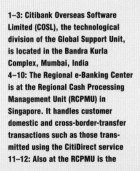

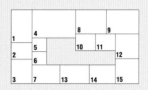

1–3: Citibank Overseas Software Limited (COSL), the technological division of the Global Support Unit, is located in the Bandra Kurla Complex, Mumbai, India

4–10: The Regional e-Banking Center is at the Regional Cash Processing Management Unit (RCPMU) in Singapore. It handles customer domestic and cross-border-transfer transactions such as those transmitted using the CitiDirect service

11–12: Also at the RCPMU is the Singapore Image Processing Center, which handles customer domestic and cross-border transfer transactions that are transmitted via written forms or fax. The forms and faxes are captured as images for processing purposes

13–15: The Asia-Pacific Processing Center (APPC) in Singapore is one of the international data centers which provide computer processing services to Citigroup businesses in 77 countries. Shown here is the Command Center of the APPC. It runs 24 hours, 7 days a week, and controls two remote hardware centers which house the bank's computers and network equipment

```
       ┌────┬────┬──────┬────┬────┐
   1   │ 4  │    │  8   │ 9  │    │
       ├────┤ 5  ├──┬───┤    ├────┤
   2   │    ├────┤10│11 │    │ 12 │
       │    │ 6  │  │   │    │    │
       ├────┼────┼──┴───┼────┼────┤
   3   │ 7  │    │ 13   │ 14 │ 15 │
       └────┴────┴──────┴────┴────┘
```

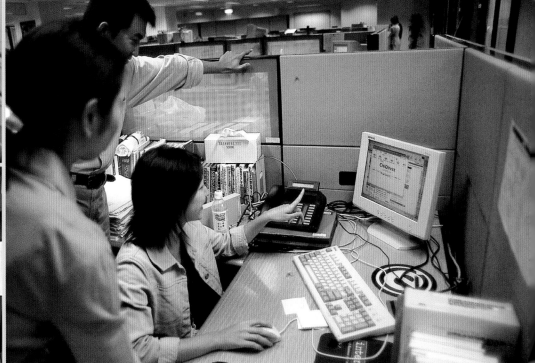

[Making Things Happen]

Software development is increasingly important to Citigroup in Asia. Technology for ATMs is developed in the Philippines. And in Japan, the rapid expansion of consumer banking activities, including the use of internet applications, has boosted the demand for new Japanese-language software.

By 1992, the number of credit cards issued in Asia was over a million. On an average day, 5,000 cards are issued in Singapore, and 25,000 checks are cleared. One of the offshoots of the processing arm of the regional card center was the Asia-Pacific computer center. It evolved to include consumer bank data processing not only for Asia but also for several other countries in the Middle East, Europe, the Caribbean and Latin America. The data centers for Citibank's consumer and corporate bank activities have since been merged, becoming one of the region's largest hubs for processing financial data.

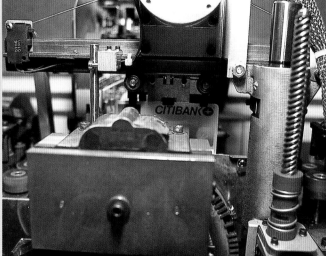

1–4: Citibank in the Philippines develops software for use in Southeast Asia as well as training modules for teaching computer literacy in the Citibank Center for Education program

5–6: Software is developed to enable internet banking for Citibank customers in Shinagawa, Tokyo, Japan

7: At the card embossing unit in Singapore, the embossing process begins with a click of the mouse

8: Before embossing, blank Visa cards are put into the input hopper

9: First the card-holder's signature and photograph are printed on the card

10: Next the card is laminated. Details such as the credit card number, expiry date and card-holder's name are then embossed, and the card undergoes tipping, which results in the glossy look of the embossed data on the card

11: The finished card is automatically placed on a card carrier that is printed with customer details. What emerges from the embossing machine is a packed envelope ready to be delivered

12–15: At Corporate Payment Services in Singapore, the contents of business reply envelopes are

neatly removed by a mail extractor and manually sorted into piles, according to various combinations of payment stubs and checks

16: The piles of checks and payment stubs are proofread—they must all have signature, payee and valid date

17: The DP500 (data processing) machine captures important data as an image and separates the stubs and checks into batches of 500

18: The stubs and checks are sent for balancing. Then the stubs are returned to the respective customers and the checks to the Automated Clearing House

1		5		7		8	9	
2				12		10	11	
		6		13				
3				14				
4				15	16	17	18	

Customer Service with Innovation

The first in the region to establish such a consistent branding, Citibank's retail branches are distinguished by their "blue wave." The bank sees a continuing role for "bricks and mortar" branches, even though its branch network may be less extensive than that of many local banks, due to banking-license restrictions. But in these days of "virtual" or electronic banking, this is less of a hindrance to the development of customer relationships than in the past.

Banking today takes on many forms. The Citigroup Private Bank was first set up in Hong Kong in 1972. Over the next few years, offices were set up in Singapore and the Philippines. By the turn of the century, it was also operating in Japan, Taiwan, Thailand, Indonesia, India and Australia. As befits the world's largest private bank outside Switzerland, its clients include many of Asia's most influential entrepreneurs, families and senior executives. They demand expert personal service in comfortable surroundings, and the Citigroup Private Bank provides it.

1: Fort branch in Mumbai, India
2: Toranomon branch in Tokyo, Japan
3: Yen San branch in Singapore
4: Wheelock House branch in Central, Hong Kong
5: Makati City branch in the Philippines
6: The Private Bank office in Otemachi, Tokyo, Japan

7–10: Clients consult with a private banker in the Hong Kong Private Bank office
11: Khar branch in Mumbai, India
12: 24-hour Citicard Banking Center at the ground floor of China Bright Chang An Building in Beijing, China
13: Chembur branch in Mumbai, India

		6	7	8
1	4		9	10
2		11		
3	5	12	13	

Over the past decade, Citibank has made it a priority to offer a full range of financial products and a high level of service for customers. Modern branches provide the choice of traditional banking and "virtual banking" via ATMs, CitiPhones and CitiDirect booths.

Many relatively affluent customers in Asia have banking needs going beyond the traditional branch. They are catered for by CitiGold Wealth Management Banking. A service targeted at clients with the equivalent of around 100,000 U.S. dollars or more to invest, CitiGold was developed in Asia and later exported to other parts of the world.

1: Inside the Citibank branch in Otemachi, Tokyo, Japan

2: Citibank customers lining up outside the Makati City branch in the Philippines to make credit card payments

3: Traditional "bricks-and-mortar" banking at Fort branch, Mumbai

4: CitiDirect Banking Center in Exchange Square, Hong Kong

5: Citibank customers receive over-the-counter service at Wheelock House branch in Central, Hong Kong

6–8: Frits Seegers and Danny Liu at the CitiGold Wealth Management press conference in Hong Kong held in July 2001

9–10: CitiGold at Wheelock House branch in Central, Hong Kong

11: CitiGold at Capital Square branch in Singapore

		3	6		7
1					8
		4	9		10
2		5	11		

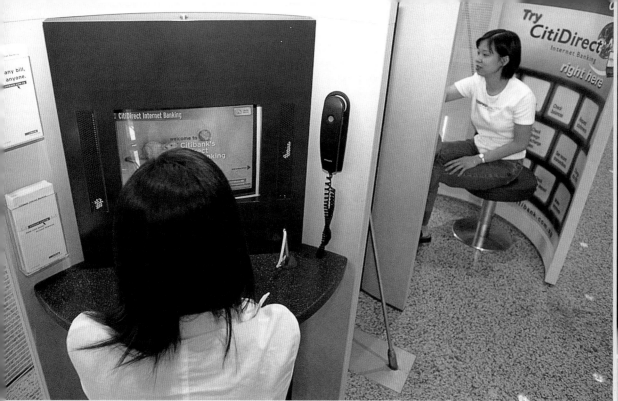

[Customer Service with Innovation]

Banking today is not restricted to the traditional branch network. Citibank has been a leader in introducing 24-hour services 7 days a week. It was among the first in Asia to open card centers and drive-in centers. When international automatic teller machine (ATM) transactions became possible, Citibank customers in Hong Kong, South Korea, Taiwan and Singapore were among the first to get the new technology. In Japan, Citibank also took the lead in extending ATM opening hours; and in China, it was the first foreign bank to offer cash withdrawals in renminbi.

Once the ATM was seen as the height of innovation; now an increasingly sophisticated range of financial services is available electronically at remote locations, from phone banking to internet banking on computers and mobile phones. The pace of innovation is quickening. Some 95 percent of the 10 million transactions performed each month are accounted for by remote channels such as telephones, ATMs and the internet. The ratio is among the highest of any retail bank in the world.

透過萬通咭，
您可在全球超過
570,000部自動櫃員機
提取現金。

花旗銀行
Citibank, N.A.

自動櫃員機中心
24小時開放
Citicard Banking Centers are
24hours, 7 days a week

請 Push

Please remember to take your Card before you leave.
請緊記於離去前取回咭

TOUCH SCREEN

1–2: Internet banking facilities at Capital Square branch, Singapore

3–4: CitiPhone banking at Capital Square branch, Singapore and Exchange Square branch, Hong Kong

5–6: Behind the scenes, corporate banking customers receive CitiService in Shanghai and Mumbai respectively

7: A Citibank officer receives a CitiPhone call from a customer

8: Dip-card technology in Singapore

9: 24-hour Citicard Banking Center at the ground floor of Peace Hotel in Shanghai, China

10: An Associates Aiku touchscreen ATM in Shimbashi, Tokyo, Japan

11: Citicard Banking Centers are open 24 hours a day, 7 days a week

12: A touchscreen ATM in Hong Kong

13: A typical Citibank ATM with the distinctive "blue wave" design

14: One of the two drive-thru ATMs in Singapore. Shown here is the drive-thru ATM at Capital Square

15: An ATM at the Hanae Mori Building ATM in Tokyo, Japan

16–17: Citicard Banking Centers in Bandra Kurla Complex, Mumbai and Makati City, Manila

			8	9	10	11
---	---	5				
1				12		
2		6			14	15
3	4	7	13		16	17

Citicard Banking Center

- Get Cash
- Make a Deposit or Payment
- Transfer Money
- Get Account Information
- Order a Statement or Checkbook
- Change ATM PIN
- Get Other Services

CITIBANK Citicard

Planning Ahead
For Retirement?

Citibank Investment Services
We have you covered

CITIBANK

24 Hour Banking

Citicard
Banking Center

- Get Cash
- Make a Deposit or Payment
- Transfer Money
- Get Account Information
- Order a Statement or Checkbook
- Change ATM Personal Identification Number (PIN)

Citicard
Banking Center

Citicard
Banking Center

[Customer Service with Innovation]

Banking for individual customers became a strategic focus for Citibank in Asia in the last two decades of the 20th century. Most of the emerging markets in Asia have relatively young and fast-growing populations in need of an increasingly complex array of financial services. The bank decided to position its products and services as a premium brand, easily distinguishable from its competitors. This meant energetic marketing.

From billboards on the busy streets of Hong Kong to signs in Japan and public transportation vehicles in Singapore, Citibank advertisements are a familiar sight to many. "Roving vans" in the Philippines and booths both inside and outside shopping malls are also used to promote the bank's co-brand credit cards.

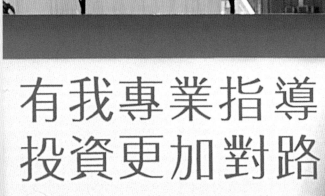

有我專業指導
投資更加對路

信我有智有謀 Citibank 投資服務

A member of citigroup

1–2: Citibank Ready Credit advertisements are a familiar sight on Singapore taxis. Credit card applications are also available inside
3: Citibank advertisements can be seen on Singapore's "bendy-bus"
4–5: Bus-stops in Central, Hong Kong and Mumbai, India are also used to advertise Citibank products
6: A CitiDirect billboard captures attention at a busy junction in Times Square, Causeway Bay, Hong Kong
7: Advertising Citibank Investment Services at the Cross-harbour Tunnel, Causeway Bay, Hong Kong

8–11: Ways of selling credit cards in the Philippines include booths inside and outside shopping malls and a "roving van." Shown here is a booth outside Tangs Departmental Store, Singapore, and staff at Glorietta Shopping Mall in Makati City, Manila
12: A Citibank sign at the Akasaka branch, Japan lists banking services offered at the branch
13: Pillars outside the Capital Square branch in Singapore are used to carry a variety of advertising
14: Window display advertisement on Century Avenue in Pudong, Shanghai

1	3		8	9	
2	4	5			10
					11
				12	13
6		7			14

Branches of International Banking Corporation and National City Bank 1902–1945

Map based on political status in 1942

Presence in major cities 1946–2001

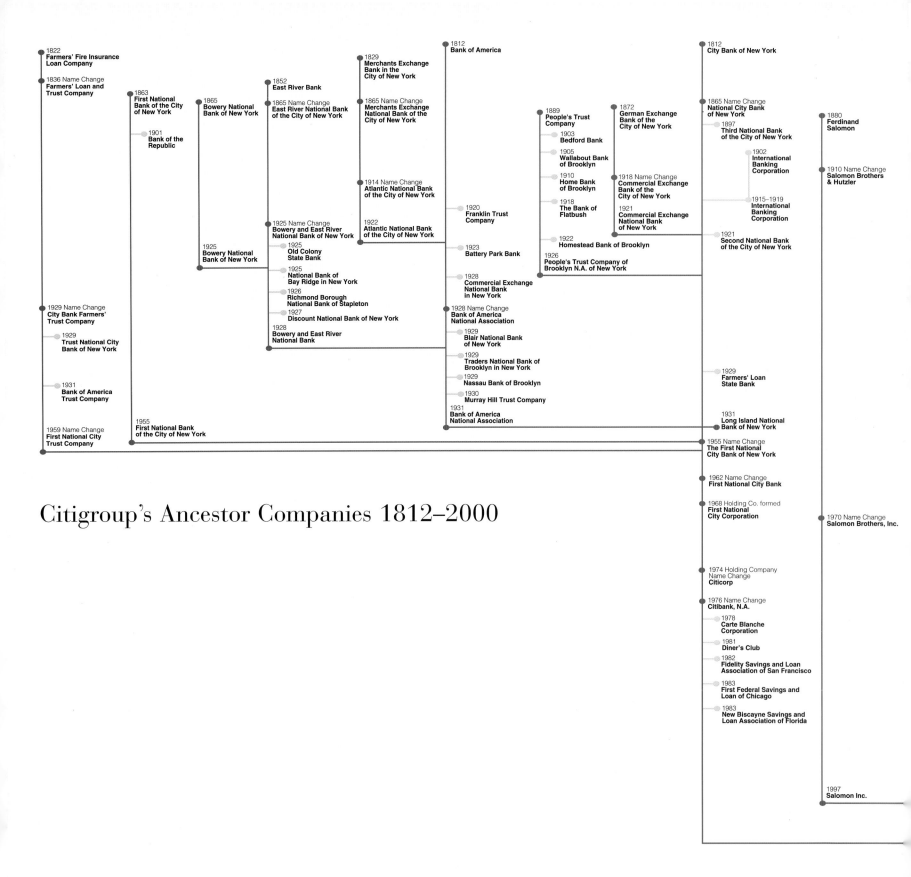

Citigroup's Ancestor Companies 1812–2000

- 1822 **Farmers' Fire Insurance Loan Company**
- 1836 Name Change **Farmers' Loan and Trust Company**
- 1863 **First National Bank of the City of New York**
- 1901 **Bank of the Republic**
- 1865 **Bowery National Bank of New York**
- 1852 **East River Bank**
- 1865 Name Change **East River National Bank of the City of New York**
- 1829 **Merchants Exchange Bank in the City of New York**
- 1865 Name Change **Merchants Exchange National Bank of the City of New York**
- 1812 **Bank of America**
- 1812 **City Bank of New York**
- 1865 Name Change **National City Bank of New York**
- 1897 **Third National Bank of the City of New York**
- 1889 **People's Trust Company**
- 1903 **Bedford Bank**
- 1905 **Wallabout Bank of Brooklyn**
- 1910 **Home Bank of Brooklyn**
- 1918 **The Bank of Flatbush**
- 1922 **Homestead Bank of Brooklyn**
- 1926 **People's Trust Company of Brooklyn N.A. of New York**
- 1872 **German Exchange Bank of the City of New York**
- 1918 Name Change **Commercial Exchange Bank of the City of New York**
- 1921 **Commercial Exchange National Bank of New York**
- 1880 **Ferdinand Salomon**
- 1910 Name Change **Salomon Brothers & Hutzler**
- 1902 **International Banking Corporation**
- 1915–1919 **International Banking Corporation**
- 1921 **Second National Bank of the City of New York**
- 1914 Name Change **Atlantic National Bank of the City of New York**
- 1922 **Atlantic National Bank of the City of New York**
- 1920 **Franklin Trust Company**
- 1923 **Battery Park Bank**
- 1925 Name Change **Bowery and East River National Bank of New York**
- 1925 **Bowery National Bank of New York**
- 1925 **Old Colony State Bank**
- 1925 **National Bank of Bay Ridge in New York**
- 1926 **Richmond Borough National Bank of Stapleton**
- 1927 **Discount National Bank of New York**
- 1928 **Bowery and East River National Bank**
- 1928 **Commercial Exchange National Bank in New York**
- 1928 Name Change **Bank of America National Association**
- 1929 **Blair National Bank of New York**
- 1929 **Traders National Bank of Brooklyn in New York**
- 1929 **Nassau Bank of Brooklyn**
- 1930 **Murray Hill Trust Company**
- 1931 **Bank of America National Association**
- 1929 Name Change **City Bank Farmers' Trust Company**
- 1929 **Trust National City Bank of New York**
- 1931 **Bank of America Trust Company**
- 1929 **Farmers' Loan State Bank**
- 1931 **Long Island National Bank of New York**
- 1959 Name Change **First National City Trust Company**
- 1955 **First National Bank of the City of New York**
- 1955 Name Change **The First National City Bank of New York**
- 1962 Name Change **First National City Bank**
- 1968 Holding Co. formed **First National City Corporation**
- 1970 Name Change **Salomon Brothers, Inc.**
- 1974 Holding Company Name Change **Citicorp**
- 1976 Name Change **Citibank, N.A.**
- 1978 **Carte Blanche Corporation**
- 1981 **Diner's Club**
- 1982 **Fidelity Savings and Loan Association of San Francisco**
- 1983 **First Federal Savings and Loan of Chicago**
- 1983 **New Biscayne Savings and Loan Association of Florida**
- 1997 **Salomon Inc.**

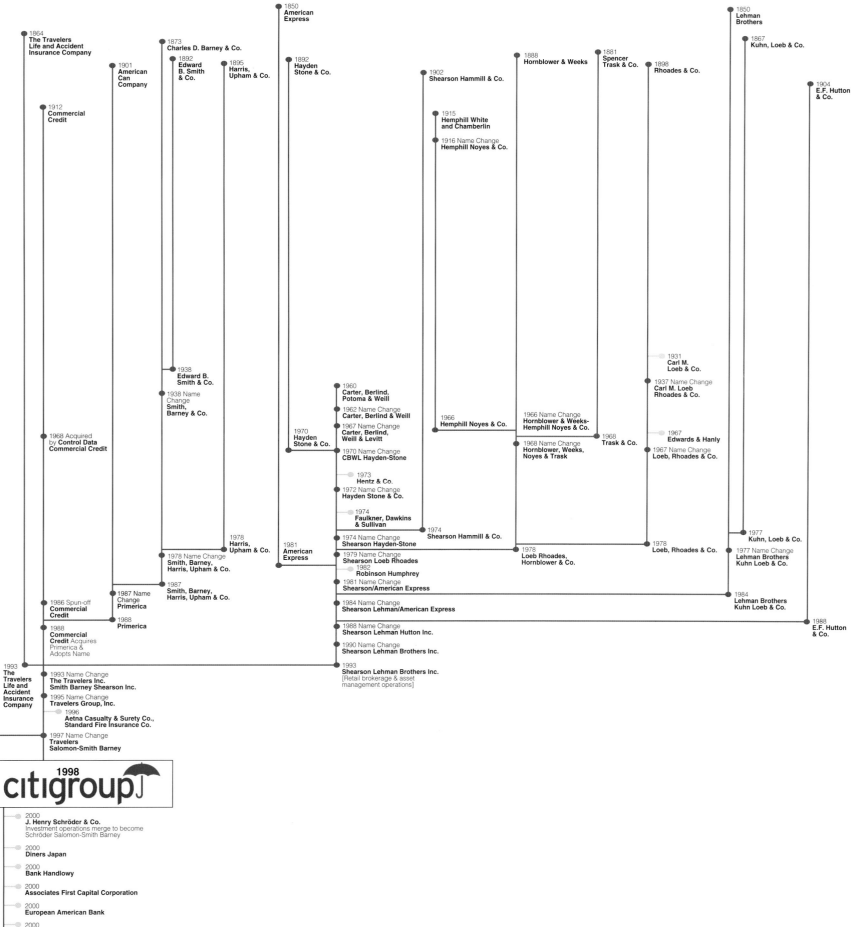

1850
**American
Express**

1850
**Lehman
Brothers**

1864
**The Travelers
Life and Accident
Insurance Company**

1867
Kuhn, Loeb & Co.

1873
Charles D. Barney & Co.

1892
**Edward
B. Smith
& Co.**

1895
**Harris,
Upham & Co.**

1892
**Hayden
Stone & Co.**

1901
**American
Can
Company**

1888
Hornblower & Weeks

1881
**Spencer
Trask & Co.**

1898
Rhoades & Co.

1902
Shearson Hammill & Co.

1904
**E.F. Hutton
& Co.**

1912
**Commercial
Credit**

1915
**Hemphill White
and Chamberlin**

1916 Name Change
Hemphill Noyes & Co.

1931
**Carl M.
Loeb & Co.**

1937 Name Change
**Carl M. Loeb
Rhoades & Co.**

1938
**Edward B.
Smith & Co.**

1938 Name
Change
**Smith,
Barney & Co.**

1960
**Carter, Berlind,
Potoma & Weill**

1962 Name Change
Carter, Berlind & Weill

1966
Hemphill Noyes & Co.

1966 Name Change
**Hornblower & Weeks-
Hemphill Noyes & Co.**

1968
Trask & Co.

1967
Edwards & Hanly

1967 Name Change
**Carter, Berlind,
Weill & Levitt**

1968 Acquired
by **Control Data
Commercial Credit**

1970
**Hayden
Stone & Co.**

1970 Name Change
CBWL Hayden-Stone

1968 Name Change
**Hornblower, Weeks,
Noyes & Trask**

1967 Name Change
Loeb, Rhoades & Co.

1973
Hentz & Co.

1972 Name Change
Hayden Stone & Co.

1974
**Faulkner, Dawkins
& Sullivan**

1974
Shearson Hammill & Co.

1977
Kuhn, Loeb & Co.

1978
**Harris,
Upham & Co.**

1974 Name Change
Shearson Hayden-Stone

1978
Loeb, Rhoades & Co.

1978 Name Change
**Smith, Barney,
Harris, Upham & Co.**

1981
**American
Express**

1979 Name Change
Shearson Loeb Rhoades

1982
Robinson Humphrey

1978
**Loeb Rhoades,
Hornblower & Co.**

1977 Name Change
**Lehman Brothers
Kuhn Loeb & Co.**

1986 Spun-off
**Commercial
Credit**

1987
**Smith, Barney,
Harris, Upham & Co.**

1981 Name Change
Shearson/American Express

1984
**Lehman Brothers
Kuhn Loeb & Co.**

1987 Name
Change
Primerica

1984 Name Change
Shearson Lehman/American Express

1988
**Commercial
Credit** Acquires
Primerica &
Adopts Name

1988
Primerica

1988 Name Change
Shearson Lehman Hutton Inc.

1988
**E.F. Hutton
& Co.**

1990 Name Change
Shearson Lehman Brothers Inc.

1993
**The
Travelers
Life and
Accident
Insurance
Company**

1993 Name Change
**The Travelers Inc.
Smith Barney Shearson Inc.**

1993
Shearson Lehman Brothers Inc.
[Retail brokerage & asset
management operations]

1995 Name Change
Travelers Group, Inc.

1996
**Aetna Casualty & Surety Co.,
Standard Fire Insurance Co.**

1997 Name Change
**Travelers
Salomon-Smith Barney**

**1998
citigroup** ☂

2000
J. Henry Schröder & Co.
Investment operations merge to become
Schröder Salomon-Smith Barney

2000
Diners Japan

2000
Bank Handlowy

2000
Associates First Capital Corporation

2000
European American Bank

2000
Banamex

Citibank country heads in Asia 1970–2002

AUSTRALIA

Shayne Elliott
2001–present

William Ferguson
1998–2001

Thomas McKeon
1996–1998

Brian Clayton
1993–1995

John Thom
1991–1993

Michael Cannon-Brookes
1985–1991

BRUNEI

Glen Robert Rase
1999–present

Page Stockwell
1996–1999

Steve Lawrence
1991–1996

David Conner
1985–1990

Douglas Hardy
1981–1984

Timothy Sounders
1979–1980

Denis Dovey
1977–1978

Peter Seah Lim Huat
1975–1976

William Serumgard
1972–1974

CHINA

Richard Stanley
1999–present

John Beeman
1996–1999

C.P. Cheng
1992–1996

HONG KONG (S.A.R. of China from 1997)

T.C. Chan
1999–present

Stephen Long
1995–1999

Antony Leung
1992–1995

Steven Baker
1986–1992

Victor Menezes
1983–1986

Kent Price
1980–1983

Richard Cusac
1978–1980

Edward Harshfield
1976–1978

Richard Freytag
1973–1976

Thomas McWeeney
1971–1973

Samuel Eastabrooks
1968–1971

INDIA

Nanoo Pamnani
1999–present

David Conner
1996–1999

Robert Eichfeld
1993–1996

Jerry Rao
1989–1993

David Roberts
1985–1989

Nanoo Pamnani
1982–1985

Victor Menezes
1978–1982

Allan Williams
1976–1978

James Collins
1974–1976

Hamilton Meserve
1971–1974

Robert Davidson
1968–1971

INDONESIA

Michael Zink
2000–present

Piyush Gupta
1998–2000

Colin Woolcock
1995–1998

Maarten Hulshoff
1994–1995

James Hunt
1987–1994

Philip Markert
1984–1987

Mehli Mistri
1978–1984

James Collins
1976–1978

Earl Glazier
1974–1976

Tom Crouse
1970–1974

Charles Stockholm
1967–1970

JAPAN

Charles Whitehead
2001–present

Frits Seegers
2000–2001

Mike de Graffenried
1997–2000

Masamoto Yashiro
1987–1997

James Collins
1984–1987

Tatsuo Umezono
1980–1984

Richard Huber
1977–1980

Robert Davidson
1971–1977

George Vojta
1969–1971

KOREA

Sajjad Razvi
1998–present

Robert Wilson
1996–1997

John Beeman
1991–1996

John Bernson
1986–1991

William Ferguson
1984–1986

Thomas Charters
1980–1984

Karl Swoboda
1978–1980

Philip Sherman
1974–1978

James Collins
1971–1974

Tor Folkedal
1970–1971

Hamilton Meserve
1967–1970

MALAYSIA

Juan Bruchou
2001–present

Robert Matthews
1998–2000

Sunil Sreenivasan
1994–1998

Aditya Puri
1993–1994

Rafael Gil-Tienda
1989–1993

N.N. Hariharan
1986–1988

Shaukat Aziz
1984–1986

Philip Markert
1980–1984

Kenneth Starger
1979–1980

Rafael Buenaventura
1976–1979

Richard Bird
1974–1976

Peter Howell
1972–1974

Edward Dunn
1969–1972

PHILIPPINES

Catherine Weir
2000–present

Suresh Maharaj
1995–2000

Stephen Long
1995–1995

William Ferguson
1989–1995

Nanoo Pamnani
1985–1989

Rafael Buenaventura
1982–1985

James Collins
1979–1982

Daniel Jacobsen
1975–1979

Samuel Eastabrooks
1971–1975

Michael Vernon Stolen
1970–1971

SINGAPORE

Sunil Sreenivasan
1998–present

Shehzad Naqvi
1997–1998

David Conner
1991–1996

David Browning
1989–1991

Bob McCormack
1988–1989

Nick Greville
1984–1987

Tom Dunton
1980–1983

Garrett Bouton
1978–1980

Eric Lawrence
1976–1978

Jonathan Graves
1974–1976

Wong Nang Jang
1970–1974

TAIWAN

Eric Chen
2001–present

Peter Baumann
1997–2001

Brian Clayton
1995–1997

Thomas McKeon
1988–1995

Frederick Copeland
1982–1988

Michael Cannon-Brookes
1980–1982

Kent Price
1978–1980

Bruce Brenn
1975–1978

Bill Yang
1973–1975

Earl Glazier
1968–1973

THAILAND

Terence Cuddyre
2002–present

Henry Ho
1997–2001

Shaukat Tarin
1995–1997

David Hendrix
1987–1995

David Mortlock
1985–1987

VIETNAM

John Beeman
1999–present

Bradley LaLonde
1994–1999

Michael McTighe
1973–1975

Robert Hudspeth
1972–1973

Reference should also be made here to the previous generation of country and regional managers, who laid the foundations for the bank's growth in Asia in the last three decades.

Some have appeared earlier in the book—they include Alexander Calhoun, Leo Chamberlain, Al Costanzo, Earle Cutting, Ken Emerson, Larry Glenn, Robert Grant, Ray Kathe, Tatsuo Kubota, Robert Morehouse, Glen Moreno, Red Newell, William Simmons, Hank Sperry, Carleton Stewart, William Taylor, Tom Theobald, David Van Pelt and Rick Wheeler. A number of other names would appear in any full list of key players. They include Bruce Baker, Jack Barrington, Robert Bennett, William Bulkeley, Jack Caouette, Frank Catterson, Marty Cooper, Louis Cullings, Thomas Davies, John Grammer, James Griffin, Sam Heffner, Richard Henry, Thomas Hitchcock, Granville Hutchinson, Donald Hykes, Richard Jackson, Johnny Johnson, Barry Mason, John Murphey, Eduardo Regala, Daniel Roberts, Irving Spering, Peter Tileston, Beau Wilson and Peter Wodtke.

Sources

Many present and former members of the bank's staff were interviewed during the preparation of this book, and their testimony is a key source. Much important financial information was taken from the bank's annual reports (including those of the International Banking Corporation), although in the earlier days these often amounted to no more than a brief Statement of Condition. Invaluable material was also gleaned from the various staff publications produced over the years by the bank, both in New York (*Number Eight* in particular) and by the various branches. In addition to *Number Eight*, their titles include *Citibank Magazine, Citibank World, Citigroup World, Emerging Markets Asia-Pacific News, Esprit, Overseas Citibanker, Overseas Division Monthly Letter, The Americas, Citibanker, Citi Balita* (a particularly lively publication produced in Manila), *Singapore Citibanker, Citibank News, Citibank Korea*—and no doubt others have been produced over the past century. The official history *Citibank 1812–1970* by Cleveland and Huertas (see below) is an important source, although its coverage of Asia is necessarily limited. Other major printed sources are listed below.

ALLETZHAUSER, AL, *The House of Nomura*, Bloomsbury Publishing Ltd., London 1990.

ASIAN DEVELOPMENT BANK, *Emerging Asia: Changes and Challenges*, Asian Development Bank, Manila, 1997.

BANGKO SENTRAL NG PILIPINAS, *Fifty Years of Central Banking in the Philippines*, BSP, Manila, 1998.

BECKER, JASPER, *The Chinese*, John Murray (Publishers) Ltd., London, 2000.

BURR, ANNA ROBESON, *The Portrait of a Banker: James Stillman 1850-1918*, Duffield & Co., New York, 1927.

CARUNUNGAN, CELSO AL., *The Citibank Story: Eighty Years of Partnership with the Philippine Republic*, Manila, 1982.

CAREW, EDNA, *Fast Money 2*, Allen & Unwin Australia Pty. Ltd., Sydney, 1985.

CAREW, EDNA, *The Language of Money*, Allen & Unwin Australia Pty. Ltd., Sydney, 1985.

CLEVELAND, HAROLD VAN B., AND HUERTAS, THOMAS F., *Citibank 1812–1970*, Harvard University Press, Cambridge Mass. and London, 1985.

CODY, JEFFREY, "Remnants of Power Behind the Bund: Shanghai's IBC and Robert Dollar Buildings," *Architectural Research Quarterly*, vol. 3, no. 4, Cambridge University Press, 1999. See also Lin Syaru's *Citicorp in China*.

DE MENOCAL, DANIEL, transcript of unpublished memoirs, 1961, Citigroup Corporate Affairs Archives, New York.

DELHAISE, PHILIPPE F., *Asia in Crisis: The Implosion of the Banking and Finance Systems*, John Wiley & Sons (Asia) Pte. Ltd., Singapore, 1998.

FAR EASTERN ECONOMIC REVIEW, *Asia 1999 Yearbook*, Review Publishing Co. Ltd., Hong Kong, 1999.

FEDERAL RESERVE BULLETIN, *Foreign Business of the National City Bank of New York*, October, 1918.

FORBES, B.C., *Men Who Are Making America*, B.C. Forbes Publishing Co., New York, 1922.

FUNATANI, KENTARO, *You Swim or Sink*, unpublished memoirs, n.d., Nagoya, Wheeler Archives, Concord.

H., J.W. *A Memoir of Marcellus Hartley*, Gramercy Park, 1903.

HART, BOIES CHITTENDEN, *Banker at Large*, unpublished memoirs, n.d., Citigroup Corporate Affairs Archives, New York.

JAPAN: AN ILLUSTRATED ENCYCLOPEDIA, Kodansha Ltd., Tokyo, 1993.

KATHE, RAYMUND A., transcript of interview with Clarence Wasson in 1979, Citigroup Corporate Affairs Archives, New York.

KEAY, JOHN, *India: A History*, HarperCollins Publishers, London, 2000.

KING, FRANK H.H., *The History of the Hongkong and Shanghai Banking Corporation* (4 vols.), Cambridge University Press, Cambridge, 1988

LEE KUAN YEW, *The Singapore Story*, Times Editions, Singapore, 1998.

LEE KUAN YEW, *From Third World to First*, Times Media Pte. Ltd., Singapore, 2000.

LEIFER, MICHAEL, *Dictionary of Modern Politics of South-East Asia*, Routledge, London, 1995.

LIN SYARU, SHIRLEY, *Citicorp in China*, Citicorp/Citibank, c. 1989. The material on the architecture of IBC was written by Jeffrey Cody, and was in part the basis of a later published article (see Jeffrey Cody's *Remnants of Power Behind the Bund: Shanghai's IBC and Robert Dollar Buildings*).

MA BODE, TANG WEIKANG, XU YUAN AND BO WEIQUN (eds.), *Currencies in Old Shanghai* (Lao Shanghai Huobi), Shanghai People's Fine Arts Publishing House, Shanghai, 1998.

MAO TSETUNG, *Quotations from Chairman Mao Tsetung*, Foreign Languages Press, Beijing, 1972.

MOORE, GEORGE S., *The Banker's Life*, W.W. Norton & Co., New York, 1987.

MORITA, AKIO, EDWIN M. REINGOLD, AND MITSUKO SHIMOMURE, *Made in Japan: Akio Morita and Sony*, E.P. Dutton, 1986; William Collins Sons and Co. Ltd., Glasgow, 1987. The text in "Accounting Lesson" on page 133 is quoted by permission of Dutton, a division of Penguin Putnam Inc.

MURPHY, CHARLES J.V., *Shanghai: Reopened Under New Management*, Fortune, February, 1945.

NAKAMURA, TAKAFUSA, *The Postwar Japanese Economy*, University of Tokyo Press, Tokyo, 1995.

NEWELL, RALPH P. ("Red"), transcript of interview with Clarence Wasson in 1980, Citigroup Corporate Affairs Archives, New York.

OZORIO, CANDIDO EMILIO DE LOPES E, *A Brief History of the Shanghai Branch of the National City Bank of New York*, Shanghai, 1940.

PEOPLE'S BANK OF CHINA, FINANCIAL RESEARCH INSTITUTE, *America's Flower Flag Bank in China: Historical Documents*, China Financial Publishing House, 1990 (Zhongguo Renmin Yinhang, Jinronggongzuo Yanjiushi, Meiguo Huaqi Yinhang Zaihuashiliao, Zhongguo Jinrong Chubanshe, Beijing, 1990).

PHELPS, CLYDE WILLIAM, *The Foreign Expansion of American Banks: American Branch Banking Abroad*, The Ronald Press Company, New York, 1926.

PRESTON, DIANA, *Besieged in Peking: The Story of the 1990 Boxer Uprising*, Constable, London, 1999.

RIES, PHILIPPE, *Cette crise qui vient d'Asie*, Editions Grasset et Fasquelle, Paris, 1998; trans. Peter Starr as The Asian Storm: Asia's Economic Crisis Examined, Tuttle Publishing, Boston, 2000.

ROBERTS, RICHARD, *Schroders: Merchants & Bankers*, Macmillan Press Ltd., London, 1992.

RODRIGO, RAUL, *Phoenix: The Saga of the Lopez Family*, Eugenio Lopez Foundation Inc., Manila, 2000.

ROY, BARUN, *Citibank in Asia: the Drama and the Dream*, Asian Finance, Hong Kong, 1983.

SAKAKIBARA, EISUKE, *Beyond Capitalism: the Japanese Model of Market Economics*, University Press of America Inc., Lanham, 1993.

SCOTT, GEORGE, transcripts of oral history interviews in 1976 and 1978, Citigroup Corporate Affairs Archives, New York

SEAGRAVE, STERLING, *The Soong Dynasty*, Harper & Row Publishers Inc., New York, Sidgwick & Jackson Ltd., London, 1986.

SEAGRAVE, STERLING, *Dragon Lady: the Life and Legend of the Last Empress of China*, Alfred A. Knopf Inc., New York, 1992; Vintage Books, New York, 1993.

SIVASUBRAMONIAN, S., *The National Income of India in the Twentieth Century*, Oxford University Press, New Delhi, 2000.

SKULLY, MICHAEL T., *Financial Institutions and Markets in Southeast Asia*, Macmillan Press, London, 1984.

SKULLY, MICHAEL T., *ASEAN Financial Cooperation*, Macmillan Press, London, 1985.

SOBEL, ROBERT, *Salomon Brothers 1910–1985: Advance to Leadership*, New York, 1986.

SUZUKI, YOSHIO, *The Japanese Financial System*, Clarendon Press, Oxford, 1987 (originally published under the title *Waga kuni no kinyu seido*, Institute for Monetary and Economic Studies, Bank of Japan, Tokyo, 1986).

TOYO KEIZAI INC., *Japan Company Handbook: First Section (Spring)*, Toyo Keizai Inc., Tokyo, 1997.

TSURU, KOTARO, *The Japanese Market Economy System: Its Strength and Weaknesses*, LTCB International Library Foundation, Tokyo, 1996 (originally published under the title *Nihon-teki Shijo-Keizai System*, Kodansha, Tokyo, 1994.

VANDERLIP, FRANK A., written with Boyden Sparkes, *From Farm Boy to Financier*, The Saturday Evening Post, Philadelphia, 1934–1935; D. Appleton-Century Company, New York, 1935.

VANDERLIP, FRANK A., *Facts About the Philippines with a Discussion of Pending Problems*, The Century, New York, 1898.

VANDERLIP, FRANK A. Jr., transcript of interview with Clarence Wasson, 1981, Citigroup Corporate Affairs Archives, New York.

VINER, ARON, *Inside Japan's Financial Markets*, The Economist Publications Ltd., London, 1987.

WASSON, CLARENCE, *Comments on My Years in Citibank*, unpublished memoirs, n.d., Citigroup Corporate Affairs Archives, New York.

WATSON ANDAYA, BARBARA, AND ANDAYA, LEONARD Y., *A History of Malaysia*, Macmillan Press Ltd., London, 1982.

WELLS, H.G., *A Short History of the World*, Revised edition, Penguin Books Ltd., Harmondsworth, 1965.

WHEELER, RICHARD W., transcript of oral history interview, Citigroup Corporate Affairs Archives, New York. Richard Wheeler was also interviewed specifically for this book.

WOLFEREN, KAREL VAN, *The Enigma of Japanese Power*, Macmillan London Ltd., London, 1989.

WRISTON, WALTER B., *Risk and Other Four-Letter Words*, Harper & Row Publishers Inc., New York, 1986. Walter Wriston was also interviewed specifically for this book.

YASHIRO, MASAMOTO, *My Career Chronicle*, Toppan Printing Co. Ltd., Tokyo, 1997 (originally published as *Watashi no rirekisho* in the Nihon Keizai Shimbun from April 1 to April 30, 1997). Masamoto Yashiro was also interviewed specifically for this book.

YOSHIHARU, KUNIO, *Asia Per Capita: Why National Incomes Differ in East Asia*, Curzon Press, London and New Asian Library, Singapore, 2000.

ZHEJIANG PEOPLE'S PUBLISHING HOUSE, *Twentieth Century Focus 1900–1999*, Hangzhou, 2000 (*Ershishiji jiujiao 1900–1999*, Zhejiang Renmin Chubanshe, Hangzhou, 2000).

ZWEIG, PHILLIP L., *Walter Wriston, Citibank, and the Rise and Fall of American Financial Supremacy*, Crown Publishers Inc., New York, 1995.

Index

213

Acknowledgements

The author and publisher thank the many current and former Citigroup staff members who helped with the preparation of this book. A detailed list appears below.

Citigroup's archival staff in New York were unfailingly helpful and we would particularly like to thank Patricia Henry, Suzanne Lemakis and Joan Silverman. Among the wives of veteran Citibankers who spent much of their lives in Asia, Ansie Lee Sperry, Betty Ann Wheeler and Jacqueline Kathe deserve special mention.

For additional assistance, the author would like to thank Ray Bashford, Roberto Coloma, Chum Samonn, Fatimah bte Basar, Adelia da Fonseca-Ries, Haji Harddy Hisysham bin Mohd. Hanafi, Janet Linggi-Anderson, Angela Mackay, Mohd. Ali bin Harddy Hisysham, Pun In-shek, Haji Razali bin Haji Kalong, Anusak Konglang, Reach Mony, Joan Orendain, Sarah Sargent, Makiko Tazaki, Yoichi Teraishi, Manami Teraishi, Kate Webb, and Yeung Ling-ling.

Thanks are also due to Dionisia C. Boro of the Asian Development Bank, and Daisy A. Navarro of the Central Bank of the Philippines; and to Jonathan Best, Jeffrey Cody, Sharada Dwivedi, John Falconer, and Professor Loh Wei Leng.

The publishers acknowledge with grateful thanks the co-operation of the following in the preparation of the photoessay Citigroup in Asia Today: 7-Eleven Japan; Eastman Chemical Pte. Ltd., Singapore; Fudan University, Shanghai; HOPE *worldwide* Center for Kids, Hong Kong; Island School, Hong Kong; Keio University, Japan; Li & Fung Ltd., Hong Kong; Manila Electric Company (Meralco); Philippine Business for Social Progress; Royal Container Carriers, Mumbai; Shanghai General Motors Co. Ltd.; Society for the Promotion of Area Resource Centres (SPARC), Mumbai; Tuloy sa Don Bosco, Philippines; and Working Women's Forum (WWF), Chennai.

This book could not have been produced without the help of many present and former members of the staff of Citigroup and the organizations which preceded it:

Nina **Aguas**, Eric **Alberto**, Leila **Almeida**, Ditta **Amahorseya**, Joji **Aonuma**, Marife **Apilado**, Nobuyoshi **Arai**, Sandeep **Arora**, Agatha **Awyong**, Shaukat **Aziz**, Bruce **Baker**, Nick **Balamaci**, D.P. **Banerjee**, Sujit **Banerji**, Richard **Beales**, John **Beeman**, Steven **Bernstein**, Ravi **Bhatia**, Meher **Bhiwandiwala**, Sir Win **Bischoff**, Anita **Boloor**, Amanda **Bowling**, Dolores **Brown**, Juan **Bruchou**, Steven **Budlong**, Rafael **Buenaventura**, Andrew **Butcher**, Judy **Carbone**, Dabney **Carr**, Frank **Catterson**, George **Chan**, Laymond Y.B. **Chan**, Sandy **Chan**, T.C. **Chan**, Deborah **Chang**, Dominic K.W. **Chang**, Philip **Chang**, Tada **Charukitpaisarn**, Myrna **Chaves**, **Cheah** Sook-lian, **Chen** Min'an, Eric **Chen**, Jennifer **Chen**, Joyce **Chen**, Ed **Cheney**, Felix **Cheng**, Frances **Cheng**, Yotin **Chenvanich**, **Cheoh** Gim Hoon, Claudia L.C. **Cheung**, Kenny **Chew**, **Chia** Chee Yoong,

Pei-Yuan **Chia**, Cleopatra **Chittalarn**, Bell **Chong**, Daniel S.L. **Chow**, Li-yee **Chow**, Deepak **Chowdhury**, Sara **Chua**, Agnes **Chun**, Brali **Chung**, Albert **Cobetto**, James **Collins**, David **Conner**, Al **Costanzo**, Daniel **Cox**, Candace **Crawshaw**, Tony **Cretaro**, Thomas **Crowse**, Francisco **Cuyegkeng**, Katherine **D'Arcy**, Mike **de Graffenried**, Vicki **de Souza**, Uma Gopal **Deb**, Ivo **Distelbrink**, Cathy **Dou**, Denis **Dovey**, Joseph **Draper**, Penny **Drapkin**, Samuel **Eastabrooks**, Maximino **Edralin**, Edmond **Eger**, Robert **Eichfeld**, Shayne **Elliott**, Ken **Fagan**, Lillibeth **Fajardo**, Christopher **Fehon**, William **Ferguson**, Vincern C. **Fernando**, Cecille **Fonacier**, Eric **Fong**, Pat **Fong**, **Foo** Tsiang Wei, Julie **Foo**, Junie **Foo**, Richard **Freytag**, Sayaka **Fujimoto**, Rajat **Garg**, Edwin **Gerungan**, Malay **Ghatak**, David **Gibson**, Tereze **Gluck**, Edward **Go**,

Pia **Gonzalez-Nazareno**, Maggie **Grady**, Robert **Grant**, Glenn **Gray**, **Gui** Fubao, Grace Y. **Guo**, Madhulika **Gupta**, Piyush **Gupta**, Caroline **Gurney**, Don **Hanna**, Alan **Harden**, Edward **Harshfield**, Mark **Hart**, Raissa **Hechanova-Posadas**, Sam **Heffner**, David **Hendrix**, Ma Eulalia **Herrera**, **Ho** Man Chiu, Henry **Ho**, Joyce **Ho**, Tejpal **Hora**, Peter **Horell**, Alma **Horn**, Teizo **Hotta**, Richard **Howe**, Scott **Hoy**, Stephanie **Hu**, Wendy **Hu**, **Huang** Xiaoguang, Robert **Hudspeth**, James **Hunt**, Yuri **Idesari**, K.V.S. **Iyer**, Penny **Jack**, Richard **Jackson**, Shital **Jain**, Richard **Janiak**, Finni **Januar**, P.S. **Jayakumar**, Yu **Jin**, Leah **Johnson**, Michelle **Jones**, Money **K**, P.S. **Kadam**, Ajit **Kanagasundram**, Mieko **Kanemoto**, **Khoo** Teng Cheong, Eddie **Khoo**, Edwin **Khoo**, Ferdy **Khouw**, Chan Souk **Kim,** Koichiro **Kitade**, Bronwen **Knight**, Emily **Ko**, Toshiharu **Kojima**, **Kong** Choy Chan, Venky **Krishnakumar**, Kiichi **Kume**, Jason **Kwok**, Aloysius H.M. **Lai**, Vasant **Lajmi**, Adrienne **Lam**, Connie **Lam**, Daisy **Lam**, Maisie **Lam**, Jonathan **Larsen**, **Lau** On, B.T. **Lau**, Ajit Kumar **Law**, **Lee** Ah Boon, **Lee** Peng Luen, **Lee** Sze Min, Joan, Adelina Y.K. **Lee**, Albert S.S. **Lee**, Hyun Jung **Lee**, Ricky O.C. **Lee**, Barry **Lesmana**, Antony **Leung**, Brace **Leung**, Kaven W. **Leung**, Raymond **Leung**, Jenny J.L. **Lim**, Victor **Lim**, Wendy **Lim**, **Liu** Zhengxing, Danny **Liu**, Stephen **Long**, Lawrence **Low**, Maureen **Low**, Doreen **Loy**, James **Lye**, Sheila **Lynch**, Kirsty **Mactaggart**, Stephen **Mann**, Dennis **Martin**, Barry **Mason**, Les **Matheson**, Robert **Matthews**, Sir Deryck **Maughan**, Edward **Melo**, Victor **Menezes**, Hamilton **Meserve**, William **Mills**, Mehli **Mistri**, Yoshie **Mitsuhashi**, Zeny **Molina**, Vaughn **Montes**, Robert **Morehouse**, Glen **Moreno**, Mark **Morgan**, Robert **Morse**, Sanjiv **Mullick**, Norberto **Nazareno**, Nicholas H.P. **Ng**, Tarrin **Nimmanahaeminda**, Midori **Nomura**, **Ong** Hui Leong, **Ow** Yew Wah, N.R. **Padki**, Alma **Padron**, Terry **Pamianowska**, Nanoo **Pamnani**, Soon-Hee **Park**, H.N. **Patil**, Lisa **Paul**, Rajesh **Peswani**, Joyce **Phillips**, Edward **Pomeroy**, Rajeev **Potnis**, G.M. **Prabhudesai**, Sheri **Ptasheks**, **Qi** Yiyu, Peter **Qiu**, Ellen **Quinn**, Ravi **Raman**, Jerry **Rao**, Pavitra **Rao**, Glen **Rase**, Sajjad **Razvi**, John **Reed**, **Ren** Zhiming, William **Rhodes**, Heinz **Riehl**, Eric **Ripp**, Mike **Robertson**, Frederick **Roesch**, Michael **Ross**, Trevor **Rowe**, Sachit **Salgaonkar**, Arora **Sandeep**, Armaity **Sanga**, Sanjay **Sarkar**, Naazneen **Sarkari**, Malik **Sarwar**, Michael **Schlein**, Frits **Seegers**, Pradipta K. **Sen**, Chiharu **Senoo**, Deepak **Sharma**, Philip **Sherman**, R.K. **Shinde**, John **Shinkle**, Manish **Shivram**, Penny **Shone**, Abbie **Shroff**, Hans Brinker **Sicat**, Joan **Silverman**, B.M. **Singh**, Richard **Smith**, Prakash **Somayaji**, Bill **Spathelf**, Henry **Sperry**, Sunil **Sreenivasan**, Richard **Stanley**, Carleton **Stewart**, Charles **Stockholm**, Narayan **Swamy**, Freda **Sze**, Rana **Talwar**, Christine **Tam**, Anusorn **Tamajai**, Andrew **Tamarkin**, **Tan** Hock Lam, Alice **Tan**, Allen K.H. **Tan**, Amy **Tan**, Christopher **Tan**, Li-Lian **Tan**, Michael A.C. **Tan**, Flor **Tarriela**, Peggy **Tay**, William **Taylor**, Tresor Anne **Teo**, Richard **Tesvich**, Peter **Tileston**, Ameer **Toor**, Pornsanong **Tuchinda**, Andrew **Tung**, Tatsuo **Umezono**, Chuyen **Uong**, K.V. **Venkaparayan**, S. **Venkatachalam**, Subramaniam **Venkatanarayanan**, K.V. **Venkataraman**, K.V. **Venkatnarayan**, Phong Kim **Vo**, George **Vojta**, Bill **Walker**, Pamela **Wardrope**, Eileen **Wee**, Susan **Weeks**, Sanford **Weill**, Catherine **Weir**, Richard **Wheeler**, Charles **Whitehead**, Illiana **Wijanarko**, Simon **Williams**, Peter **Wodtke**, **Wong** Kwan Ling, **Wong** Nang Jang, **Wong** Wai Ling, Jimmy K.H. **Wong**, Norman C.W. **Wong**, Virginia **Wong**, Y.S. **Wong**, Walter **Wriston**, Bonnie **Wu**, Yukinori **Yamamoto**, Lyn **Yang**, Masamoto **Yashiro**, Freda **Yeo**, Mei-Yi **Yong**, **Zhang** Mei, Henry **Zhang**, **Zheng** Yifei, Mona **Zhong**, Michael **Zink**.

Thanks are also due to Sharmini **Blok**, Patrick **Cranley**, Louise **Harris**, Jessica **Low**, Jane **Rogers**, Matthew **Ward**, and Estelle **Xiang**.

Picture credits

The publishers would like to thank the following for permission to reproduce photographs and other illustrations:

A.L. SYED 65 left
AFP PHOTO 107 right, 125 below
BANGKO SENTRAL NG PILIPINAS 24 center right, 34 center
BILL RAY 142 top right
BILL WALKER 106 center and below
BLACK STAR 5 ©1997 Ray Cranbourne, 139 © 1992 Swapan Parekh, 151 top © 1992 Eiji Miyazawa, 156 top © 1999 Mike Wilbur, 164 below right © 2000 Ray Takei
BOARD OF COMMISSIONERS OF CURRENCY, SINGAPORE 24 center, 55 center
CARLETON M. STEWART 93 top left
CURRENCY MUSEUM, BANK OF JAPAN 23 center right, 23 below left
D.P. BANERJEE 96 left, 98 center, 118 center right
DENNIS DOVEY 35 top, 102 top, 103, 110 top right, 121 top right, 131
EDITIONS DIDIER MILLET 55 left and right
ENRICO TEDESCHI 133 right
EUGENIO LOPEZ FOUNDATION 19 below left, 19 center right, 29 below
GEORGE CHAN 131, 116 below left and center, 121 top left and center, 123 top right, 124 top and below, 126 nos. 1, 2 and 18
GUI FUBAO 71 below
HANK AND ANSIE LEE SPERRY 2, 58 top, 60 below, 66 top, 69 top, center and below left, and center right, 82, 90 left and center right, 93 center below
HONG KONG MUSEUM OF ART COLLECTION 19 top
JOHN FALCONER 16, 20, 21 top left and below
JONATHAN BEST 40 right, 78 top left
KIRK RAMOS 152 top
LUCA TETTONI PHOTOGRAPHY 112 top
LUIS AND MATHESS SAN PEDRO 126 no. 11
MARLENE B. PICCIO 115 top left
MING PAO DAILY NEWS, Hong Kong 144 below

MYRNA CHAVES 130, 131
NATIONAL ARCHIVES AND RECORDS ADMINISTRATION 19 middle right
NATIONAL ARCHIVES, SINGAPORE 21 top right
NATIONAL MARITIME MUSEUM, LONDON © Duncan E. 18
NEPTUNE ORIENT LINES 161 below right
THE NEW YORK PUBLIC LIBRARY 27 top
THE NEW YORK STOCK EXCHANGE 162 top right
NORBERTO C. NAZARENO 143 below
PANA PHOTO 109 top
PAT FONG 114 top right, 147 top
RAFAEL B. BUENAVENTURA 102 below
REUTERS 123 top left, 145 below
RICHARD W. WHEELER 30 top left, 31 below, 37 top, 41 left, 47, 48 left and center, 56 below, 59, 61, 63 top, 65 right, 69 right, 71 top, 74, 75 below, 87 below left, 88 left, 91 below left, 97 below left, 101 below left and right, 110 below right, 111 left
ROBERT H. MOREHOUSE 99
SAM TATA 85 top left and below left
SINGAPORE HERITAGE SOCIETY, 1992, 72 left © Chandra Mohan
SONY CORPORATION 133 left
THE STRAITS TIMES, SINGAPORE 35 below left, 114 below, 123 center right, 141 top
SVEN SINDING 162 top right
TATSUO UMEZONO 136 left
VICKI DE SOUZA 115 top right, 116 top, 117 left
VICTOR J. MENEZES 119 below , 129 top left, 129 center right
WILLIAM R. RHODES 137 center left, 155 top
WONG NANG JANG 114 top left

If any due acknowledgement or copyright clearance has been inadvertently overlooked, the publishers will be pleased to make good the omission in any subsequent printing.

Thanks are also due to staff in the following Citigroup offices for their kind assistance in lending archival photographs and other illustrations.

CITIGROUP, AUSTRALIA 125 top, 165 top right
CITIGROUP, CHINA Front cover, 1, 31 top, 37 below, 39 below, 43 top, 49 top right, 56 top, 58 below, 63 below, 79 below, 107 left, 126 no. 16, 149 top left, 167 top
CITIGROUP, HONG KONG 32 top, 36 left, 67 below, 89 below, 104, 116 below right, 126 no. 17, 146 below right
CITIGROUP, INDIA 118 top right, 119 top, 156 below, 161 top left, 165 top left, 167 below
CITIGROUP, INDONESIA 157, 161 center right
CITIGROUP, JAPAN 44 below right, 57 below, 60 top, 76, 94 left, 95, 100 left, 101 top left, 108 top left, 110 top left, 150 center right, 150 below right
CITIGROUP, KOREA 110 below left and center, 155 below left and right
CITIGROUP, MALAYSIA 93 center right, 148 below
CITIGROUP, PHILIPPINES 87 top left, 91 center right, 101 top right, 114 top right, 121 below, 122, 126 nos. 3, 9, and 19, 137 below left and center right, 145 top
CITIGROUP, SINGAPORE 126 nos. 4 and 10, 129 below, 160 top left
CITIGROUP, TAIWAN 160 below right
CITIGROUP, THAILAND 138, 150 top right
CITIGROUP ART COLLECTION, NEW YORK 6–7, 17 below, 28, 30 below, 32 below, 33 top, 35 top right, 38, 39 top, 40 left, 41 right and center, 42, 43 below, 45, 46 left and top right, 49 top left, center right, below left, center and right, 50, 51 left, 52, 73, 78 below, 79 top left, 79 right, 81 center, 83 below, 86, 88 top right, 94 below right, 97 right, 126 no. 14
CITIGROUP CORPORATE AFFAIRS ARCHIVES, NEW YORK 8, 25, 26, 27 below, 34 top left, 34 below left, 44 top left, center and right,

46 center right, 48 right, 51 right, 53 below, 54, 62, 66 below, 70, 75 top left and right, 77 below, 78 top right, 80 top left, 81, 84 top left, 87 top right, 87 below right, 88 below right, 89 top, 90 top right, 91 top left, 92, 97 top right, 98 below, 105 below, 106 top left, 108 top right, 108 below, 111 right, 113 below, 115 below, 117 right, 126 nos. 6, 7, 8, 12 and 13, 129 top right, 131 top left, 134, 142 top left, 147 below left, 150 left, 153
CITIGROUP INC. 146 top left
CITIGROUP PRIVATE BANK 146 below left, 149 below
CITIGROUP REGIONAL CORPORATE AFFAIRS ARCHIVES, SINGAPORE 113 top, 123 below left, 124 center, 126 nos. 5 and 15, 128, 131, 135 below, 136 right, 151 below, 152 below right, 153 below, 160 center
NIKKO SALOMON SMITH BARNEY LTD. 143 top, 144 top, 161 top right, 164 below left
SALOMON SMITH BARNEY 143 top, 144 top center, 164 top right

SPECIAL PHOTOGRAPHY

Photography for the photoessay *Citigroup in Asia Today* was undertaken by LUIS ASCUI (Singapore), AMIT ASHER (India), JON BURBANK (Japan), CHIRODEEP CHAUDHURI (India), GARETH JONES (Hong Kong), HILDA TING (China), and PRESCIANO YABAO (Philippines).

Additional photography by TIMOTHY AUGER, BABU, TONY CRETARO, PATRICK CUMMINS, SAYAKA FUJIMOTO, LAWRENCE LIM and ZHANG CHUNHAI.